This polemical work presents to the English-speaking world one of the most original philosophical thinkers to have emerged within post-war Europe. Sebastiano Timpanaro is an Italian classical philologist by training, an author of scholarly studies on the 19th century poet Leopardi, and a Marxist by conviction. With great force and wit, *On Materialism* sets itself against what it sees as the virtually universal tendency within Western Marxism since the war, to dissociate historical materialism from biological or physical materialism. Whereas the philosophical legacy of the later Engels has been decried by most prominent Marxists since the 1920's, Timpanaro eloquently defends its essential purpose and relevance, by unfashionably re-emphasising the permanent weight of nature within history. In doing so, he returns to the heritage of Lucretius and Leopardi, and argues for a consistent materialism that is at once more pessimistic and more hedonistic than any other contemporary version of Marxism. Timpanaro emphasises the insuperable limits of frailty and mortality as unalterable conditions of human life under the yoke of nature. At the same time, he combines this with an insistence on emancipation as pleasure, within the alterable conditions of society whose transformation is the goal of revolutionary socialism. Timpanaro vigorously attacks what he regards as the widespread entente between a diluted Marxism and a fashionable idealism in the West, whether in the form of an 'existentialist' or a 'structuralist' union of the two. The aversion of the former to the work of Darwin and Engels receives a spirited refutation, no less than the indulgence of the latter towards the work of Saussure or Levi-Strauss. A special introduction written for this English edition deals with the phenomenon of the recent revival of 'vulgar materialism' in the Anglo-Saxon world, in the fields of psychology and anthropology, and its relationship to racism. *On Materialism* will be one of the central focuses of cultural and intellectual controversy within and beyond Marxism in the next decade.

# Sebastiano Timpanaro

Verso

# On Materialism

*Translated by Lawrence Garner*

First published as *Sul Materialismo*
Nistri-Lischi, Pisa 1970
'Karl Korsch e la filosofia di Lenin'
Belfagor, XXVIII, 1, 1973

This translation first published, 1975
© NLB, 1975

Verso Edition first published, 1980
NLB and Verso Editions, 7 Carlisle Street, London W1

Printed and bound in Great Britain by Redwood Burn Ltd,
Trowbridge and Esher

ISBN 0 902308 03 3 (cloth)
ISBN 0 86091 721 5 (paper)

# Contents

*to Luciano Della Mea*

# Foreword

I am only too well aware of what might be termed the pre-scientific and pre-philosophical nature of these essays. In them, requirements are stated and a polemical position taken up; but their theoretical stance is neither rigorously grounded nor fully developed. My decision, despite this, to publish them together in book form is based on the belief that, at the present stage of Marxist discussion, they can fulfil a provisional function of critical stimulus.

In recent years, in connection with the crisis of the official communist parties, the Chinese cultural revolution and the rise of new revolutionary currents in the West, we have seen a revival of theoretical interest. The need to struggle against reformism has clearly shown how essential it is not to simply entrench oneself in a defence of Marxist-Leninist orthodoxy, but to rethink Marxism in the light of everything new that has occurred in the capitalist West, in China and in the third world. Unfortunately, however, the two main interpretations of Marx which have come to influence the revolutionary left in the West in recent years – one furnished by the Frankfurt school and its various offspring, the other by Althusser – allow very little of Marxism to survive. Moreover, and this is far more grave, they represent in many respects a step backwards: the former because, following in the path of tendencies which were already very widespread in the Western Marxism of the twenties and thirties, it ignores the need to found a 'scientific socialism' and sees in science only bourgeois false objectivity; the latter because, although it does proclaim most emphatically the scientific character of Marxism, it takes from twentieth-century epistemology a Platonist concept of science which is not that of Marx and Engels and which makes it impossible to pose correctly the relation between theory and practice.

Anyone who saw these interpretations simply as intellectual errors, without understanding that they reflect objective difficulties facing the working-class movement in the advanced capitalist countries, would be a very poor Marxist indeed. The main way to defeat these tendencies, in other words, is not through philosophical discussion alone, but through a study of contemporary capitalism, the contemporary proletariat and the nexus between capitalism and imperialism: a study, it goes without saying, linked to and constantly verified by political action. And yet, at the same time, it would be just as unMarxist to seek to reduce Marxism to a revolutionary sociology, purging it of those aspects of a general conception of reality which are not a residue of nineteenth-century metaphysics but an essential component of a doctrine which, in the broadest sense possible, poses the problem of the real liberation of mankind.

This is why, in my view, it is necessary to reconfirm and develop materialism; in other words, on the one hand to reassert the need to found communism scientifically and on the other to reject all those conceptions of science which emerged from the idealist turn of the late nineteenth century. The reactionary character of this turn was perceived at the very beginning of this century, with admirable clear-sightedness, by Lenin. This book says too little about Lenin's philosophical thought and its relation to his political thought and action – though it dwells at greater length on a closely related problem, the evaluation of Engel's contribution to Marxism. But even from the little that is said here it will be clear that I do not share the facile anti-Leninism which is currently fashionable in large sections of the revolutionary left in the West. I do not share it either as far as the relation between party and class is concerned (a problem which, although it is certainly posed in very different terms today from those of *What is to be Done?* and the practice of the pre-Stalinist Bolshevik party, nevertheless cannot be resolved by a *fuite en avant,* by a denial of the necessity – however provisional and perilous – for a party), or with respect to the specifically philosophical part of Lenin's work. One aspect of Lenin's greatness consists precisely in having understood that voluntarism, subjectivism and the refusal of science may constitute a momentary 'revolutionary stimulus', but cannot be the basis of a solid revolutionary doctrine. This does not imply that we should await the mythical 'spontaneous collapse' of capitalism, or conceal behind a scholastic profession of Leninism an acceptance in essence of reformism, as the official communist parties do in the West. It does not mean that we should underestimate the indispensable role of the subjective element in the struggle against capitalism. What it does mean is understanding that the formation of these subjective conditions themselves (with all the problems which arise from the unequal development of revolutionary consciousness, from the difficult relationship between intellectuals and masses, etc.) is the result of objective processes, not of some miraculous act of will.

For the same reason, I cannot agree with that particular form of 'Western Maoism' which not merely, as is perfectly correct, stresses the extremely novel elements in the Maoist approach to the relationship between party and masses, but interprets Maoism in terms of a break with the ideas of Lenin – and ultimately those of Marx. This is simply the $n$th return of that subjectivism to which – incurably – the 'revolutionary with a degree in Arts' of our time always tends. The main problem, in my view, requiring clarification through further discussion is the following: even if one acknowledges (as one certainly should) that any inner-party democracy which does not extend to the relation between party and masses is insufficient, and therefore acknowledges a limitation in the conception and practice of the Bolsheviks, must one not at the same time recognize that no democracy is conceivable at the base which does not also reach the very highest levels of the party and – just for a start – imply, as a condition which though *absolutely not sufficient* is nonetheless necessary, that debates should be made public and their exact terms known?

Let me make it clear: if I consider it important to study this problem, this is not because I want to be in a position to pronounce a negative or limiting judgement on the Cultural Revolution (which occurred in the conditions permitted by a specific historical situation, and nevertheless represented a grandiose attempt to create a socialist 'new man', repudiating the road which carried the USSR to its Stalinist and post-Stalinist involution), but because it will assist discussion on the model of party and society which we set ourselves. It is in the context of this discussion that it will be necessary to re-examine the thought of a revolutionary who to this day, with grave injustice, is generally passed over in silence or simply excommunicated: Leon Trotsky. This thought too, of course is historically dated and conditioned; nor is it free from contradictory aspects. But it cannot be evaded, if one does not wish to continue a perpetual oscillation between spontaneism and an ecclesiastical conception of organization.

Once voluntarism and Platonist scientism (for a critique of the latter, see, in particular, 'Structuralism and its successors' below) have been rejected, the task is to go beyond the indications given by the Marxist classics, fundamental as they are, and to construct a 'theory of needs' which is not, as so often, reduced to a compromise between Marx and Freud, but which confronts on a wider basis the problem of the relation between nature and society. The accusation of 'biologism' or 'vulgar materialism' is, at this point, obvious and foreseen. If this label refers to an immediate reduction of the social to the biological and a failure to recognize the radically new contribution made by the appearance of labour and relations of production with respect to merely animal life, then I hope that these essays are already forearmed against any such error (see, in particular, pp. 63, 82, 102, 208 and 216 below). If, however, as is too frequently the case in the Western Marxism of our century, what is meant is denial of the conditioning which nature continues to exercise on man; relegation of the biological character of man to a kind of prehistoric prologue to humanity; refusal to acknowledge the relevance which certain biological data have in relation to the demand for *happiness* (a demand which remains fundamental to the struggle for communism); then these pages are deliberately 'vulgar materialist'. From this point of view, they take as their point of departure certain hedonist and pessimistic themes which were widespread in eighteenth-century thought and which reached their highest point in Leopardi. They thus represent the continuation of a line of thinking first adumbrated in my earlier book *Classicismo e illuminismo nell'Ottocento italiano*.

Nor has this line of thinking – any more than what I said earlier about Maoism – reached a definitive conclusion. At the start of the fifties, it was difficult to speak of pessimism with Italian Marxists. In almost all cases, they were too full of historicist faith in human progress, and tended too much – as a consequence of their Crocean origins – to ignore the relation between man and nature. From that climate, my initial and fragmentary Marxism-Leopardism (if I may so term it for brevity's sake) contracted an original flaw from which, perhaps, it is still striving to free itself. This resulted from the juxta-position of a historical and social optimism (communism as a now certain goal of human history, even if the price paid with Stalinism seemed even at that time excessive to many of us, despite our inability to see any alternative to Stalinism other than a social-democratic one) and a pessimism with respect to nature's oppression of man, which would continue to be a cause of unhappiness even in communist society.

Today the situation has changed. As a result of the increasingly monstrous developments of 'capitalist rationality' on the one hand, and the crisis of the world communist movement on the other, that tranquil faith in historical progress as a certain bearer of communism has vanished. Indeed, contemporary Marxism (especially through the agency of the thinkers of the Frankfurt school) has to a considerable degree taken on an apocalyptic hue. Certain Leopardian themes involving a critique of 'progress' and 'modern civilization' must be accorded greater attention than was done in that earlier period by Marxists. But in the face of the 'Adornian' interpretations of Leopardi which have already begun to appear and which are no doubt destined to develop further, it is necessary to recall that Leopardian pessimism, precisely because of the materialist and hedonistic basis which is most explicit in its final formulation, is immune from the Romantic and existentialist dross which gravely contaminates the thought of Horkheimer and Adorno – and even the later works of Marcuse, despite their far more political and secular character. Leopardi was able to work out for himself a complex relationship to the ideas of the Enlightenment (a relationship that involved criticizing the myth of progress, but strengthening hedonistic and materialist themes and hence refusing the Romantic restoration) which was far more correct than that in which the above-mentioned thinkers situate themselves. As far as the still crucial problem of what position to adopt vis-à-vis the Enlightenment is concerned, he is much more and much better than a precursor of the Frankfurt thinkers: indeed he helps to explain their limitations and provide a critique of them.

The real way to overcome the initial flaw in my approach, referred to above, does not consist either in dreams of escaping from science or in a confident belief that man has already won the struggle to dominate nature and need only make a communist use of his domination. It consists rather in an ever more accurate definition of the links between the struggle for communism and the struggle against nature – without, however, identifying the two in a simplistic way. This also requires a new type of scientist. Today, while the reactionary or the apolitical still predominate by far among physicists, biologists and doctors, a new type of revolutionary biologist or psychiatrist has begun increasingly to appear. These consider it their prime duty to reject their role as biologists or psychiatrists, and to resolve biology or psychiatry immediately into political action. This, in my view, is an incorrect attitude. Marxist scientists must certainly reject the corporative aspect of their own science and refuse the barrier between those who are experts in the field and those who are not. But Marxism would be impoverished if, instead of bringing to it their experience as researchers into nature, they helped to confine it within a merely 'humanist' ambit or reduce it to simple activism. If Norman Bethune, instead of using the 'lancet' as well as the 'sword', had limited himself to explaining to sick Chinese comrades that their illnesses were due to imperialism, if he had believed that a doctor can only become a true revolutionary by ceasing to concern himself with medicine, then his contribution to the revolutionary cause would have been a lesser one.

1970

# Introduction to the English edition

I think it is necessary to supplement my original foreword, translated above, with some brief clarifications for the English and American reader and a number of observations which the experience of the intervening years has suggested.

It is stated in this book, notably in the first essay written as long ago as 1966, that there is no danger in contemporary bourgeois culture of a revival of vulgar materialism. Consequently, my polemical fire is entirely directed against idealist infiltrations into Marxism. When, however, the comrades of *New Left Review* published the essay in question in NLR 85, they pointed out in the 'Themes' that there does indeed exist a danger from reactionary biologism in the ideology of the British and still more the North American bourgeoisie. Reading certain recent works has convinced me that they are right. The fields in which this new offensive of reactionary biologism is unfolding are basically three in number, closely interlinked.

First, there is a straightforward rebirth of racist theories. These present themselves as being more 'sophisticated' and up-to-date than the old colonialist racism of the late nineteenth century or Nazi and Fascist racial doctrines. They claim to base themselves on the most recent achievements of genetics. However, in reality, they reveal their ideological and non-scientific character precisely on the terrain of biology itself. Books such as Baker's *Race* and Eysenck's *Race, Intelligence and Education* are typical of this new trend, all the more insidious in that the brutal ferocity of National Socialism is now succeeded by an unctuous paternalism.[1] It is no fault of ours, these authors (especially Eysenck) seem to say, if the

[1] John R. Baker, *Race*, London 1974; H. J. Eysenck, *Race, Intelligence and Education*, London 1971.

unfortunate blacks have a lower IQ than ours; moreover, it does not justify our exterminating or oppressing them; it is simply a question of educating them to the extent that this is possible, and of treating them with the humanity owed even to inferior beings – without, however, seeking to deny the 'scientific truth' of their inferiority. It is really hard to say whether this hypocritical tone is more or less odious than a more patent racism. Certainly *today* it is more dangerous. Moreover, appearances notwithstanding, it is just as erroneous and inconsistent from a scientific point of view.[2]

Educational psychology is a second field in which we can see a revival of reactionary vulgar materialism, with the views of Skinner and others. It is highly instructive, in this respect, to read Oettinger's *Run Computer, Run*.[3] On the one hand, this book contains an impressive phenomonology – and condemnation – of pedagogic methods which replace the teacher by the 'teaching machine' and combine this dehumanization of teaching with an increasingly authoritarian technocratism. On the other hand, it is not clear whether Oettinger really wants to combat root and branch this depersonalization of the pupil, or simply to achieve the same objective with methods which are *outwardly* less abrasive, in order to provoke a lesser reaction from schoolchildren and teachers. It should be pointed out that these ideological aberrations have been facilitated by a theoretical error to which I have occasion to refer below in another context (see p. 167): the false identification of materialism with behaviourism.

Finally, a third field susceptible to similar ideological aberrations is animal ethology. But here the issue must be posed in very different terms. Animal ethology is a fascinating science, which has already made and will continue to make great advances in our understanding both of the animality of man and of the rudiments of 'culture' to be found in other animal species. We are indebted to

[2] This is very effectively demonstrated, for example, by Steven Rose, John Hambley and Jeff Haywood, in 'Science, Racism and Ideology', *The Socialist Register*, 1973, pp. 235–60. This article also demolishes the crude mystification involved in the concept of IQ. The only minor rectification I would suggest concerns the passage dealing with nineteenth-century racism (pp. 237ff.): the authors derive the colonialist and slave-owning racism of the last century too exclusively from social Darwinism, whereas in fact (as I suggest, though in too cursory a manner, on p. 50 n. 21 below, and as I intend to demonstrate more fully in a forthcoming study) evolutionism initially met with fierce hostility precisely from racist and colonialist biologists.

[3] Anthony G. Oettinger, *Run Computer, Run*, Cambridge Mass. 1969.

ethological research, moreover, for the knowledge that no other species presents, in so widespread and generalized a form as man, phenomena of aggressivity among members of the same species – nor, we may add, tendencies to destruction of the natural environment (the questions of inter-specific human aggressivity and ecology seem to be increasingly closely linked).[4] But both animal ethology and ecology become transmuted from sciences into reactionary ideologies if, as often occurs, they leap over or circle around the fundamental moment of the establishment of social relations of production, the division of society into classes, the class struggle and the new rhythm which the historical development of mankind has taken on since then and which has replaced that of biological evolution (remoulding even if not suppressing it). If all this is ignored, only two roads remain open and neither leads very far: either an immediate biologization of human history, which excludes any perspective of liberation for the oppressed class or creation of a classless society; or else an ingenuous (but not too ingenuous!) philanthropism which entrusts to scientists the solution of social problems. Moreover, it is worth adding – since this is too often forgotten even by comrades of the revolutionary left – that this oscillation between brutal ethics of force and naive philanthropism can be found not only in the positivists of the late nineteenth century and the biologists of today, but also in Freud: a subject to which I intend to return elsewhere.

However, while acknowledging that I underestimated the danger of this new wave of reactionary biologism, I think I can safely claim that there is nothing in the essays collected here which could give even the slightest justification or support, however involuntary, for its mystifications. I remain convinced that pseudo-materialism must be fought with a scientifically founded materialism, and not with a return to antediluvian forms of voluntaristic spiritualism, as is too often the case.[5]

---

[4] On ecology and the falsity of ecological planning entrusted to capitalists and their governments, see Dario Paccino, *L'imbroglio ecologico*, Turin 1972, and Jean Fallot, *Exploitation, pollution, guerre*, unpublished MS.

[5] A wrong way of combating reactionary biologistic ideas, in my opinion, is that followed by Chomsky (see pp. 199–209 below). It is surprising that an economist of Joan Robinson's merit should have been so easily convinced by it. Her *Freedom and Necessity: an Introduction to the Study of Society*, London 1970, especially so far as its later chapters are concerned, is a mélange of naive moralism, Chomskyism and 'anti-Marxist Maoism'.

I have read with great interest, and with far more agreement than disagreement, the interview with Lucio Colletti in NLR 86. I regard it as highly positive that the 'Enlightenment' Marxism of Colletti should be known outside Italy: acquaintance with it can do nothing but good to the Althusserian and Frankfurt Marxists. I admire greatly the intellectual and political courage with which Colletti criticizes and goes beyond certain of his previous positions. I share his judgement on Trotsky. I share his diagnosis that 'in the West, Marxism has become a purely cultural and academic phenomenon' and that 'if Marxists continue to remain arrested in epistemology and gnoseology, Marxism has effectively perished': a bitter diagnosis, expressed (as Colletti himself warns) in somewhat over-simplified terms, but one that is fundamentally correct.

However, I do not think that the objection Colletti makes to my book is correct, when he accuses it of revealing 'a type of naturalism that remains somewhat ingenuous'. What does materialism require in order to free itself from 'ingenuousness'? To recognize that man is a social being and, as such, has a 'second nature'? In that case, our disagreement would be based simply on a misunderstanding because, I repeat, I think it is very hard to find in what I have written hitherto any sign of a refusal to acknowledge this 'second nature'. The point which requires discussion is a different one. Has this second nature, this 'artificial terrain' (as Labriola called it), *entirely* absorbed within itself the *first* nature? Is it to be foreseen that such an absorption, if it has not yet taken place, might occur with the establishment of communist society? Is a conception of nature as mere object of human labour exhaustive, or must nature not also be seen as a force which conditions, consumes, destroys man and – in a long-term perspective – all humanity? Colletti says: 'The specificity of man as a natural being is to refer to nature in so far as he refers to other men, and to refer to other men in so far as he refers to nature.' He further adds: 'Otherwise, any discourse on man could equally be applied to ants or bees.' But Colletti does not say whether the specificity of man as a social being suppresses or includes within itself entirely his genericity as an animal. In my view, to reduce man to what is specific about him with respect to other animals is just as one-sided as to reduce him (as vulgar materialists do) to what he has in common with them. Marx and Engels are absolutely right to stress the specificity of man: but this emphasis is necessary because the most urgent task for humanity (and especially for the oppressed class, the proletariat) is the social revolution and the achievement of a classless society. For too long the ruling classes have attributed to 'nature' (i.e. to a secular version of the 'inscrutable decrees of Divine Providence') the iniquities and sufferings for which the organization of society is responsible – including certain 'natural' calamities (from floods and earthquakes to sicknesses and deaths) which would not have occurred, or would have been much less serious and premature, if the quest for maximum profit and the subordination of public powers to capitalist interests had not caused (and certainly not simply through technical 'incompetence') the most obvious measures of security and prevention to be neglected.

However, one-sidedness, in the long run, is always a source of weakness in polemics against the class enemy, who will take advantage of such exaggerated reduction of *all* the 'biological' to the 'social' to relaunch reactionary scientistic or out-and-out religious ideologies. Marxists themselves, faced with the problem of 'physical ill', have hitherto proposed two mutually contradictory replies. On the one hand, they have maintained that in communist society sickness, old age and death, although they will continue to exist, will no longer be *experienced* as ills. Man will be stripped of his own individualism and feel at one with society, eternal through it, strong with the strength that comes from identification with young healthy comrades even if, as a single individual, he himself is infirm and in pain. Antonio Labriola expressed the wish that 'in a future mankind made up of men almost transhumanized, the heroism of Baruch Spinoza may become a petty everyday virtue, and myths, poetry, metaphysics and religion may no longer encumber the field of consciousness'.[6] A noble wish. But it belongs to a pre-Marxist, a stoic and idealist way of overcoming physical ill, which instead of eliminating it in practice denies it in the realm of ideas. If such a line of argument was valid, it could equally well be applied to social ills: men 'almost transhumanized' would maintain the heroic imperturbability of Spinoza before the spectacle of slavery, poverty and exploitation as well – and would feel no need to suppress social ills *in reality*. It should be clear to everybody how alien such an ethics is to Marxism.

The second reply given is based on faith in scientific progress

[6] *Discorrendo di socialismo e di filosofia* (open letters to Sorel), Naples 1895, Letter VI.

when it is no longer at the service of one class, but rather of the classless society as a whole. Certainly, extraordinary progress is to be expected so far as man's physical and psychic health is concerned, not just as a result of the invention of new therapies, but above all through the establishment of a new environment in which physical ills are prevented before they need to be cured. And yet it remains very doubtful whether a radical elimination of the biological limits of the individual – and potentially of the human species as a whole – is in fact possible. (I continue, despite the smiles of many comrades, to believe that Engels was perfectly right not to consider futile the problem of the 'end of humanity', not merely as a result of catastrophes provoked by capitalist madness, but due to 'natural causes'.)

It is to further elucidate this problem of man's biological frailty that I consider it particularly important to study the thought of a poet and philosopher who is very little known outside Italy,[7] and who even in Italy is often more admired than understood: Giacomo Leopardi (1798–1837). And while I certainly would not claim to be able to give my English and American readers, in a few words, any adequate exposition of Leopardi's thought and poetry, I must provide at least a few essential points of clarification.

European culture of the last two centuries is full of pessimists, from Schopenhauer to Kierkegaard (and in many ways Nietzsche), from Horkheimer to Adorno; there are powerful pessimistic themes in Freud too, especially in the last phase of his thought, when Eros was joined by the death wish. If this book were to propose yet another marriage of Marxism and 'Frankfurt' pessimism, of existentialist or Freudian ancestry, it would no doubt appear far more in conformity with the present orientations of much of Western Marxism.

Why then go back to Leopardi? From a provincial and nationa-

---

[7] On knowledge of Leopardi in England, see G. Singh, *Leopardi e l'Inghilterra* (with an essay on the poet's fortunes in America), Florence 1969. See too the lively and intelligent book by John Whitfield, *Giacomo Leopardi*, Oxford 1954. Whitfield, however, though he polemicizes effectively against Croce's essay on Leopardi, totally ignores the 'new course' in Leopardi studies which by 1954 had already been under way for several years, with Cesare Luporini's 'Leopardi progressivo', in *Filosofi vecchi e nuovi*, Florence 1947, pp. 183ff., and Walter Binni's *La nuova poetica leopardiana*, Florence 1947. Moreover, Whitfield's 'vitalist' interpretation, although it represents an advance over the reduction of Leopardi to an 'idyllic' poet, nevertheless still fails to give adequate emphasis to Leopardian materialism.

listic desire to be able to say that Italy too has its pessimist, to be exhumed and inserted willy-nilly into Marxist culture? By no means. Leopardi's pessimism is radically different from the romantic and existentialist variety which characterizes the thinkers mentioned above (only in the case of Nietzsche should a *certain* distinction be made). These pessimists of *Mitteleuropa* all have an anti-materialist, anti-Enlightenment, anti-jacobin orientation; and all end up in, or at least tend towards, more or less explicitly religious positions. What is involved is for the most part a 'religion of the shadows', a mystical desire for annihilation, rather than a banal religion of consolation; but through their despair, however sincere, there peeps a faith in an 'other reality' to be attained not on this earth but in a metaphysical world.

The itinerary of Leopardi's thought – and of his poetry, which though never banally pedagogic, indeed one of the most purely lyrical in any language, was neverthelsss, like that of Lucretius, born of the courage of truth, recognizing the revivifying power of illusions without ever accepting to make use of them as an escape from harsh human reality – was quite different. Leopardi too felt deeply, from the morrow of Napoleon's fall, what has been called the 'historic disappointment' which followed the collapse of Enlightenment faith in progress. However, unlike the greater part of the Italian and European bourgeois intelligentsia, he neither slipped back into religious positions nor into a 'reasonable' form of Enlightened thought, suitably castrated and purged of its subversive charge. In a first phase (roughly from 1817 to 1823) he professed a kind of secular Rousseauism: it is necessary to return to nature (and to the Greek classics, not as academic models to be imitated in scholastic fashion, but because they are closer to us), to nature still virgin and uncorrupted; it is necessary to struggle against a false and mortificatory civilization which identifies 'modernity' and 'popular character' with Christianity, as the Romantics did. Christianity, for Leopardi, is not genuine primitiveness, inseparable from a proclamation of man's inherent need for happiness, but *barbarie,* i.e. corrupted civilization, which aggregates within itself the ills of the excess of civilization which preceded it (distance from nature, mortification of hedonistic impulses) and those of ignorance and superstition. This demand for a return to nature, against a society which claims to educate the spirit while neglecting the body, Leopardi maintained to the end. But, first spasmodically, later with increasing vigour, there developed in his thought another line, which derived not from Rousseau but rather from the Voltaire of the *Poème sur le désastre de Lisbonne*, from the more radical of the French materialists (especially d'Holbach and Volney), and from hedonistic pessimists such as Maupertuis and Pietro Verri. Especially from 1825 on, the most intransigent materialism, the denial of any notion of providence or anthropocentrism and the refusal of all myths, 'humanistic' as well as religious, were taken by Leopardi to their ultimate conclusions. These conclusions, moreover once the joy inherent in every conquest of truth and every liberation from prejudice passed, revealed far more clearly than in Leopardi's eighteenth-century precursors their pessimistic complexion. If nature is 'good' in contrast to a repressive and ascetic education or a progress which perpetually creates new false needs in us, not natural and not necessary, it nevertheless reveals itself to be a limit on the human need for happiness. 'Physical ill', as I mentioned earlier, cannot be ascribed solely to bad social arrangements; it has its zone of autonomous and invincible reality.

Hence, no romantic and existentialist pessimism, but a materialist pessimism. Also, however contradictory the notion may at first sight appear, an 'Enlightenment' pessimism. The later Leopardi, while he did not believe that the growth of knowledge would produce a growth of happiness (and in this sense he was not and never had been an Enlightenment thinker, at least in the more narrowly defined sense of the term), was neverthelsss convinced that it was necessary, against the Italian and European 'moderates', to develop a materialist and pessimistic culture *for all*. That it was necessary to cease 'pacifying' the masses with the opium of religion, and instead to found a *common* morality, based on the solidarity of all men in the struggle against nature: a struggle that is, in the final analysis, a desperate one, but which alone can make all men brothers, outside all paternalist hypocrisy and all the foolish pride of those who will not acknowledge that men 'are no more than a tiny part of the universe'.

I must make it clear that I have never sought to fabricate a Leopardi 'precursor of Marxism'. Leopardi had no clear idea of the antagonism between social classes, even to the limited extent that this was possible before Marx and Engels. His cultural ancestry was profoundly different from that of Marx: he neither had experience of English classical economics nor of Hegel and the Hegelian left; he did not even have any direct political experience. (Though the malice with which clericals and reactionaries denigrated and persecuted him and the efforts which liberals made to circumscribe his greatness by presenting him as simply an 'idyllic' poet, belated follower of a bad philosophy, show that the politically dangerous character of his thought – albeit indirect – was well understood.) Thus the point is not to seek in Leopardi what one can find much better in Marx, Engels and Lenin. It is to gain, through Leopardi, an awareness of certain aspects of the man-nature relationship which remain somewhat in the shadows in Marxism, and which nevertheless must be confronted – and confronted materialistically – if Marxism is to be not simply the replacement of one mode of production by another, but something far more ambitious: the achievement of the greatest possible degree of happiness (in the full, strong sense which this word had in the eighteenth century, when it denoted a need which, though it could never be fully satisfied, was nonetheless impossible to suppress).

Theories of human needs are once again beginning to be discussed by Marxists, and a pupil of Lukács, Agnes Heller, has recently devoted an extremely acute and moving essay to this subject.[8] However, she still seeks a solution in a 'Westernizing', anti-materialist Marxism. Her work too, therefore, despite its merits, confirms my conviction that it is necessary to go back to Leopardi. The same can be said with respect to Freudian Marxism. This again is on the one hand too crudely biologistic, on the other too concerned to detach psychology from neuro-physiology; the pessimism of the later Freud lays emphasis more on man's 'wickedness' than on his 'unhappiness'. From this point of view as well, Leopardian pessimism has its own specific characteristic: it is uncompromisingly hostile to misanthropy (apart from a few rare occasions which Leopardi soon transcends). 'My philosophy not only does not lead to misanthropy, as might appear to a superficial observer, and as many claim against it; instead, by its nature it excludes misanthropy . . . My philosophy renders nature guilty for everything and, totally exculpating men, diverts hatred – or at least lamentation – towards a higher source, towards the true

[8] 'Theory and Practice in Function of Human Needs', originally published in *Uj Iràs*, Budapest, April 1972; French translation in *Les Temps Modernes*, August–September 1974.

origin of the ills of the living.' In this reflection of 2 January 1829 (see *Zibaldone*, page 4428 of the manuscript) there is contained the germ of what, in more heroic tones and with greater awareness, Leopardi will say in one of his last poems, *La Ginestra*.[9]

Finally, a few words on some of the political implications of this book. It is the work of a comrade of the proletarian, anti-reformist left who formerly belonged to the left wing of the PSIUP and now – after the inglorious demise of that party, which had nevertheless aroused not unjustified hopes when it first emerged – is a member of the *Partito di Unità Proletaria per il Comunismo*.[10] The book has enjoyed a certain success in Italy; it can perhaps claim some small part of the credit if Marxists now speak more than they used to in terms of materialism. Its call for a return to materialism was seen by the author as an attempt to correct extremes of voluntarism and pragmatism which can hardly serve as a basis for refounding a communism at once 'scientific' and revolutionary. Hence the author's unconcealed sympathy for Engels, Lenin and Trotsky, who do not receive a very good press these days from the revolutionary left in the West, which prefers to go back to the early Lukács, Korsch or Rosa Luxemburg (interpreted in a voluntarist sense which does not correspond to her real thought). Indeed, in Italy the book has achieved more success with the traditional than with the revolutionary left – apart from comrades who are members or sympathizers of the Fourth International. This would not matter much as a fact in itself, since it could be attributed simply to the limitations and modest theoretical level of these essays of mine. But it seems to me that one can discern in this 'success' or 'lack of success' of my book, an indication of a more worrying fact. There is a danger of a constantly growing divergence between, on the one hand, a reformist (and not even seriously reformist) Marxism, which concedes a certain space to materialism provided it remains confined to high scientific culture and does not disturb the policy of collaboration with the Christian Democrat Party, and, on the other hand, a revolutionary Marxism which relegates Lenin to a position among the 'left Kautskyites'

[9] Both the section in question of the *Zibaldone* and *La Ginestra* are included in Giacomo Leopardi, *Tutte le opere*, W. Binni and E. Ghidetti (ed.), Florence 1969, II, p. 1199, and I, p. 43.

[10] Party formed in 1974 through a fusion of the PDUP (part of the PSIUP which refused to liquidate itself into the Communist Party) and the *Il Manifesto* group.

and deludes itself, as happened in the twenties, that idealism and voluntarism, ideologies of an aggressive bourgeoisie or (at best) residues of utopian socialism, can serve as revolutionary stimulants. The attacks which some militants of the revolutionary left have made on Geymonat and his school are inspired by an idealist activism which would not have displeased Giovanni Gentile. Geymonat's school in its turn, however, risks being satisfied with admiring Lenin as the world's best epistemologist, while casting Lenin the revolutionary into the shade. Moreover, those followers of Geymonat who are members of the various 'Marxist-Leninist' groups seem to content themselves with taking their distance from Stalinism on a purely cultural plane, while swallowing on the political plane the idea of a 'continuity' between Lenin and Stalin – an idea which represents one of the crudest mystifications current today.

The discussion has undoubtedly been rendered more difficult and confused by the attitude of much of the revolutionary left in Europe towards People's China. Unquestionably, a revolutionary militant faced with a choice between the USSR and China must unhesitatingly opt for the latter. The Soviet Union is a static reality today – and will remain such for a future which, although it will certainly not be eternal, will last for a span of time which cannot at present be predicted. It can and indeed must be preferred to capitalist states; it is essential to reject those simplistic and false theories according to which capitalism has been, or is in the process of being, restored there. But it no longer constitutes a point of reference for the revolutionary forces of the world. It is not a reality *moving towards communism*. The grave aspects of authoritarianism, suffocation of all freedom of discussion and anti-egalitarianism which continue to characterize it can no longer be considered mere 'residues' of Stalinism on the way to being eliminated; they must be seen instead as proof of a bureaucratic involution of which so-called de-Stalinization only eliminated certain of the more brutal and tyrannical manifestations, not the substance.

China is a reality still in movement. The desire not to come to the same end as the USSR, to oppose bureaucratic sclerosis, to create a communist democracy at the base, to develop elements of egalitarianism, is still alive and open to new developments; indeed, a great deal has not remained a mere desire, it has been accomplished. However, the attitude of much of the revolutionary left in the

West to events in China has been one of mystical and acritical identification, or of sophistical justificationism, or (when certain facts have been clearly unjustifiable) of over-prudent reticence. It is correct to praise the democracy at the base which has continued to prevail in the Chinese agrarian communes and factories, despite some very harsh trials. But there has been a refusal to see that democracy at the base only develops to the full and creates a real guarantee against relapses into authoritarianism if it rises from the base to involve the upper levels of Party and State as well. During the Cultural Revolution, byzantine distinctions were made with respect to the concept of 'cult of personality', in order to prove that it could in no way be applied to the clamorous exaltation of 'Mao Tse-tung thought'. The question was not posed whether, whatever name one gives it, the belief that the communist 'new man' can arise from a study of one man's thought, reduced to a collection of maxims and memorable sayings mostly dating from times long past, is not profoundly anti-Marxist. Nor was the question posed whether the publication of leadership debates is not a necessary condition for the development of a real discussion at the base, not only in China but throughout the international proletariat. It is very likely that Liu Shao-chi did represent a rightist, 'economistic' tendency, oriented towards a repetition of the errors made in the USSR; but who has ever been able to read an article by Liu, since the attacks on him began? It is very likely that Lin Piao – to judge by his writings and speeches – did contribute to giving the Cultural Revolution that mystical, heavily pedagogic character which constituted one of its most negative aspects; but it certainly would not have been excessive to expect him to be defeated *politically,* for what his real political positions were. Instead, we had on the one hand moral accusations which explain nothing ('plot', 'treachery' and so on), on the other the identification of Lin Piao 'right disguised as left' with his political adversary Liu – or even with Confucius! Both techniques are, it must be said, typically Stalinist: political disagreement, before it can even be expressed by *both* sides in the debate and discussed at the base, is immediately reduced to a phenomenon of criminality and desertion to the class enemy; and the 'opposed extremisms', right and left, are as immediately identified with one another, since left deviations not only have to be criticized, they cannot in the last resort even exist, they must always be a dishonest provocational form of the right deviation.

No one should be mythicized, not even Lenin. However, I think it is necessary to say that, so far as inner-party democracy is concerned, it was Leninism which – although not immune from criticism (under-estimation of the function of the soviets and their dialectical relationship with the party) – has hitherto attained the highest level. Maoism probably represents a progress so far as the relationship between party and masses is concerned: not, I repeat, with respect to democracy at the higher levels. Moreover, we cannot consider irrelevant what takes place at the higher levels of Party and State, so long as these institutions exist. We must aim, as we well know, at their elimination; but it would be too easy to 'consider them eliminated' in order to avoid a distasteful discussion. It would also be too easy to entrench oneself behind the assertion (indubitably true as it is) that we know too little about what goes on at the top in China. Precisely the fact that the Chinese leadership lets us know so little – and the same goes for their own base, even when there are certainly no security considerations concerning either the class enemy within or imperialist aggression without to justify such reticence – is a demonstration of poor communism and poor internationalism.

It does not escape me that the excessive reluctance of comrades of the revolutionary left in the West to criticize aspects of China's internal and external policy involves a 'moral question'. Does someone who, though claiming to be a sincere revolutionary, has not yet been able to make the revolution have the right to criticize those who have been able to do so, in such difficult conditions, with such admirable heroism, and who now have to confront the (in some ways even more arduous) problems involved in constructing a socialist society and introducing, even at the present stage, ever greater elements of communism? Does the Western proletariat, which when the revolution comes will have the best possible chance of avoiding the objective dangers of Stalinism, have the right, without making the revolution, to criticize that quota of 'obligatory Stalinism' which is inherent in the construction of socialism in a single backward country? The question is indeed a serious one; and the less one has contributed in action to the struggle against capitalism, the more seriously one should take it. But democracy at the base is inseparable from the right – of even the least intelligent, active and courageous comrades – to raise objections and express doubts. These comrades in their turn may be criticized, even severely, for their inadequate contribution to the struggle; but one cannot respond to their objections with sophistries, since this *damages the whole movement*.

Materialism also means respect for the truth, refusal to substitute moralistic pseudo-explanations of disagreements and political conflicts for political and social explanations. For this reason too, while conceding nothing to false bourgeois and reformist democracy, problems which interest the entire world proletarian movement must be treated with greater frankness.

I have dedicated these essays to Luciano Della Mea, both because they essentially originated in a continuous dialogue with him (a dialogue which did not abate in the slightest when we happened to become members of different political organizations) and because very few militants on the revolutionary left, I think, have felt with the same intensity as he has always done the need for a democracy at the base that is really practised – rather than merely theorized, with an intellectual aristocratism which ends up by constituting its involuntary negation.

This book is indebted to many other friends for ideas and stimulation: to Antonio La Penna, who just as he became a Marxist before I did, so too felt dissatisfied before I did with generic and ambiguous appeals to 'historicism' and 'humanism'; to Mario Mirri, who was already speaking of the irreducibility of science to ideology at a time when Italian Marxism had not yet accepted this distinction (and without the theoreticist distortions by which Althusser spoiled it, in the very act of so meritoriously re-emphasizing it); to Sergio Landucci, whose historiographical and theoretical comments helped me to correct in part the first essay and to write the others. More recently, I have been greatly assisted by discussions with Luca Baranelli, Franco Belgrado, Marcello Buiatti, Giuseppe Giordani, Romano Luperini, Carlo Alberto Madrignani, Pierluigi Tedeschi and others referred to in the course of the book. The fact that the first three essays were published in a preliminary version and stimulated a whole debate was due to the friendship of Piergiorgio Bellocchio and Grazia Cherchi, the moving spirits of a review – *Quaderni Piacentini* – which represents the free-est and liveliest meeting-ground for the various groups of the revolutionary left in Italy. For the fact that the essays were republished as a book, I must once again thank Lanfranco Caretti, who wanted this book and in particular gave me extremely valuable suggestions for the fourth essay.

In preparing the second Italian edition on which this translation is based, I was helped, apart from many of those already mentioned above, by Perry Anderson, Furio Cerutti, Attilio Chitarin, Tullio de Mauro, Giulio Lepschy, Vittorio Rossi and Ernesto Carletti. I must also express my gratitude to Larry Garner, who diverted valuable time from his work on Gramsci to produce this meticulous translation.

# Considerations on Materialism

Perhaps the sole characteristic common to virtually all contemporary varieties of Western Marxism is their concern to defend themselves against the accusation of materialism. Gramscian or Togliattian Marxists, Hegelian-Existentialist Marxists, Neo-Positivizing Marxists, Freudian or Structuralist Marxists, despite the profound dissensions which otherwise divide them, are at one in rejecting all suspicion of collusion with 'vulgar' or 'mechanical' materialism; and they do so with such zeal as to cast out, together with mechanism or vulgarity, materialism *tout court*. Much of the polemical debate between various Marxist groups turns precisely on the selection of the most effective safeguard against the danger of falling into vulgar materialism: whether this safeguard is to be the dialectic or historicism, an appeal to Marxist humanism or an association of Marxism with an empirio-critical or pragmatist or Platonist epistemology.

The present division within the workers' movement of the West between a majority that conceives socialism as the integration of the working class into the capitalist system, and a minority, or rather a number of minorities, which pose in various ways the task of world socialist revolution, is much clearer today than it was ten years ago. But if contemporary reformists are anti-materialist, because of the understandable influence of bourgeois culture on them, it cannot be said that the new levy of revolutionary Marxists which has emerged since 1960 has restored any emphasis on materialism. These new revolutionary groups are indubitably hostile to *certain* forms of idealist Marxism – in Italy, especially to the Gramscian form; but their sympathies seem to oscillate between a Hegelian Marxism with strong existentialist overtones, and a pragmatist scientism. This is visible even in their language, which is frequently inaccessible to comrades at the base for two reasons: on the one hand an excess of Hegelian philosophical notions, on the other, an excess of neo-positivist technicism. Often one and the same article in *Quaderni Rossi* or *Classe Operaia*[1] or one of the journals descended from them would contain manifest elements of both. It is probable that the revolutionaries of the sixties feared that any accentuation of materialism might lead to a relaxation of voluntarist tension, a return to *attentiste* expectation of the 'spontaneous collapse' of capitalism, and also a loss of contact with modern scientific thought, which is in such large measure hostile to the old materialism of the nineteenth century.

This anti-materialism is not, in fact a new phenomenon in revolutionary thought in the West. In the period after the First World War, Leninists in Germany and Italy professed, in philosophy, ideas very different from those of Lenin: for them, the main enemy in the sphere of philosophy was not idealism, but materialism, which they considered a positivist and social-democratic deformation of the thought of Marx. Whereas Lenin was already fighting in 1908 against the triumphant *new* bourgeois ideology of reborn idealism, the Leninists of the twenties and thirties were seeking to bring Marxism up to date with the development of idealism, by accepting a formulation of gnoseological problems and of relations between structure and superstructure that was in step with the contemporary bourgeois ideologies: Karl Korsch's *Marxism and Philosophy* is one of the clearest expressions of this orientation. Their philosophy was thereby defined as a radicalism of the intelligentsia rather than a doctrine of the revolutionary proletariat.

Thus today not even the antithesis between reform and revolution coincides on the philosophical plane with the antinomy between idealism and materialism. On the contrary, in Western Europe, both political camps are situated within the ambit of anti-materialism. It is significant that in a long debate between Marxist philosophers in Italy that occurred in 1962 in the pages of *Rinascita*, the only point on which all contending parties were in agreement from the outset was the need to emancipate Marxism from the

---

[1] Italian Marxist journals of the sixties, which have since ceased publication. (NLB).

'incrustations of vulgar materialism'.[2] It should be added that the initiator of this discussion, Cesare Luporini, had the year before formulated a limpid and rigorous materialist position in his essay *Verità e Libertà*, conspicuous for its originality and courage in the philosophical panorama of the last few decades.[3] Subsequently, however, the pressure to bring Marxism up to date and enrich it intellectually (in other words to make contact with dominant currents in Western culture, such as psychoanalysis and structuralism) prevailed over him, so that he no longer persisted in that direction.

It is true that in themselves polemics against vulgar materialism in no way constitute an idealist deviation from Marxism, but rather, as is well known, form part of the original nucleus of its doctrine. But the strange thing is that the insistence on this polemic has for many decades now no longer corresponded to any important influence or even effective presence in the West of vulgar materialism, which has never recovered from the crisis it underwent at the end of the last century. Today the struggle within bourgeois culture is – to put it very schematically – between two idealisms: a historicist and humanist idealism and an empirio-criticist and pragmatic idealism. The 'two cultures' so much bruited are – broadly speaking – indentifiable with these two idealisms. The victory of the second is the victory of modern technocracy over the antiquated humanism characteristic of backward bourgeois classes. Humanism has, however, in the countries of advanced capitalism been subordinated but not destroyed, since its services are to a certain extent still necessary. For every exploiting class always needs a discourse on 'spiritual values': even the old positivism of the nineteenth century left room for agnostic and religious escape, and the same phenomenon is repeated today in contemporary American philosophy, with the spiritualist overtures of many pragmatists, methodologists and more or less 'critical' naturalists.[4]

---

[2] This debate is now reprinted in Franco Cassano, *Marxismo e Filosofia in Italia*, Bari 1972. (NLB).

[3] In the symposium of the same title, containing the reports to the XVIII Congress of the Italian Philosophical Society, Palermo 1960, pp. 139ff., and now included in C. Luporini *Dialettica e materialismo*, Rome 1974, pp. 77ff.

[4] See Sergio Landucci, 'Metodologismo e agnosticismo', in *Belfagor*, 1961, pp. 637–40. How little American 'critical naturalism' is naturalist is evident from the pertinent account by G. de Crescenzo, *P. Romanell e l'Odierno Naturalismo Statunitense*, Florence 1966.

Thus the diagnosis which underlay Lenin's determination to write *Materialism and Empiriocriticism* still seems to retain its validity today: a situation of disequilibrium dominated by idealism, dictating a need to direct polemical attack more against idealism than against vulgar materialism. Instead, contemporary Marxism in the West seems intent above all on demonstrating to itself and to its adversaries that it is not 'crude'. Under the ensign of anti-materialism (together with a repudiation of some of the most backward metaphysical positions) a philosophical ecumene is now emerging, in which Marxists, Neopositivists, modernized Existentialists, and Catholics disposed to dialogue, converge and can often be confused.

This ostensible self-purification of Marxism is typically concretized and symbolized by a devaluation of Engels, who for many holds prime responsibility for the decline of Marxism from its true philosophical heights to the depths of a 'popular philosophy'. Because of its dramatically contradictory character (which deserves a more profound study), Engel's work is particularly liable to attack from both main contemporary Marxist currents, Hegelian and empirio-pragmatist. On the one hand, Engels was much more sensible than Marx of the necessity to come to terms with the natural sciences, to link 'historical' materialism (in the human sciences) to physical and biological materialism – all the more so, at a time when Darwin had finally opened the way to an historical understanding of nature itself. On the other hand, in his effort to reject any reduction of Marxism to a banal evolutionism or eclectic positivism, Engels undertook to apply the Hegelian dialectic to the sciences with a certain punctilio, and to translate phenomena of physics or biology into the language of the 'negation of the negation' and the 'conversion of quantity into quality'. It is for this reason that he can be accused in turn of archaic Hegelianism and contamination by positivism, abandonment of the great German philosophical tradition and neglect of the pragmatist hints in the *Theses on Feuerbach*, scientism and a retrogressive and superficial scientific culture.

It might be argued that polemics against the deformations of vulgar materialism are justified by the need to struggle against Stalinist dogmatism and to restore its free creative force to Marxism. It is true that in Stalin's opuscule *On Dialectical and Historical Materialism*, which became the most widely diffused elementary text on Marxism, not merely in the USSR but throughout the world communist movement, it is easy to find extremely schematic and crude assertions, especially as regards relations between structure and superstructure. But a crude conception and exposition of Marxism does not necessarily mean an accentuation of its materialist aspect. In fact, Stalin's brochure, as well as his other writings, lack any specific interest in the natural sciences or the relationship between man and nature; there is a complete absence of any emphasis on the 'passive side' of consciousness, on the way in which man is conditioned by his own physical structure and the natural environment. Indeed, certain of Stalin's positions, such as his patronage of Lysenko, or his very theory of socialism and even communism in one country, can well be defined as idealist and voluntarist. It is no mistake that critics have spoken of 'Stalinist subjectivism'. The so-called dogmatism of Stalin and his followers did not in reality consist of a coherent materialist position, but rather of a 'politicization' (in the pejorative sense) of Marxist theory – in other words an immediate reduction not only of science to ideology, but of ideology itself to an instrument of propaganda and petty justification of adventitious political positions, whereby the most abrupt changes of policy were in each case legitimated with pseudo-theoretical arguments and presented as congruent with the most orthodox Marxism.[5]

But if it is not the case that Stalinism involved any accentuation of the materialist aspect of Marxism, it is nevertheless true that destalinization – because of the confused way in which it was prosecuted and the potentially social-democratic character which it all too soon acquired – led to a reflorescence of 'Westernizing' tendencies in the Communist countries as well. The stupid persecution to which students of formal logic, physics or psychoanalysis were subjected in the Stalinist era has created a strong reaction of sympathy today, not only towards the scientific achievements of these disciplines, but also towards the ideological conceptions to which they have given rise in the West. Robert Havemann's lectures, *Dialectics without Dogma,* are very significant

---

[5] This aspect of Stalinism was first analyzed by Trotsky: see especially *The Revolution Betrayed,* New York 1965, pp. 32–5. Note also Lukács's comments in *Nuovi Argomenti* No. 57–8, July–October 1962, pp. 120–4.

in this respect.[6] This courageous Communist scholar from East Germany was certainly right to lay claim, against an incompetent and dogmatic party bureaucracy, to freedom of expression and of scientific research. But it cannot be overlooked that what Havemann calls 'mechanical materialism' is simply *any* materialism whatsoever, and that he tends to give a veneer of twentieth-century science to antiquated spiritualist concepts.

But what are we to understand by materialism? Moreover, how is materialism to escape from the accusation of itself being a metaphysic too, and one of the most naïve ones at that?

By materialism we understand above all acknowledgement of the priority of nature over 'mind', or if you like, of the physical level over the biological level, and of the biological level over the socio-economic and cultural level; both in the sense of chronological priority (the very long time which supervened before life appeared on earth, and between the origin of life and the origin of man), and in the sense of the conditioning which nature *still* exercises on man and will continue to exercise at least for the foreseeable future. Cognitively, therefore, the materialist maintains that experience cannot be reduced either to a production of reality by a subject (however such production is conceived) or to a reciprocal implication of subject and object. We cannot, in other words, deny or evade the element of passivity in experience: the external situation which we do not create but which imposes itself on us. Nor can we in any way reabsorb this external datum by making it a mere negative moment in the activity of the subject, or by making both the subject and the object mere moments, distinguishable only in abstraction, of a single effective reality constituted by experience.

This emphasis on the passive element in experience certainly does not claim to be a theory of knowledge – something which in any case can be constructed only by experimental research on the physiology of the brain and the sense organs, and not by merely conceptual or philosophical exercises. But it is the preliminary condition for any theory of knowledge which is not content with verbalistic and illusory solutions.

This implies a polemical position towards a major part of modern

[6] For Havemann's 'Westernizing' political conceptions – which, in my view, are not unrelated to his philosophical and scientific ideas – see Cesare Cases, in *Quaderni Piacentini* No. 27, June 1966, pp. 15ff.

philosophy, which has entangled and exhausted itself in the setting up of 'epistemological traps' to catch and tame the external datum, in order to make it something which exists solely as a function of the activity of the subject. It is important to realize that epistemology has undergone such an enormous (and sophistical) development in modern thought because it has not only corresponded to the need to understand how knowledge arises, but has been charged with the task of founding the absolute liberty of man, by eliminating everything which commonly seems to restrict that freedom. Whether this task has been executed in the direction of a romantic idealism of the absolute ego, or in that of a critical empiricism, whether the subject-object relation is conceived as relation of creation, or scission within an original unity, or reciprocal action or 'transaction', or any other variant, certainly implies a whole series of important differences in cultural formation and social ambience, and explains the fierce polemics of both past and present among the proponents of these various idealisms. It does not, however, alter their common character as illusions. It should be added that the attacks on epistemologism by pragmatists and actualists of the left also serve, indeed in exasperated form, the same purpose of 'annihilating external reality' and founding human freedom which generated epistemologism itself. They thus form a type of polemic which irom our point of view can be situated within the general orientation that we hold must be rejected.

It will be said that if the idealism of the absolute ego is the expression of a culture strongly imbued with romantic and anti-scientific irrationalism, empirio-criticist and pragmatist positions arose precisely from reflections on science, and that it is therefore illegitimate to counterpose a materialism based on the sciences of a century ago, or even on naïve common sense, to these conceptions as 'more scientific'.

But it is on this very point that mistakes are particularly easy to make. It is true that scientific knowledge is the only exact and rigorous form of knowledge. But if philosophy displaces all its attention from the results and objects of scientific research to the research as such, and if, omitting to consider man's condition in the world as it is established by the *results* of scientific research, it confines itself to a methodology of the activity of the scientist, then it relapses into idealism, because it then suggests that there is only one reality – not nature, but man the investigator of nature and constructor of his *own* science. The results of scientific research teach us that man occupies a marginal position in the universe; that for a very long time life did not exist on earth, and that its origin depended on very special conditions; that human thought is conditioned by determinate anatomical and physiological structures, and is clouded or impeded by determinate pathological alterations of these; and so on. But let us consider these results as mere contents of our thoughts as it cogitates or of our activity as it experiments and modifies nature, let us emphasize that they do not exist outside our thought and our activity, and the trick is done: external reality has been conjured away, and not by an antiquated humanism hostile to science, but instead with all the blessings of science and of modernity!

The moment philosophy is reduced without residue to epistemology or methodology (in the more or less openly subjective sense mentioned above), it becomes simply narcissistic theorization of the activity of the scientist – who, producing phenomena in order to understand them, conceptually developing and systematizing the results of his experiments, deludes himself into thinking that he is the 'legislator of nature'. It then becomes, not the systematization of everything that science has taught and is teaching us about man and the world, but the sectoral, corporative expression of a restricted category of man: scientists, whose situation and activity are improperly assumed to be paradigms of the human condition in general. Philosophy thereby loses not merely the imaginary 'universality' of the metaphysical tradition, but also that minimum of general or global outlook to which it can never by definition cease to aspire.

From this viewpoint neither the vaunted 'unification of the sciences', nor even closer junctures between knowledge and action or the sciences of nature and the techniques of transforming nature, are sufficient to avoid the sectoralism just discussed, for it is a sectoralism *a parte subiecti*. A philosophy which is, even in the broadest and most comprehensive sense, a methodology of human *action*, always runs the risk of evading or underestimating that which is passivity and external conditioning in the human condition.

There are certainly not lacking in contemporary thought serious currents of opposition to methodologism and neopositivism, critical of their agnostic and idealist bias. Unfortunately, such opponents, while correctly re-emphasizing once again the necessity of a

*Weltanschauung*, nevertheless remain tied to a cultural formation which is indifferent if not hostile to science. They are in general Hegelians (or Marxists for whom Marx did no more than render explicit what was already in Hegel) : that is, exponents of a system whose conception of nature was regressive at birth (think of the Hegelian idea of nature as an eternal circle, by comparison with Kant's openness towards evolutionism), and of a dialectical method whose only valid function today is a polemic riposte to philosophies which deny historicity or interpret it in a key of anti-revolutionary gradualism – but which provides no positive deeper insight into the real ways in which the historicity of nature and of man are to be explained. The force and fascination of Hegelian Marxism lie in its anti-eclecticism, its refusal to follow the latest philosophical or scientific fashion (though certain contaminations between Hegelianism, existentialism and psycho-analysis qualify this trait). But the price paid for this avoidance of eclecticism is an ostentatious archaism, a devaluation not only of how much is new in Marxism by comparison with Hegel, but also of how much in pre-Hegelian culture, and in particular in the Enlightenment, is more advanced than Hegel.

Thus Hegelians and methodologists both elude, in different ways, the need for a philosophy that is a vision of the world based on the results of the sciences : the former, since they substantially identify the world and history with the human world and human history, the latter since they consider science formalistically and thus recede into subjectivism.

It is nevertheless necessary to note that among the various sciences of nature there are some more and some less exposed to the errors of idealism. If physics has played a primary role as an incubator of idealism and of methodologism in the twentieth century (thanks to the ambiguity of the concept of experience), the biological sciences have continued to show themselves much more tenaciously materialist, and particularly the historical sciences of nature, from geology to paleontology to evolutionary biology, which pose directly the problem of the late appearance of man on earth and hence of the very long period of time during which there existed – to put it with deliberate and appropriate crudity – object without subject. It is not for nothing that these sciences have always been the *bête noire* of all idealism and all pragmatism : nor that the idealist reaction which started in the late nineteenth century and still persists today has always made one of its principal objectives a struggle against Darwin, or at least a neutralization of Darwinism.

This neutralization has been attempted in two different ways. On the one hand, the classical subjectivist sophism has been applied to the historical sciences of nature in their turn: nature before man (or after the future disappearance of the human species) is, it is said, merely a construction of our science: to attribute ontological reality to it would be metaphysics; accordingly, Darwinism yes, but a purely 'methodological' Darwinism! The only snag is that this argument, if it proved anything, would prove too much: it is not, in fact, possible to deny ontological reality to the history of nature without denying it also to the whole of the past – human or extra-human, close or remote – and thus also to the whole of reality outside oneself, including other human beings. From an idealist point of view, Gentile was perfectly right to observe that the admission of any kind of reality (even human, even 'spiritual') outside the thinking mind is naturalism. The value of Gentile's actualism lay precisely in the consistency with which it developed the premises of idealism to their extreme limit and so reduced them to absurdity. If Croce thus had good reason to draw back from the identification of history with historiography, *res gestae* with *historia rerum gestarum*, he was nevertheless manifestly wrong not to see that the rejection of that identification implied the rejection of all idealism. Now if *res gestae* are distinct from *historia rerum gestarum*, there is in fact no reason to believe in the battle of Waterloo as something which 'really happened', while denying the same credence to the formation of the solar system or to any other cosmic episode preceding the origin of man. 'Purely methodological' Darwinism is thus revealed as fraudulent. Nor are attempts at relationist or 'transactionist' solutions ('experience is in nature *but also* nature is in experience')[7] really capable of eliminating these errors. The two propositions linked by *but also* are both true, but at quite different levels of fundamental significance and determination. The 'mirror' theory of knowledge, though certainly inadequate, has at least the merit of expressing, if only metaphorically, this discrepancy: the mirror exists in a determinate ambience and the image of this ambience exists 'in the mirror', but the two terms

[7] See, for example, A. Visalberghi, *Esperienza e Valutazione*, Florence 1966, chaps. I and VI.

do not have the same degree of dependence on each other: the circle between them is not perfect.

The other axis of reaction to Darwinism lay in various attempts to attribute an objective spirituality to nature, without entering into too obvious conflict with the results of modern science, and even seeking in twentieth-century science grounds for rehabilitating spiritualism, in counterposition to the 'antiquated' materialist science of the nineteenth century. The 'flat' evolutionism of the nineteenth century was rejected in the name of an evolutionism 'by leaps' corresponding to the legitimate acknowledgement of rhythms of development in the evolution of natural organisms (let alone of human society) very different from the smooth and gradual tempo which Spencer and others claimed to be inevitable on the political and social planes too. But this criticism soon fell into miraculist conceptions of evolution, presenting the 'leap' as an absolute unshackling of the superior from the inferior, a suppression of all conditioning. Bergson's *Evolution Créatrice,* Sorel's social developments of it, and Bergson's own final religious involution are the clearest examples of this false response, not revolutionary but adventurist, to social Darwinism.

At the same time, a polemic against the 'reductionist fallacy' (the hobby-horse of Dewey and his followers) took up the defence of the autonomy of the various 'levels' – physical, biological, social and so on. It is true that the hasty and clumsy monism of a Haeckel rendered a defence of the *relative* autonomy of the higher levels from the lower ones necessary. But along this road it proved a short step, from Boutroux[8] onwards, to making this autonomy into an absolute, and thence to restoring vitalism in biology (it is enough to recall the reactionary use made at the beginning of the twentieth century of Mendel's and Morgan's genetics against Darwinism), and spiritualism in the human sciences. Finally, quantum mechanics and the indeterminacy principle were also to be used to give an up-to-date scientific stamp to 'free will' once again, as if indeterminacy and freedom of self-determination were the same thing, or Heisenberg's principle could serve to cancel the conditioning of so-called free will by pathological states of the human organism, heredity, environment, and social or

---

[8] Emile Boutroux (1845–1921): French spiritualist philosopher of 'contingency'. (NLB).

cultural formation.[9]

All these attempts to neutralize the materialist thrust of the historical sciences of nature only confirm by their sophistical character the efficacy of this thrust itself. It remains, however, to be asked whether the materialist polemic which we have so far sought to develop is directed only against idealist 'deviations' from Marxism, or calls in question some aspects of Marxism itself, above all concerning the relationship between man and nature.

The very uncertainty which has always existed within the camp of Marxism as to the way in which materialism should be understood, and the ease with which versions of Marxism have prevailed that have attenuated or directly denied its materialist character, are undoubtedly due to the influences of bourgeois culture (as we have sought, albeit rather rapidly, to demonstrate). But I also believe that they have found a propitious terrain because of a lack of clarity that goes right back to the origin of Marxist theory and was perhaps never completely overcome even in Marx's mature thought.

Marxism was born as an affirmation of the *decisive primacy* of the socio-economic level over juridical, political and cultural phenomena, and as an affirmation of the historicity of the economy. It might be said that in the expression 'historical materialism', the noun was a polemic against Hegel and a whole philosophical tradition which affirmed the primacy of the spirit over any economic structure, whereas the adjective was a polemic against Feuerbach and English classical economics, in short against any statically naturalist conception of human society.

If a critique of anthropocentrism and an emphasis on the conditioning of man by nature are considered essential to materialism, it must be said that Marxism, especially in its first phase (up to and including *The German Ideology*) is not materialism proper. Physical and biological nature is certainly not denied by Marx,

9 It is astonishing to note that even serious philosophers calmly identify *freedom* (which, if it is not understood mythologically, means a capacity for planning, and subordinating means to ends) with *indeterminacy*, merely because both are commonly counterposed to causal determinism. 'Me-ti said: physics has just declared that the fundamental particles are unpredictable; their movements cannot be foreseen. They seem to be individuals, endowed with free wills. But individuals are not endowed with free will. Their movements are difficult to predict, or cannot be predicted, only because there are too many determinations, not because there are none.' Brecht, *Me-Ti: Buch der Wendungen*, Frankfurt 1965.

but it constitutes more a prehistoric antecedent to human history than a reality which still limits and conditions man. From the time when man started to labour and to produce, it appears that he enters into relationship with nature (according to a famous passage in *The German Ideology*) only through work. This was to relapse into a pragmatic conception of the relationship between man and nature which illegitimately annuls the 'passive side' of this relationship itself; to pass over in silence the fact that man enters into relation with nature also through heredity and, even more, through the innumerable other influences of the natural environment on his body and hence on his intellectual, moral and psychological personality. To deny all this by affixing the label of positivism or of vulgar materialism to it is not possible, whether for the fundamental reason that facts do not allow themselves be vanquished by labels or because, even historically, materialism has not been a privilege or a blemish only of the positivist age (among positivists, indeed, it has been a minority position), but characterized a whole strand of the eighteenth-century Enlightenment (not to speak of earlier philosophical positions, or later ones such as those of Leopardi or Feuerbach) which cannot be liquidated with a couple of polemic strokes.

Marx in his maturity – who admired Darwin and wanted to dedicate the second volume of *Capital* to him, who declared in the preface to *Capital* itself that he 'viewed the evolution of the economic formation of society as a process of natural history' – was certainly much more materialist than the Marx of the *Theses on Feuerbach*. But the gigantic labour to which he had dedicated himself in the field of political economy did not permit him to develop a new conception of the relation between man and nature which would fully replace that outlined in his youthful writings.

Even more than by Marx – though evidently not in dissent from him – the need for the construction of a materialism which was not purely socio-economic but also 'natural' was felt by Engels, and this was a great merit of his. The impulse to deepen their materialism in this way came not only from the general philosophical and scientific climate of the second half of the nineteenth century, but more specifically from the radical change which Darwinism introduced in the natural sciences, by its definitive demonstration (against the concept of nature accepted by Hegel and materialists of Hegelian derivation such as Moleschott) of the historicity of nature. The task was now no longer to counterpose the historicity of human society to the ahistoricity of nature, but to establish both the linkage and the distinction between the two historicities. Engels contributed to this task most especially in his splendid book on *The Origin of the Family*, as well as in his general expositions of Marxism. However, as we have already mentioned, he remained torn between a tendency to develop physical-biological materialism and a tendency to counterpose the last great 'classical' philosophy of Hegelianism to the 'eclectic soup' of positivist professors. I should say that the most significant testimony to this contradiction is the passage in Chapter I of *Ludwig Feuerbach*: 'It is not necessary, here, to go into the question of whether this mode of outlook is thoroughly in accord with the present state of natural science, which predicts a possible end even for the earth, and for its habit-ability a fairly certain one; which therefore recognizes that for the history of mankind, too, there is not only an ascending but also a descending branch. At any rate we still find ourselves a considerable distance from the turning point at which the historical course of society becomes one of descent, and we cannot expect Hegelian philosophy to be concerned with a subject which natural science, in its time, had not at all placed upon the agenda as yet.'[10] Some-one who writes like this certainly does not consider nature as a mere 'object of human labour', and does not confer on the concepts of progress and dialectic any absoluteness (the final cosmic catas-trophe would be a typical case of a 'non-dialectical negation', of true destruction of values, not of negation with conservation). Yet elsewhere Engels continues to celebrate the advent of socialism as a passage from necessity to absolute liberty, and to consider human unhappiness as due only to causes of an economic and social order.

Another serious battle for materialism was fought by Lenin with his *Materialism and Empirio-Criticism*, the value of which is in no way affected by the ten or fifty errors in physics which can be found in it. It remains a lasting merit of Lenin to have discerned the reactionary character of the idealist renaissance of the early twentieth century, even where it was presented as a revival of revolutionary activism against social-Darwinist quietism. It is nevertheless plain that a deeper study of the relation between man and nature lay outside the range of Lenin's interests, given the

[10] Marx-Engels, *Selected Works* in one volume, London 1970, pp. 58–89.

urgency of the revolutionary tasks to which he was called.

What was in Engels a complex position, an *odi et amo* towards the materialism of the natural sciences, indubitably became an outright hostility in the Western Marxists of the twentieth century, even among those who might seem most immune to any subjectivist regression. In this hostility, correct theses and sophisms have been closely intertwined.

When Marxists affirm the 'decisive primacy' of economic and social structures, and therefore designate this level and not the biological level underlying it as the 'base' of human society and culture, they are right in relation to the great transformations and differentiations of society, which arise fundamentally as consequences of changes in economic structures and not of the geographical environment or physical constitution of man. The division of humanity into social classes explains its history infinitely better than its division into races or peoples; and although, as a given fact, racial hatreds and national conflicts have existed and continue to exist, and although the ambiguous and composite concepts of nation and of homeland always have a racist component, there is nevertheless no doubt that these conflicts, at least from the end of prehistory onwards, are fundamentally disguised or diverted economic and social conflicts (increasingly so), not 'genuinely' biological or ethnic contrasts. Hence the immense methodological superiority of Marx's historiography by comparison, not merely with a vulgar racist historiography, but even with an ethnic historiography such as that of Thierry.[11]

By comparison with the evolutionary pace of economic and social structures (and of the superstructures determined by them), nature, including man as a biological entity, also changes, as evolutionism has taught us, but at an immensely slower tempo. 'Nature is ever green, or rather goes/by such long paths/that she seems still', says Leopardi.[12] If therefore we are studying even a very long period of human history to examine the transformations of society, we may legitimately pass over the physical and biological level, inasmuch as relative to that period it is a constant. Similarly, we may agree it is permissible for a Marxist, when writing the history of political or cultural events within the restricted context

[11] Augustin Thierry (1795–1856): French historian who concentrated on national conflicts in European history. (NLB).

[12] *La Ginestra*, lines 292–4. (NLB).

of a fundamentally unitary and stable socio-economic situation, to take the latter as a constant and study the history of the super-structure alone. Engels, and later Gramsci, warned that it would be naïve to think that each single superstructural fact was the reper-cussion of a change in the infrastructure. Luporini has recalled that Marx himself, in the 1859 preface to *A Critique of Political Economy*, explicitly affirms the dependence of the superstructure on the structure only 'in its macroscopic and catastrophic aspects, so to speak, that is, in relation to social revolutions'.[13]

But if, basing ourselves on this relatively immobile character (over a certain period) of the economic and social structure, we were to conclude that it has no conditioning power over the super-structure, or even no real existence, we should be committing a typical 'historicist' fallacy. Now, it is a precisely similar sophism to deny the conditioning which nature exercises on humanity in general, just because this conditioning does not conspicuously differentiate individual epochs of human history. Marxists put themselves in a scientifically and polemically weak position if, after rejecting the idealist arguments which claim to show that the only reality is that of the Spirit and that cultural facts are in no way dependent on economic structures, they then borrow the same arguments to deny the dependence of man on nature.

The position of the contemporary Marxist seems at times like that of a person living on the first floor of a house, who turns to the tenant of the second floor and says: 'You think you're independent, that you support yourself by yourself? You're wrong! Your apart-ment stands only because it is supported on mine, and if mine collapses, yours will too'; and on the other hand to the ground-floor tenant: 'What are you saying? That you support and condition me? What a wretched illusion! The ground floor exists only in so far as it is the ground floor to the first floor. Or rather, strictly speaking, the real ground floor is the first floor, and your apartment is only a sort of cellar, to which no real existence can be assigned.' To tell the truth, the relations between the Marxist and the second-floor tenant have been perceptibly improved for some time, not because the second-floor tenant has recognized his own 'depen-

13 Engels, letters to Bloch and Schmidt, Marx-Engels, *Selected Correspondence*, Moscow 1965, pp. 417–25; Gramsci, *Prison Notebooks*, London 1971, pp. 407ff. See also C. Luporini, 'Realtà e Storicità: Economia e Dialettica nel Marxismo', in *Critica Marxista*, IV, 1966, p. 105, and now in *Dialettica e materialismo*, p. 207.

dence', but because the Marxist has reduced his pretensions considerably, and has come to admit that the second floor is very largely autonomous from the first, or else that the two apartments 'support each other'. But the contempt for the inhabitant of the ground floor has become increasingly pronounced.

The historicist polemic against 'man in general', which is completely correct as long as it denies that certain historical and social forms such as private property or class divisions are inherent in humanity in general, errs when it overlooks the fact that man as a biological being, endowed with a certain (not unlimited) adaptability to his external environment, and with certain impulses towards activity and the pursuit of happiness, subject to old age and death, is not an abstract construction, nor one of our prehistoric ancestors, a species of pithecanthropus now superseded by historical and social man, but still exists in each of us and in all probability will still exist in the future. It is certainly true that the development of society changes men's ways of feeling pain, pleasure and other elementary psycho-physical reactions, and that there is hardly anything that is 'purely natural' left in contemporary man, that has not been enriched and remoulded by the social and cultural environment. But the general aspects of the 'human condition' still remain, and the specific characteristics introduced into it by the various forms of associated life have not been such as to overthrow them completely. To maintain that, since the 'biological' is always presented to us as mediated by the 'social', the 'biological' is nothing and the 'social' is everything, would once again be idealist sophistry. If we make it ours, how are we to defend ourselves from those who will in turn maintain that, since all reality (including economic and social reality) is knowable only through language (or through the thinking mind), language (or the thinking mind) is the sole reality, and all the rest is abstraction?

We have spoken of the importance which the biological level has in determining the characteristics of the human condition in general. But it must be added that although the biological level has virtually no importance in determining traits distinguishing large human groups (there is, for example, no correlation between membership of a certain race and the possession of certain intellectual or moral gifts), it does again have a conspicuous weight in the determination of individual characteristics. Humanity is not made up of individuals who are all equal in psycho-physical constitution, differentiated only by the social environment in which they happen to find themselves.[14] As well as differences in socio-cultural formation (differences which should in turn be translatable into determinate 'acquired characteristics' of the brain and nervous system), 'constitutional' differences derived from a multiplicity of other biological factors come into play. The grotesque naïvetés and racist extrapolations of the Lombrosian school and other such tendencies certainly induce us to shelve attempts at 'biological' interpretation of this or that historical personage until study of relations between physiology and psychology is at a far more advanced stage than it has reached at present. It is obviously more scientific to renounce a scientific explanation, for lack of reliable evidence, than to abandon oneself to science-fiction. Let us not forget, however, that this will not be a permanent renunciation, since any denial in principle of the existence of those relations would signify a return to the concept of the 'soul', with all its absurdities. Nor must it be forgotten that, at the limit, nature affects human history through the death of the various actors in that history. We do not become converts to the cult of 'heroes', nor abandon Marxism, if we say that the death of Lenin, due to illness, had a notable (even if not pre-eminent) effect on certain degenerations of the Bolshevik Party and of the Russian Revolution; and this is also true to a lesser extent for each of the lesser and least personages in the human drama. Human history is continually crossed by 'natural' accidents (which, of course, are not only deaths). I know that to this remark it may be replied that the protagonist of history is the absolute Spirit (or the human species, or classes) and that empirical individuals have no true reality. But it is also common knowledge that this conception renders the absolute Ego transcendent over empirical subjects, that is, it restores a platonic dualism between sensible appearance and true reality, at the very moment that it proclaims a stentorian monism.

This conditioning which – to express it in Labriola's language – the 'natural terrain' exercises over man even after the formation and development of the 'artificial terrain', must be borne in mind

14 This was, as is well known, one of the issues of dispute between Diderot and Helvétius; and here Diderot, basing himself on his biological studies, was more materialist than the mechanist Helvétius, even if in other respects Diderot's *Réfutation* ran risks of relapsing into spiritualism (because of an absolute anti-reductionism, inspired by a polemic, in itself correct, against over-hasty reductionism).

when we consider the vexed question of the relations between structure and superstructure, and more generally, of the role to be assigned to so-called 'spiritual' or cultural activities.

It is certainly necessary to warn that the dependence of the superstructure on the structure must not be conceived in a simplistic way. It is still more necessary, as Luporini has recently observed,[15] not to content oneself with generic refutations of simplism and mechanism ('reciprocal action between structure and super-structure', 'dependence of the superstructure on the structure, but only *in the last instance*'), but finally to proceed to deepen actual study of the processes by which the superstructure acquires auto-nomy (always within certain limits) of the structure, and exercises a reaction on it, which will yet remain secondary by comparison with the action exercised on it by the structure. However, it seems to me that the concept of superstructure, *even understood non-mechanically,* cannot include the totality of cultural activities.

Interest in mathematics or physics or philology only arises, it is true, in a definite social environment; the adoption of particular techniques of research is only conceivable in a particular society; furthermore ideology itself (this is aimed specifically at the many modern historians who consider themselves immune from all 'practical political' interests) is a perilous but irreplaceable instru-ment of research, at least as long as a perfectly classless society has not been achieved. But the *objective* truths which the sciences have already attained in pre-socialist societies (sometimes the work of politically and socially conservative scientists) are not reducible to slave-owning or feudal or bourgeois ideology. Otherwise we should really fall into a debased historicism, into a relativist concep-tion of knowledge and, at the end of the day, into a denial of external reality or of its knowability.[16] Thus, just as scientific knowledge

---

[15] 'Realtà e Storicità', pp. 104–6.

[16] It must be remembered that the concept of superstructure historically arose from a critique of religion and law, that is to say, of constructions which were both eminently devoid of objective validity, and especially profuse in univer-salistic pretensions, vaunting a divine or 'natural' origin. The concept of super-structure played an extremely important role in demystifying these claims. But transferred without modification to the domain of scientific knowledge, it risks making the latter as relative and subjective a phenomenon as religion or law; that is, it can have an anti-materialist and anthropocentric effect. The very theory of knowledge as a mirror-reflection, which appears to be a *ne plus ultra* of objectivism, can acquire a relativist character if it is only historical and social reality, and not also natural reality, that is taken as the object of the reflection:

is not *sic et simpliciter* superstructure (although, we repeat, it is necessarily connected with elements of the superstructure), so the *instrumental,* ideologically neutral and therefore extra-class dimensions that exist in all human institutions – in language more than in legal, political and cultural institutions in the strict sense[17] – are not reducible without residue to superstructures.

I believe, however, that the reduction of cultural activities to superstructures should be limited in another sense also. It is not only the social relations between men, but also the relations between men and nature that give rise to scientific and philosophical reflection, and to artistic expression. Philosophy, science and art do not draw stimulus and nourishment solely from the 'artificial terrain' of society, but also from the 'natural terrain'. Too little account has been taken in discussions of superstructural problems of an observation by Antonio Labriola which seems to me illuminating. After remarking that art, religion and science are determined by economic structures *'in large part* and *by indirect ways'*, Labriola explains that by his second qualification he means to recall that 'in works of art and religion the mediation between the conditions and the products is fairly complicated' (this is the warning that is continually repeated today, which Luporini justly demands be made less generic); while by the first qualification he wishes to emphasize that 'men, living in society, do not thereby cease also to live in nature, and to receive occasion and material from it for their curiosity and fantasy'.[18] A little later, he returns to the same idea: 'Men, living socially, do not cease to live also naturally. They are certainly not bound to nature as are animals . . . But nature is always the immediate subsoil of the artificial terrain of society, and is the ambience which envelops us all. Technique has interposed modifications, diversions and attenuations of natural influences between

---

Kepler's laws or Pascal's principle then become mere expressions of the socio-cultural ambience in which their authors were reared, and not also formulations of *objective* relations between phenomena – relations which antedate their discoverers. There is a way of writing the history of science as the history of culture, and of equating science with the history of science, which may represent a major advance over historical or literary idealism, but itself remains too humanistic.

[17] See Stalin's only writing of any theoretical interest, *Marxism and Linguistics,* and my comments on it in *Belfagor,* XVIII, 1963, pp. 9–14.

[18] Antonio Labriola, *Essays on the Materialist Conception of History,* New York 1966, p. 217 (translation modified).

ourselves as social animals and nature; but it has not thereby destroyed their efficacy, which on the contrary we experience continuously. Just as we are born naturally male and female, die nearly
always in spite of ourselves, are dominated by a reproductive
instinct, so we also bear within our temperament specific conditions,
which education in the broad sense of the word, or accommodation
to society, may certainly modify within limits, but can never
eliminate. These conditions of temperament, repeated in many
individuals and developed through many individuals over the
centuries, constitute what is called ethnic character. For all these
reasons, our dependence on nature, however diminished since prehistoric times, persists amidst our social life; as does the matter for
curiosity and fantasy furnished by the spectacle of nature itself. Now
these effects of nature, with the mediate or immediate sentiments
which result from them, though refracted, since the dawn of
history, only through the angle of vision provided by social conditions, never fail to find reflection in works of art and religion;
and this complicates the difficulties of making a full and realistic
interpretation of either.'[19]

This passage allows us to see how seriously Labriola (who may
himself be considered in certain respects a too impatient adversary
of 'vulgar materialism') took certain of the demands of the positivism he was concerned to combat. In the very extract we have
quoted there is an unwarranted concession to positivism (or perhaps, more probably, an undue fidelity to Humboldt and Steinthal[20]
and the German philology which was so impregnated with ethnic
preoccupations) – the allusion to 'ethnic character'.[21] Belief in the

[19] Ibid. pp. 220–21.
[20] Wilhelm Humboldt (1767–1835): Prussian educationalist and philologist;
Heymann Steinthal (1823–1899); German linguist and psychologist of 'national
character'. (NLB).
[21] It is, of course, entirely correct to single out racism and colonialism as the
most negative aspect of positivist culture. However, there is today a tendency to
consider too summarily the whole of positivism as infected with racism, and
above all, virtually to identify positivist racism with 'social Darwinism'. In reality,
positivist racism found its major European and American exponents in anti-
evolutionist and Cuvierian ethologists and linguists, who considered the various
human races as so many zoological 'species', distinct *ab origine*. Darwinism, by
destroying the notion of the fixity of species and thereby establishing a genetic
affinity between the various human races or species, dealt a serious blow to racism,
and was therefore greeted with hostility not only by spiritualists but also by
racists. It was only later that a racism on Darwinist, or rather pseudo-Darwinist,
foundations was reconstituted. Moreover, it should not be forgotten that,
although before the spread of Darwinism polemics against racism were often left

scientific validity of this ambiguous category probably contributed to provoking those colonialist aberrations which remain the most disconcerting and negative aspect of Labriola's thought and action. But once the inconsistency of race and nation as biological and cultural categories has been clearly exposed, the impact of nature on culture remains very real in the triple sense of the influence of biological constitution on psycho-intellectual character in each individual, of stimulus to scientific-philosophical and artistic activity, and of object for these same activities. Labriola, while explicitly acknowledging the mediation exercised by social ambience, is wholly correct to deny that this mediation cancels or renders nugatory impulses and conditions which come from nature.

To give a banal example: love, the brevity and frailty of human existence, the contrast between the smallness and weakness of man and the infinity of the cosmos, are expressed in literary works in very different ways in various historically determinate societies, but still not in such different ways that all reference to such constant experiences of the human condition as the sexual instinct, the debility produced by age (with its psychological repercussions), the fear of one's own death and sorrow at the death of others, is lost. On the other hand, one poet's way of feeling love or of lamenting old age differs from that of another poet not only because of differing social and cultural formation, but also because of differing 'nervous temperament', in which straightforwardly biological elements play a part. Affinities may come into play on this basis even across very diverse social and cultural environments. Leopardi's affinity with the epic poet Torquato Tasso is certainly to be explained by the literary education of Leopardi himself and perhaps by certain analogies between the atmosphere of the Counter-Reformation and of the Restoration; but it is also related to the affinities of poor health and melancholy disposition shared by Tasso and Leopardi, which led both to single out and express with especial intensity certain dolorous aspects of the 'human condition'.[22]

---

to idealist thinkers (in Italy, for example, Lambruschini), there were still some who felt the need to defeat racism on the terrain of science itself: one need only think of Cattaneo in Italy. I hope to discuss this more fully elsewhere. [Raffaello Lambruschini (1788–1873): liberal catholic publicist and educationalist. Carlo Cattaneo: radical-democratic leader of the 1848 Revolution in Milan, who was also a prominent writer on history, philology and psychology. NLB]

[22] The error of those positivists who raised similar themes (and brought discredit

The constant dimensions (hardly modified hitherto, and perhaps scarcely modifiable in the future) of the human condition are not, be it clearly understood, metaphysical or metahistorical. 'Man in general' as we understand it – who is none other than natural man – is not 'eternal man'; so much so that he has an origin and will have an end (or a transformation by Darwinian evolution). But though they are not actually eternal, these aspects are nevertheless *long-lasting*: that is to say, they have, relative to the existence of the human species, much greater stability than historical or social institutions.[23] To attempt to reduce them to the latter is merely to provide an easy polemical target for those who will exploit the inevitable failure of such a reduction to reaffirm once again the existence of 'eternal man' – just as any attempt to derive religion exclusively from economic and social conditions, overlooking the

---

on such studies) was to believe that certain pathological conditions were necessarily an obstacle – and not, in certain cases, an incentive – to objective knowledge of the human condition. The experience of illness and weakness, if it does not lead to escape into irrationality and mysticism, may aid a better understanding of the 'passive aspect' of the relations between man and nature, just as the experience of poverty and exploitation can aid understanding of the negative aspects of a socio-economic system (see my study *Classicismo e Illuminismo nell' Ottocento Italiano*, Pisa 1969, pp. 156–8). A particularly obvious example is Leopardi. I would like to add that consideration of the relation between man and nature may help to explain the contrasts between ideological involutions and poetic progress which we encounter, for example, in poems of the late Parini or late Carducci. A poet in full political or ideological involution may in some cases suffer, as it were, a complete decadence of cognitive (and hence also poetic) faculties; but in other cases, he may maintain, or even increase, his capacity for expressing certain 'natural' aspects of the human condition which are *relatively* independent of his economic and social situation. [Guiseppe Parini (1729–99) was an Enlightenment poet who welcomed the French Revolution, and then turned against its extension to North Italy, saluting the Austro-Russian counter-revolutionary armies before he died. Giosue Carducci (1835–1907) was a radical-democratic politician and poet of the Risorgimento period, who eventually rallied to the monarchy after 1878. NLB]

[23] Of course, there are also very considerable differences in the duration of historical and social superstructures. Marx and Engels noted in *The Communist Manifesto* that certain forms of consciousness were common to all successive civil societies hitherto, since they were all societies divided into classes. Probably basing himself on this passage from the *Manifesto*, the Triestine writer and scholar Guido Voghera sought to develop from a Marxist point of view the idea that certain moral principles correspond to the inherent needs of any society (including communist society), and are therefore certainly superstructures, but superstructures 'of sociality in general'. Although the dangers of a regression to an ahistorical conception of ethics are evident, I think that this notion neverthelsss deserves close consideration.

fact that religion is also an illusory compensation for the fear of death and in general for the oppression which nature exercises on man, plays into the hands of those who exalt the independent and privileged value of the 'religious experience'.[24] The problem of 'historical and cultural inheritance' and of the 'permanence and transmission of values' through successive and variant forms of society (the importance of which is rightly emphasized by Luporini in the article we have already had occasion to cite) will doubtless find a large measure of its solution in a more articulated conception of the relations between structure and superstructure and in a closer study of the function of intellectuals as bearers of the continuity of culture. But we should not forget either that this cultural continuity – through which, as Marx observed, we feel so near to the poetry of Homer – has also been rendered possible by the fact that man as a biological being has remained essentially unchanged from the beginnings of civilization to the present; and those sentiments and representations which are closest to the biological facts of human existence have changed little.

At this point it will, I think, be sufficiently clear in what respect one can, from a materialist point of view, agree or disagree with recent orientations which may be summarized by such formulas as 'Marxism plus psychoanalysis' or 'Marxism plus structuralism plus psychoanalysis'. These trends must be conceded the merit of rejecting the reduction of Marxism to 'historicism' (with all the idealist and intuitionist errors connoted by this term),[25] of emphasizing the need for scientific study of historical and literary dis-

[24] It may be noted that the role of the relationship between man and nature in the genesis and perdurance of religion was precisely perceived by Lenin in a letter to Gorky of December 1913: 'God is (in history and in real life) first of all the complex of ideas generated by the brutish subjection of man both by external nature and by the class yoke.' Lenin, Collected Works, Moscow 1966, Vol. 35, p. 128.

[25] See Louis Althusser, Reading Capital, London 1970, and Luporini, 'Realtà e Storicità' already cited. However, it should be said that the profession of historicism by Italian Marxists did not merely have the inferior humanist or intuitionist connotation that is rightly repudiated today; it also had the sense of a polemic against the metaphysical or 'actualistic' aspects of Italian neo-idealism. Especially in the field of literary history, historicism meant a rejection of the aesthetics of pure intention, and of monographic essays, in other words, what was summarily defined as a 'return to De Sanctis'. It should also be noted that well before Althusser or Luporini, there were Italian Marxists who denounced the ambiguities inherent in the notion of 'historicism': see especially A. La Penna in La Riforma della Scuola, VI, No. 2, February 1959.

ciplines, and finally of seeking to connect the study of historical man with the study of natural man (hence their interest in psychology, in anthropology, and in language as a more or less intermediate formation between natural organisms and social institutions).

However, psychoanalysis and structuralism, if they contain an appeal to science against the claims of a purely humanistic culture, are at the same time deeply permeated with anti-materialist ideology. The attacks to which psychoanalysis has been and is subjected 'from the Right' should not lead us to forget the fact that this scientific current arose in polemical opposition to materialist psychology, and sought to render psychic phenomena independent of anatomical and physiological data. That linguists with a Crocean or Vosslerian background[26] attack structuralism in the name of an identification of language with art, does not alter the fact that structuralism makes the 'system' it studies into something closed and intrinsically coherent, and reveals no interest in its genesis 'from below', or in the relations between human activities and their material determinations – whether socio-economic or biophysical. Its truly Cuvierian concept of 'system' is inherently ahistorical, not merely anti-historicist. Polarization of the distinction between synchrony and diachrony, and contempt or indifference towards diachronic studies, are essential characteristics of structuralism, which cannot be overcome by any eclectic blending of it.

Surveying these two tendencies, it is more necessary than ever to separate their scientific achievements from all that is ideological and unverifiable in them (I refer in particular to psychoanalysis), or even tantamount to charlatanry (I refer, as a limiting case, to the colossal presumptions and ridiculous coquetries of a Lévi-Strauss). What is needed is an ideological confrontation between Marxism and these tendencies, an antagonistic and not merely receptive stance: antagonistic not only in the sense of a critique of their lack of interest in economic and social facts and in the link between theory and practice, but also in the sense of a critique of their anti-materialism. Failing this, any *rapprochement* with structuralism or psychoanalysis will merely end in yet another 'modernization' of

[26] Karl Vossler (1872–1949): German linguist and follower of Croce, who equated language and poetry. (NLB).

Marxism, through which it will be culturally enriched but will always remain subaltern.

It is also wrong, in my view, to assume that a Marxist interest in linguistics or psychology today must obligatorily be directed towards the *latest* schools within these disciplines. If we are convinced (and as a matter of principle we should all be) that the development of bourgeois culture does not follow a trajectory of absolute progress, but of progress-and-involution (progress in methodological refinement and in certain areas of knowledge, involution in ideology and therewith partial falsification or misinterpretation of properly scientific results), then it may be that Pavlov will have more to tell us than Freud, at least in certain respects, and Ascoli[27] more than Roman Jakobson. It may also be that the vanguard role within the sciences at present assigned by bourgeois culture to linguistics and psychology will prove debatable, and a more important position be attributed to the historical sciences of nature. But of course all these options depend on a choice for or against materialism.

[27] Graziadio Ascoli (1829–1907): the greatest Italian linguistic scholar of the last century, a specialist in neo-latin and celtic languages. (NLB).

# 2

# Praxis and Materialism

I am intervening again in this discussion on materialism not with any pretension to draw conclusions, but simply in an attempt to clarify certain points for the sake of a future renewal of the discussion itself.[1]

One point on which there has been almost unanimous disagreement was my assertion that it is necessary to recognize 'the element of passivity in experience'. This statement has been seen as the beginning of a general theory of human powerlessness, of man's resignation before the existing situation, etc. Ciafaloni simply termed the kind of materialism defended by me 'passivism'. In point of fact, not only did I not formulate any theory of this kind, but I did not at all say that knowledge *is passivity*. I simply said that there exists in knowledge – even in its most elementary form, sensation – *an* element of passivity, irreducible to the activity of the subject. There is, in other words, a stimulus coming from the external world which is precisely the 'given'. The knowing process is certainly not a mere passive reception of the given. As everyone knows, it entails elaboration of that given and a search for determinate objects of experience, spurred on by the needs and the interests of the subject. Why, therefore, should one emphasize the element of passivity? It is because a great deal of modern philosophy (including certain forms of Marxism) is characterized by a particular *ideological use of epistemology,* which tends to claim an illusory and mystified freedom for man on the basis of a belittling of external reality, and thereby skirts the problem of the

---

[1] The present essay is a reply to comments on 'Considerations on Materialism' by Giovanni Jervis, Fiamma Baranelli, Francesco Ciafaloni, Paolo Cristofolini, Massimo Aloisi, and Marzio Vacatello (see *Quaderni Piacentini* No. 29, pp. 37–9; No. 30, pp. 110–20, 121–7, 127–31; No. 32, pp. 107–12, 112–15).

real liberation of man. In order to oppose this ideological practice it is necessary to stress that the 'active side' of experience is precisely only one side and not the entire process. Furthermore, one should bear in mind that the 'active side' itself is not an unconditioned principle. Rather, it in turn must be accounted for, both historically (that is, within the framework of the evolution of inorganic matter into life and thereby into thought) and presently (within the framework of a scientific study of the knowing mechanism, its organs and functions).

In the light of these requirements, the formula so dear to Jervis (and also to Ciafaloni, who on other points argues effectively against Jervis) is altogether inadequate: 'Praxis as the foundation of the knowing activity'. It is inadequate even as a simple postulate for future research, since it already possesses a fundamental tendentiousness in its way of formulating the problem.

I know very well that the word 'praxis' exerts a strong power of suggestion today, due in part to its very vagueness and multiplicity of meanings. In it can be found echoes of the *Theses on Feuerbach,* American pragmatism, Gramscism, and even of the philosophical consequences which some people have believed could be drawn from Heisenberg's principle. More particularly, the appeal to praxis often represents, within the Marxist camp, a way of not talking about or of talking very little about materialism. Those very people who today are busy burying Gramsci take over from Gramsci precisely that characteristic most closely linked to the cultural contingencies of the milieu in which he lived: his attenuation of materialism, which found expression, among other things, in his definition of Marxism as the 'philosophy of praxis' (a definition which, as is generally recognized now, was not due only to the prison censor, and which moreover antedated Gramsci himself).

Thus, it is necessary first of all to show that a reference to praxis can have quite different meanings, according to whether one is declaring the inability of pure thought to make man happy and free ('The philosophers have only *interpreted* the world differently, the point is, to *change* it'), or declaring that knowledge itself is praxis *tout court*. In the latter case, since *to know reality is already to transform it,* one retrogresses from Marxism to idealism – i.e., to a philosophy of *thought as praxis,* which makes action seem superfluous. In the first case, however, although one may not have abandoned the idea of enlarging the dimensions of knowledge's 'active side', and although one may not make any absolute distinction between knowing and doing, it is acknowledged that knowledge by itself does not provide a complete domination of reality. True liberation can be attained only through the practical transformation of reality. This amounts to rejecting the idea that knowledge is purely and simply praxis, thereby recognizing that element of passivity which Jervis dislikes so much. An unmediated identification of knowing with acting is not Marxism; in its most coherent form, it is Gentile-ism, i.e. a philosophy equally open to an irrational activism and to a mysticism of pure thought. On the other hand, every distinction (empirical distinction and not simply a contraposition of categories) between knowing and acting must necessarily base itself, ultimately, on the more receptive, less integrally active, character of knowing with respect to acting. By way of indirect proof of this point one can cite the insurmountable difficulties encountered by Croce when he attempted to distinguish, as against Gentile, knowledge from action while still adhering to the idealist proposition that knowledge is pure activity.

Once the problem of knowledge is freed from its ideological extrapolations, it becomes a scientific problem which concerns, in the first place, neurophysiology and the sciences connected with it, from biochemistry to cybernetics. To Jervis this statement seemed to indicate 'a resolute methodological naiveté'. I do not know if he includes the applications of cybernetics to the study of the knowing processes in this hasty judgment. A reading of the essays which Vittorio Somenzi has devoted to this engrossing problem and to its philosophical implications, as well as a look at the feeble objections raised against Somenzi at the twenty-first national philosophy convention,[2] should make it clear where the 'naïveté' lies! Massimo Aloisi's remarks are also illuminating in this regard. They confirm how cybernetics' contribution to biology has struck the final and decisive blow against vitalism. Jervis is overconfident in his belief in a completely anti-materialist modern science and in a material-

[2] See Somenzi's paper, with the objections and replies, in 'L'uomo e la macchina', *Atti del XXI Congresso nazionale di filosofia*, Turin 1967, I, pp. 51ff., 122ff. Among the numerous works of Somenzi devoted to this subject, see in particular 'Dalla materia inerte alla materia vivente e pensante', *De homine*, No. 15/16, 1965, pp. 143ff.; 'Forma, informazione e vita', *Archivio di filosofia*, 1967, pp. 31ff.; 'Materialismo e cibernetica', *Nuovi argomenti*, July–December 1966, pp. 252ff. (with very interesting remarks on the 'vulgar materialism' of the second half of the nineteenth century).

ism 'relegated to the simplicities of the uneducated'. That could be true only if one's vision were confined to the physical-mathematical sciences and excluded biology.

Undoubtedly, there is something positive in that kind of *noli me tangere* which Jervis proclaims in relation to neuro-physiology, and which is not to be confused with the traditional anti-materialist phobia. Jervis is right in rebelling against a psychology and a psychiatry which proclaim their socio-political neutrality and at the same time seek to impose a particular vision of human relationships, drawn from the interests and the mentality of the ruling class, as an objective model of normality. He sees the risk of a de-politicization (actually an insidious and reactionary politicization) of his discipline as a result of the excessively close connection between psychology and biology. But the most effective way to oppose apolitical or reactionary psychology is not to accept the dilemma 'socio-political science or biological science?' and opt for the former alternative against the latter. Rather, it is to deepen one's study of the influence of the environment on the development and the pathology of the nervous system, bringing out the enormous importance of class relations in determining the 'environment'. Recognition of this reality does not, however, alter the fact that the explanation of the knowing process as such belongs to the realm of neuro-physiology, because it is the brain that feels and thinks, acquires knowledge of the external world and reacts upon it, and not some mythical spirit or equally ill-defined 'social being'. Otherwise, following the line of reasoning that Jervis tends to adopt, we could even deny that the study of the digestive process belongs to physiology, on the indisputable basis that what man digests depends on agricultural production and its distribution, on particular techniques in preparing the food, on the preference (this too is far from being 'natural' without any social mediation) which people have for some food rather than other, etc. – in short, on a particular social setting and, therefore, on particular relations of production. If we were to apply a similar line of reasoning to all the other functions of the human organism, we could immediately demonstrate that human physiology does not exist, or that it is a reactionary fabrication. And by the end of this scintillating cultural operation we would not have politicized science, but instead spiritualized socialism and made it utopian.

The argument against traditional psychoanalysis, for example, should be carried out from two sides. It is correct to criticize it for its indifference towards the socio-economic dimension of human relationships; but it is equally necessary to criticize it for its limited interest in the anatomical-physiological study of the nervous organism. This *two-fold* disconnection, from biology and from 'politics' in the broad sense, is what has made psychoanalysis more a myth of European decadent thought than a science.

The position adopted by Fiamma Baranelli with regard to the problem of knowledge is much more correct than that of Jervis. She remarks that man, in his encounters/collisions with external reality, selects, from among all the sensations which his sense organs are capable of receiving, those which *interest him*. 'On the other hand', she remarks, 'one must not forget that man's activity puts him in contact with *certain parts* of nature, varying with the different periods of his history. A *choice* – i.e. an active intervention by the subject in the knowing process – is thus possible at two levels at least: regarding which phenomena, and given a particular phenomenon which features of it, to address.'

This represents a much more concrete line of argument than a generic appeal to praxis. I should like to add one bit of clarification, however. Knowledge does not develop solely as knowledge of what responds to a need or interest of man, but also as knowledge of what distresses, harms and oppresses man. If one includes also this second type of experience in the concept of 'interest', and if therefore one understands by 'interest' everything that *concerns us* – whether in a favourable or unfavourable sense – then Baranelli's statement is perfectly correct. But in that case the concepts of 'choice' and 'the subject's active intervention' come to lose that somewhat one-sidedly pragmatist intonation which they tend to take on in her argument.

This pragmatist intonation can be readily accentuated if one regards scientific knowledge as knowledge *par excellence*. Here a problem arises which I touched on partially, but incompletely, in my first essay: the problem of the relationship between scientific knowledge and everyday experience.[3] If the former were distinguishable from the latter solely on the basis of its much greater exactitude, it would then be legitimate to regard it as simply

[3] In recent philosophy the treatment of this problem has been limited to the question of language, and this restriction has formalized it and made it difficult to see all of its implications.

representative of human knowledge in general. However, from the standpoint of the 'power relationship' between subject and object, scientific knowledge represents an altogether one-sided and atypical case, since the subject's activism enjoys a particularly privileged position within it. Of course, even within the context of scientific theory the various forms of idealism and semi-idealism are erroneous, because they render the concept of experimental verification void of any real meaning (such verification implying that one enters into contact with an objective reality against which our theoretical constructions are to be compared), and they undermine the basis of the concept of scientific progress itself, as Ludovico Geymonat has shown.[4] Nevertheless, the scientist still finds himself in a privileged position, in an activist sense, since he plans his research, selects his own experimental objects or at least their field, and therefore is in a way the producer of his own experiment. Quite different is the situation in which the average person finds himself, i.e. man in the experiences of his everyday life (and therefore also the scientist himself as an everyday man). In everyday life external reality, the existing situation, often presents itself as unplanned and undesired, as an external occurrence that blocks and interferes with other practical and knowing experiences which the subject intended to undertake.[5]

Let us consider an extreme case, and one that is therefore particularly clear-cut. Sickness has a very different meaning for the clinician or the pathologist, who regards it with scientific interest (and therefore chooses to concern himself with it, incorporates it within his own research plan, 'dominates it intellectually' even in

---

[4] See L. Geymonat, *Filosofia e filosofia della scienze*, Milan 1961, pp. 156–9. The concept of scientific progress, says Geymonat, 'allows us to talk about a link between science and something that eluded humanity before the distant beginnings of scientific research, and that now, however, is being gradually and surely overtaken'; an object that 'manifests itself as something *other* than the subject, i.e. as something irreducible to the processes by which humanity progressively attempts to elucidate and dominate it'. These remarks are all the more significant in that they come from a philosopher of science who could hardly be accused of 'naive realism' and who arrived at materialism from a scientific-philosophical background that is far removed from any simplistic empiricism. These remarks appear to clarify also in what sense one has to distinguish between 'method' and 'results' in scientific research (see above) – not in the sense of a dogmatization of the results, but in the sense of a refusal to reduce science to its methodology *tout court*.

[5] It should be noted that in Italian the same word (*esperienza*) means both 'experience' and 'experiment'. (NLB).

instances in which he fails to cure it), and for the patient, who experiences it only as an obstacle to his other interests, to other experiences which he cannot undertake precisely because of the sickness. This is obviously not merely a difference in cognitive precision (the patient who, as one of the 'profane', is to be distinguished from one who knows), but corresponds to a difference in their respective needs and interests. This is further demonstrated by the fact that even the clinician or pathologist experiences sickness on a quite different level when he himself is the patient.

I have taken the example of sickness only because of its self-evident quality; but it would be a great mistake to think that experiences in which the subject is in an unfavourable power relationship vis-à-vis external reality are confined to sicknesses or other biological mishaps narrowly defined. In the sphere of affective relationships, as well as in that of social and political life, man often finds himself compelled to live through such experiences. Thus, it would also be erroneous simply to identify the biological level with the realm of passivity and necessity, and the socio-economic level with the realm of activity and freedom. On both levels there are real situations in which men find themselves and there are efforts made by men to transform these to their advantage. On both levels these efforts at times succeed (for example, when one succeeds in overcoming an illness or in overturning an oppressive socio-political relationship), and at other times fail. With regard to certain relatively short-term prospects, there are socio-political situations just as 'blocked' as some biological situations are. The elimination of slavery at the time of Spartacus or the realization of agrarian communism at the time of Babeuf was almost as impossible as the elimination of old age or death. The difference is considerable, however, in the case of long-term prospects, which are more favourable for 'social ills' than for 'physical ills'. While it is possible to foresee a future in which man's oppression by man will be eliminated (even if one cannot afford any idle confidence in the certainty of this prospect), one cannot imagine a future in which the suffering caused by the disparity between certain human biological limits and certain human aspirations (in the final analysis, hedonistic ones, but which have been greatly complicated and enriched by culture) can be radically eliminated. Of course, many individual diseases will be cured, the average length of the human life will be prolonged, technical means will be developed which increase man's power in particular areas (and in a society of equals these technical means will no longer be, as they are today, the source of greater and greater alienation and enslavement). But these will always be reformist, and not revolutionary, forms of progress. Man's biological frailty cannot be overcome, short of venturing into the realm of science fiction.

Marx himself, and Engels to an even greater extent, often remarked that human history remains, and will continue to remain till the advent of communist society, a history that is in large part 'natural' – i.e. a history in which the conscious activity of men still has a limited part. If an initial emancipation of man from nature was begun when man began to work and to produce (and continues to develop *pari passu* with developments in technical progress), a second and qualitatively different emancipation will take place only with the creation of a society of equals – i.e. with that famous leap from the realm of necessity into the realm of freedom. But even this second emancipation will not free man from his biological limits.

These remarks should help to clarify the meaning of the division into two levels, the 'natural' and the socio-economic, which I dealt with in my first essay. To dwell on the point that there is nothing, or almost nothing, in contemporary man that has not been mediated and shaped in some way by his social being is to dwell on the obvious. At the most, it could be helpful against those who rigidify and schematize the distinction between the two levels. It becomes a sophistical ploy, however, if one then claims to reduce the natural to the socio-economic, without further ado. One then lapses back into the sophistry of those who deny . . . the physiological character of digestion. The fact is overlooked that the socio-economic mediation does not have the same depth and the same decisiveness at all times and all places. A phenomenon like capitalism arose on the socio-economic level; it belongs to that form of historicity with an accelerated rhythm which is characteristic of human history alone and which is related to the new mode of transmitting experiences through learning (and not through biological heredity), unknown or known only in a very limited way by the other animal species. Only the most distant premises of capitalism are biological: certain general conditions of the environment and of the constitution of the human organism, without which capitalism, like all other socio-economic formations, could not exist. But the explanation of the specific functioning of this mode of production is to be sought on the socio-economic level, and it is on this level that one must operate in order to destroy it and replace it with a more advanced mode of production and an egalitarian society. A phenomenon like old age, however, arose and continues to persist on the biological level. Its 'sociality' concerns certain of its far from marginal features (one need only think of the inhuman shunting-aside of old people which present-day capitalism increasingly favours). Nevertheless, even in the most gerontophile or gerontocratic society – or, in more serious terms, even in a society which eliminates both the unjust authoritarianism of the aged and the equally unjust notion that a man is worth only as much as and as long as he produces and earns a living – old age remains a highly unpleasant fact. And no socialist revolution can have any *direct* effect on the fundamental reasons which account for its unpleasantness. Diverse social orders give, of course, a very different direction to the 'struggle against nature'; they may favour resignation or, contrariwise, action to overcome biological conditioning. But such action cannot go beyond certain limits. Communism does not imply, in and of itself, a decisive triumph over the biological frailty of man, and it appears to be excluded that such a triumph could ever be attained (unless one wishes to indulge in science-fiction speculation).

A problem that has been touched on a number of times in our argument concerns the relationship between materialism and Leopardian pessimism. For Vacatello, this is the hidden presupposition of the entire materialist argument I tried to develop, and precisely for that reason it is all the more insidious and distorted. My apparent scientific interest in materialism is supposedly only a veil for a subjective propensity for pessimism.

To begin with, I have to stress that, in my opinion, the value of materialism is not at all confined to its usefulness as an introduction to pessimism. Its value is cognitive, at once philosophical-scientific and cultural-political. Unless it confirms and deepens materialism (in the way that Engels sought to achieve in the Marxist field), Marxism becomes a philosophy confined to arts graduates or pure philosophers. As such, it remains effective as a polemical vehicle for denouncing the myths of the welfare state, but is incapable of shedding light on the problem of the subject of the revolution and the forces which lead to the revolution itself (forces which cannot be purely voluntaristic ones). At the same time, science becomes ever more methodologistic and departmentalist with the fading of materialism. Of course, departmentalism is valid within certain limits; an individual science can and, in certain phases of its development, must move ahead for a good part of the way without heeding inter-disciplinary problems and the relationships between the different levels. Materialism does not entail a denial of the relative autonomy of the individual sciences or of the relative legitimacy of specialization. It does, however, entail a rejection of any absolutizing of this autonomy, as well as a rejection of any attempt to represent the unity of the diverse levels as an ascendency of the 'spiritual' or even as a 'reciprocal conditioning' with equal determining power and intensity distributed among the upper and lower levels.

These expressions, relative autonomy, conditioning, etc., are still too general. But greater exactness can be obtained better through the study of concrete cases than through purely theoretical manoeuvring. In this sense, while I find very interesting Fiamma Baranelli's remarks on the organic/inorganic relationship and on the renewed discussion between supporters of preformation and supporters of epigenesis,[6] I do not find the speculative constructions of Althusser to be very fruitful. Althusser has carried out his speculations with a great deal of Theoretical Ostentation and

---

[6] See *Quaderni Piacentini*, No. 30, pp. 114–20. I maintain, however, that it is not very useful to continue to use the term 'dialectic' to indicate processes and phenomena which are completely devoid of notions of 'supersession', 'rationality of history', etc. The statement by Lenin cited by Baranelli ('the scientist makes use of the dialectic without knowing so') presupposes the idea that, just as Marxism in general is an overturning and realization of the truth of the Hegelian dialectic, similarly modern science is an overturning and realization of the truth of *Naturphilosophie* – an idea that is one of the least valid contained in Engels's *Dialectics of Nature*. I find, therefore, that it is more accurate to state, as Aloisi does, that modern biological materialism is substantially unrelated to the dialectic. For the same reason I remain unconvinced by the suggestion of Leo Apostel – *Materialismo dialettico e metodo scientifico* (translated from the French), Turin 1968 – that one can identify the dialectic with 'feedback'. What is to be gained by translating into metaphysical language a quite precise scientific term which, apart from anything else, does not even have a relationship of cultural-historical filiation with respect to the dialectic?

[Preformation refers to the embryological theory according to which the offspring is already present in all of its parts in the unfertilized germ cell, growth being merely the quantitative enlargement of the germ cell; epigenesis is the theory that the embryo is a qualitatively new creation resulting from fertilization. NLB]

flaunting of his new terminology, but with a disturbing inability to come down to the concrete – a fact which derives from Althusser's exaggerated anti-empiricism, of which his anti-historicism is only one aspect.[7] In fact, one point that deserves attention is that the anti-historicism propounded by Althusser is not only an attack on historical apologetics or on the exaltation of the unrepeatable event above all laws, but is also and above all an expression of his supreme disdain for the empirical. This fact detracts greatly from the value of the argument he advances for the separation of Marxism from Hegelianism and for a rigorous distinction between science and ideology. The science he appeals to is a science which, like much of modern-day epistemology, is essentially Platonizing and accords little importance to the experimental moment.

Furthermore, I remain convinced that many (though not all) of the difficulties one encounters in any study of the relationship between structure and superstructure, difficulties which have often provided an inducement to regard the superstructure as completely autonomous and lapse back into idealism, can be overcome by taking into account the persistence of certain biological data even in social man. This does not at all mean that one can 'explain what capital is by taking man's biological constitution as one's point of departure'. Rather, it means that one can regard, for example, certain features of literary, philosophical and religious phenomena as determined not only by a given socio-economic situation but also by reflection on certain general characteristics of human existence. On the whole, I think that one can see how every failure to give proper recognition to man's biological nature leads to a spiritualist resurgence, since one necessarily ends by ascribing to the 'spirit' everything that one cannot explain in socio-economic terms.

Thus, I see materialism as a criterion for the unitary explanation of reality, and not as a prop for emotional reactions. Having said

[7] Very interesting remarks are to be found in the recent article by Nicola Badaloni, 'Gramsci storicista di fronte al marxismo contemporaneo', *Critica marxista*, No. 3, 1967, pp. 96ff. See, in particular, p. 117: 'Althusser's mistake lies in having forced this theoretical dimension to commune with itself, to feast with itself.' Perhaps, a critical analysis of the Althusserian concept of science should be undertaken even before the discussion about historicism or socialist humanism. In my opinion, one should not concede to Althusser that his *Théorie* is the true alternative to 'lived experience', to *Erlebnis* in the vitalist and immediatist sense. Between the one and the other there lies experimental science!

that, I must add, however, that I do not accept the definition of Leopardian pessimism – i.e. materialist pessimism, quite different from the various romantic-existentialist pessimisms which the European bourgeoisie has given birth to over the last two centuries – as an emotional disposition beyond the realm of science. As I have attempted to show elsewhere, the agreement between materialism and Leopardian pessimism has its basis in hedonism; and hedonism is the basis of all scientific systems of ethics. The problem of 'pleasure and pain', to use Pietro Verri's words,[8] is a problem that is scientific to the highest degree. That old age, sickness, etc. are causes of unhappiness for the great majority of persons afflicted with them is an objective fact, just as the suffering produced by social and political oppression is an objective fact. To cite as a counter-argument the heroic calm with which so many men have confronted suffering and death means that one has not taken into account the high price paid for the attainment of such calm. Of course, in addition to heroes there are fakirs: there are those who enjoy living on nails and there are 'social fakirs' who feel completely comfortable under the most oppressive regimes. But it still seems unwarranted to conclude that physical and social ills are a matter of 'subjective taste'.

Nor do I think that the question can be glossed over by pointing out, as Vacatello does, that Leopardi and Stendhal drew different axiological consequences from materialism. First of all, Stendhal's *Weltanschauung* is not at all the 'opposite' of Leopardi's; in both of them there is the same headlong rush of vitalism into pessimism, and even if the vitalism is more accentuated in Stendhal, his vision of life is just as tragic. Furthermore, the question has to be considered at an earlier stage, going back at least to the eighteenth century. One can then see that (as has already been noted) pessimistic themes were already present in Voltaire, Maupertuis,[9] Pietro Verri and other writers of the period, and that it is only because the

----

[8] The reference is to Pietro Verri's *Discorso sull'indole del piacere e del dolore* (Discourse on the Nature of Pleasure and Pain), written in 1773. Verri (1728–97), as an enlightenment polemicist, wrote against the retrogressive nature of the family, against out-dated cultural and literary forms, and against forms of economic and administrative organization which impeded the development of a market economy; as a student of human sensations, however, he held to the less than optimistic notion that all pleasures derive simply from a sudden lessening or cessation of pain. (NLB).

[9] Pierre Louis Moreau de Maupertuis (1698–1759): French mathematician, known for the principle of Least Action as applied to optics. (NLB).

element of struggle against the old obscurantist forces and the joy in being emancipated from religious prejudices still has the upper hand that these themes do not occupy a larger space. In Leopardi himself this element is not altogether absent: the 'bitter truth', when it is affirmed against degrading superstitions and errors, is a source of Enlightenment pride. Nonetheless, the general equilibrium has shifted in a pessimistic direction because Leopardi belongs to a different personal and cultural-political situation, which accords more space to the recognition of the unhappiness in which man finds himself *after* the destruction of religious and humanistic myths.[10]

With regard to socio-political oppression, a millennial philosophical tradition (represented in ancient times primarily by Stoicism, and in more recent times by idealism) has proffered 'inner freedom' as recompense. The man of culture is always free, even if he is subject to enslavement or torture, because he lives in a world of ideas over which external restrictions have no power. Marxism represents the most decisive and coherent refutation of this *consolatio philosophiae*. It contends that, except in those cases where the notion of inner freedom represents an extreme defensive posture designed to hold out the prospect of a future resurgence, so-called inner freedom is a poor substitute for true freedom, which cannot exist apart from man's actual emancipation from oppressive social relationships. But this refutation, if it is correct, is also valid for 'physical ills'. One cannot reject *consolatio philosophiae* as illusory in relation to socio-political oppression and at the same time regard it as completely valid and sufficient unto itself in relation to nature's oppression of man. In my opinion, this is the most valid aspect of Leopardian pessimism: its coherent refutation of all 'consolations', not only the crudely mythological ones provided by religion, as is obvious, but also those of an idealistic or stoical nature.

If the eighteenth-century theme 'of pleasure and of pain' was too much neglected by Marxism, that was a result of the fact that Marx and Engels had early on identified hedonism with bourgeois individualism in too summary a fashion. The polemic against 'robinsonades', despite a wealth of just arguments, carries with it the risk of denying the individual – not the individual as a 'persona'

---

[10] With regard to the delay in recognizing certain of the clearly pessimistic consequences of eighteenth-century materialism, see Giuseppe Paolo Samonà, *G. G. Belli: la commedia romana e la commedia celeste*, Florence 1969, pp. 117ff.

in a spiritualistic sense, whose revival is certainly not to be wished for, but the individual as a psycho-physiological reality. What in Marx and Engels is only a dangerous tendency (indeed in Engels's *The Origin of the Family* one can even find hedonist motifs which display great insight and polemical force), has become an actual feature of modern-day Marxism. The result has been that the revindication of the individual, denied on the materialist-hedonist level, has re-emerged in an altogether equivocal fashion: either as an acritical acceptance of psychoanalysis or, even worse, as 'socialist humanism'. Althusser is correct in rejecting this category of 'socialist humanism'. But the trouble is that with him this rejection culminates in an out-and-out rejection of the 'empirical individual', no better than that carried out by the idealists, which leaves unresolved the problems which the Marxist-Freudians and Marxist-humanists sought – however incorrectly – to confront.[11] I think that one can also begin to resolve the major problem of a materialist grounding for the world of values through a revival and a deepening of the 'epicurean' tradition of the seventeenth and eighteenth centuries – a tradition which is not limited to an abstract individualism and which rejects the equally abstract view that society or classes are the 'sole reality'. I shall elaborate on this question below.

Since my argument has already brought up the question of Engels on a number of occasions, I should like to clarify a point brought out by Cristofolini. We are probably in greater agreement than Cristofolini thinks. I do not at all think that the dialectic in Engels is a result of Marx's bad influence, nor that *The German Ideology* is a text that can be attributed entirely to Marx. I also recognize that certain 'pragmatist' germinations can be found in *Ludwig Feuerbach*. I merely contend that there is a departure from this in the mature Engels. This departure was not the result of some enfeebling of his thought – for Engels was not merely 'talented' but a man of genius – but corresponded to the objectively difficult situation Engels found himself in, both because he lived in a full-blown positivist era longer than Marx, and because he had an intense and specific interest in the natural sciences. On the one hand,

[11] Even Cesare Luporini, who has a largely favourable judgment (too favourable, in my opinion) of Althusser, remarks that his anti-humanism, 'to be frank about it, manifests itself in a tendency to make man disappear as much as possible from the theoretical framework of the so-called human sciences' (see the Introduction to the Italian edition of Althusser's *For Marx: Per Marx*, Rome 1967, p. xxiii).

Engels took greater account than Marx of the cosmic setting against which human history unfolds. He was cognizant, therefore, of the irreducibility of nature to a mere object of human labour or a mere pre-historical antecedent of a reality which is now entirely social-human. He sensed how even the prospect of communism as the realization of the 'realm of freedom' had its limitations in the future extinction of the human species – this being a theme which was strongly felt throughout positivist culture. On the other hand, he was correct in pointing out the serious danger of dissolving Marxism into a simple-minded Spencerian evolutionism or into a mindless empiricism, and he reacted with a hardening of his Hegelianism and with a polemical upgrading of the most obsolete part of Hegelianism, the Philosophy of Nature. This led him to an often excessive downgrading of English empiricism and to an equally excessive vindication of the merits of Oken and the *Naturphilosophie* of the early nineteenth century,[12] which he saw, somewhat one-sidedly, as the precursor of Darwinism (a precursor that, if anything, is rather to be sought in Buffon and the French materialism of the eighteenth century[13]). The obsolescence of these elements of archaic Hegelianism must be recognized; nevertheless, the work of the late Engels remains a brilliant attempt to fuse 'historical materialism' with the materialism of the natural sciences – an attempt to which one must still always refer back.

Finally, a few words about Cristofolini's proposal to define materialism as the philosophy of revolution and idealism as the ideology of the ruling class. According to this view, to debate the question of the primacy of matter or spirit is to remain in the realm of ideology. It is much more materialist to struggle against capital than to assert the primacy of the biological over the social or over the cultural. And even in the field of culture, every contribution to the demystification of bourgeois values and to the analysis of capitalist society 'is materialism (and science) to a higher degree than all the writings in defence of materialism from the Greeks to the present day; just as *Imperialism, The Highest Stage of Capitalism*

[12] Lorenz Oken (1779–1851): founder of the German school of 'nature philosophers', who speculated on the origin of life and generally ascribed it to a life force beyond the ken of empirical scientific investigation. (NLB).

[13] George Louis Leclerc de Buffon (1707–88): moving force behind the thirty-volume *Histoire naturelle* (1749–88) and author of *Epoques de la nature* (1778), which gave an impetus to later evolutionist theories with its claim that the universe is the result of a slow process of transformation. (NLB).

is more materialist than *Materialism and Empirio-Criticism'*.

If this is a declaration of the greater urgency of the revolutionary task with respect to cultural tasks; if it means that the revolution, even if carried out by those who have not attained a fully materialist consciousness, lays the groundwork for materialism to an infinitely greater degree than anybody's reflections on materialism, because it provides the impetus to create a new socio-cultural situation in which all forms of spiritualism will lead a hard life – if this is all that is meant, then it is perfectly correct.

If, however, one were to maintain that there is a complete identity between materialism and philosophy of revolution, then I cannot agree. The struggle for an integrally secular and demythologized vision of the world is certainly intimately connected with the struggle for a society of equals, but there have been and there still remain major disjunctures between the two levels.[14] Without dwelling on historical examples, I shall simply call to mind the particularly meaningful contrast between Rousseau and his French materialist contemporaries. While far more advanced on the socio-political level, Rousseau is at the same time far more closely linked to religious prejudices and far less interested in the fight for a modern science of nature. If one wishes, one may certainly say that Rousseau is *more materialist* than Diderot or Baron d'Holbach, in that he is more revolutionary. But it is clear that this is true only in a paradoxical sense, and that the disjuncture between the two levels is undeniable. An analysis in depth of this problem would probably show that the first source of this disjuncture resides in the division of society into classes. Liberation from myth and fallacy is more easily attainable, on the scientific level, by individuals of the ruling class – who are precisely those with the greatest stake in the mystification of social relationships. Those, on the other hand, who have nothing to lose but their chains, and are therefore in the best position to elaborate a scientific vision of the world, are precisely those least equipped with the specifically cultural preparation necessary to elaborate it, as a consequence of the state of oppression in which they are held by the ruling class.

Certainly, Marxism represents the highest synthesis of philosophical-scientific clarity and liberating movement of the oppressed to have emerged till now. Nevertheless, the full practical unification

[14] See, in this regard, the remarks of Antonio La Penna in an article on Lucretius, *l' Unità,* 3 November 1963.

of the two poles can take place only with the realization of communism on a world-wide scale, precisely because it implies the abolition of all inequalities in development among men – i.e. an end not only to the division of society into classes but also to its consequences on the cultural level. In the present situation, one cannot simply define as 'ideological' (in the pejorative sense) a polemic against philosophic idealism, just as it would make no sense to address such an accusation to a polemic in defence of evolutionism and declare that those who make the revolution are more Darwinian than those who argue against the anti-evolutionists on a philosophical or biological level. Otherwise we would lapse, ultimately, into a total indifference towards the natural sciences, which would then make the very construction of communist society impossible.

# 3

# Engels, Materialism and 'Free Will'

Two recent works by Lucio Colletti (the introduction to the Italian edition of Bernstein's *Evolutionary Socialism* and the book on *Marxism and Hegel*, to which could be added Iring Fetscher's *Marx and Marxism* and Alfred Schmidt's *The Concept of Nature in Marx*, the latter introduced by Colletti in its Italian edition[1]) make it necessary once again to re-examine a characteristic common to a great deal of contemporary Western Marxism: anti-Engelsism.

This is not merely a historiographic question to be left to specialists; it is also a political and theoretical problem of contemporary relevance. The downgrading of Engels implies a particular mode of understanding Marxism today. During the twentieth century, each time that a particular intellectual current has taken the upper hand in bourgeois culture – be it empirio-criticism, Bergsonism, Croceanism, phenomenology, neo-positivism or structuralism – certain Marxists have attempted to 'interpret' Marx's thought in such a way as to make it as homogeneous as possible with the predominant philosophy. This did not at all mean that there was not a sincere, and often fruitful, desire for discussion and mutual encounter. But it did mean a wish for the mutual encounter to take place on common ground; a wish that Marxism should appear as the philosophy which had already satisfied in advance the requirements of the most avant-garde

[1] Colletti's introduction to Bernstein now appears as an essay entitled 'Bernstein and the Marxism of the Second International' in *From Rousseau to Lenin*, NLB 1972; the second part of *Il Marxismo e Hegel* has also been translated – see *Marxism and Hegel*, NLB 1973; see also Iring Fetscher, *Marx and Marxism*, New York 1971, and Alfred Schmidt, *The Concept of Nature in Marx*, NLB 1971. (NLB).

With regard to the question of materialism, I find myself in much greater agreement with an essay written by Colletti before his anti-Engelsian 'shift'; see 'Il materialismo storico e la scienza', *Società*, No. 11, 1955, pp. 785ff.

elements of bourgeois culture, or which was at least able to incorporate them within itself without distorting itself. Above all else, it was feared that Marxism might appear to be a naïve, simplistic, and out-dated philosophy. This situation has continued into the present; indeed, the rapid pace with which cultural fashions succeed one another in the West forces certain Marxists to undergo ever more rapid metamorphoses. Althusser's structuralist-leaning Marxism represents, for the time being, the latest in these modernizing operations. No sooner have you begun to rejoice at the refutation of the 'humanist' and 'historicist' version of Marxism than you realize that it is bourgeois culture itself, in its advanced technocratic phase, that has repudiated humanism and historicism. Now that one cannot win anyone's ear unless one translates the most commonplace things into structuralist language, the task of Marxists appears to have become one of proving that Marxism is the best of all possible structuralisms.

In all of these operations, there is a need for somebody on whom everything which Marxists, at that particular moment, are asking to get rid of can be dumped. That somebody is Friedrich Engels. Vulgar materialism? Determinism? Naturalistic metaphysics? Archaic and schematic Hegelianism? Marx turns out to be free of all these vices, provided one knows how to 'read' him. It was Engels who, in his zeal to simplify and vulgarize Marxism, contaminated it. Thus, whereas Engels is loaded down with materialist ballast, Marx can take on that physiognomy of a profound and subtle (and still uncomprehended) great intellectual which is *de rigueur* in our cultural world.

As I have had occasion to note at other times, this is the story not only of reformist Marxism but also, to a large degree, of contemporary revolutionary Marxism in the West. In a situation in which the extra-parliamentary Left has been represented till now, for a variety of reasons, primarily by intellectual vanguards, even the revolutionary intellectual is wary of crude formulations; he too, therefore, has something with which to debit Engels. If the reformist of our day sees primarily a blameworthy denial of 'humanism' and the 'freedom of the spirit' in Engels's materialism and determinism, the revolutionary sees the denial of voluntarism and the illusion of a spontaneous collapse or gradual reform of the capitalist system.

Colletti comes close to this second type of anti-Engelsian

sentiment; but he has his own distinct characteristics, which lend to his position a particular interest and congeniality, despite the disagreements we shall be frank about expressing. In the first place, what is particularly pleasing in Colletti is the great lucidity of his thought and exposition, something exceedingly rare in contemporary European Marxism. We are confronted with an Enlightenment mind, full of healthy dislike for any form of existentialistic vapouring. At last we find a Marxist who defends the claims of the *intellect* as against those of ambiguous *reason*.[2] This is the root not only of Colletti's anti-Hegelianism, but also of his hostility towards Horkheimer and Adorno (whose obscurantist characteristics, partially revived in Marcuse, are fully brought to light by Colletti) and towards Althusser (in whose case the lines of the counter-argument are perhaps drawn up too sketchily, even though they tend in the right direction, in my opinion). This accounts also for his clear-cut denunciation of the intrinsically idealist nature of the Hegelian dialectic and of the impossibility of transforming it into a materialist device simply by 'turning it upside-down'. We shall return to this point below.

In the introduction to Bernstein, the socio-political side of Colletti's Marxism comes out more clearly. Here too one has to acknowledge two important points: an interpretation (both original and persuasive) of 'abstract labour' as *objectively* abstract labour and thus as alienated labour, and an elucidation (not new, but developed in a very lucid and timely fashion) of the necessary connection in Marx's thought between the slavery of the wage-labourer and the juridical-political freedom and equality of the citizen in the bourgeois state.

Given writings so rich in theoretical and polemical insights, it would obviously be senseless to become upset at every little stretching of the argument or historiographic inaccuracy. Someone who puts forward a theoretical argument with contemporary political implications has every right to overlook certain philological niceties (i.e. remit them to another forum or other thinkers). But the problem is that we can find in these writings arbitrary historical judgments which, in the final analysis, are such as to impair the theoretical argument as well. It is here that we find ourselves faced again with the phenomenon of anti-Engelsism, in an exasperated

---

[2] The 'intellect' refers to the German term *Verstand* in its Hegelian meaning. See explanatory note, *Marxism and Hegel*, p. 9. (NLB).

form. The anti-Engels operation, which was begun as a repudiation of the burdensome patrimony of Hegelianism and as a rediscovery of an authentic materialism, ends by seriously compromising the materialism itself, as a consequence of the simplistic manner in which it has been carried out.

According to Colletti, 'dialectical materialism' is a crude misunderstanding of which Engels alone was guilty – a misunderstanding thoroughly alien to the true thought of Marx. Under the illusion that he was founding a superior form of materialism, Engels supposedly reproduced, in a banalized form, the 'dialectic of matter' already present in its entirety in Hegel – quite unaware of the anti-materialist function that Hegel had explicitly assigned to it. From Engels there supposedly sprang a pseudo-Marxist tradition encompassing *all* of Marxism. The Lenin of *Materialism and Empirio-Criticism*, who in the first part of *Marxism and Hegel* (dating back to 1958) was still partially exonerated from the indictment, is fully implicated by the time the second part is written in 1968. So-called Western Marxism, from Korsch and the early Lukács down to Marcuse, despite its anti-materialist *and anti-Engelsian* polemic, also supposedly betrays its line of descent from Engels's fallacious Marxism.

Whereas in *Marxism and Hegel* the most negative feature of Engels's thought is ascribed to his acritical adoption of the Hegelian dialectic, in the introduction to Bernstein (published just a year earlier) more prominence is given to the other accusation traditionally made against Engels: contamination of Marxism with vulgar materialism, Darwinism, and 'fatalism'. Colletti would probably say that there is no contradiction between the two accusations. One could even trace back a Hegelian bent in vulgar materialism (one need only think of Moleschott's background[3]) to a misunderstanding of Hegel. One could also say that this wavering between vulgar materialism and archaic Hegelianism exists in Engels himself, and that both of the accusations against him are, therefore, warranted. The fact remains, however, that the anti-Engelsism of the introduction to Bernstein and the more virulent kind to be found in *Marxism and Hegel* remain two unintegrated lines of argument. As we shall see, this contributes to the lack of understanding of Engels's personality and what Engels still

[3] Jakob Moleschott (1822–93): Dutch physiologist and philosopher, who interspersed materialism and Hegelian idealism in his writings. (NLB).

has to teach Marxists, despite all his undeniable (though not commonplace) contradictions.

Marx is supposed to have been a witness to the decimation of his philosophy by his closest friend and collaborator without batting an eyelash. As can be shown by the correspondence between the two of them, Marx followed closely the germination of the *Dialectics of Nature*; he read all of the *Anti-Dühring* before its publication and collaborated on it by writing a chapter for it; and yet he supposedly never felt the need to disassociate himself from a metaphysical construction that was the antithesis of his own thought! This objection may not have the merit of being new, but it does have the merit of never having received a satisfactory reply.[4] Nor do I think that it could ever receive one. Those, like Schmidt, who still talk about the difference between Marxism and Engels-ism in somewhat obscure terms, may *perhaps* be content to remark that 'it cannot be established how far Marx was conscious of this difference between his concept of nature and that of Engels'.[5] Those, like Colletti, who sharpen the difference to the point that it becomes a matter of Engels's complete misunderstanding, take away any likely explanation for Marx's silence.

Everyone who begins by representing Engels in the role of a banalizer and distorter of Marx's thought inevitably ends by finding many of Marx's own statements too 'Engelsian'. The upshot is that one attempts either to go from the mature Marx back to the Marx of the *Economic and Philosophic Manuscripts of 1844* and the *Theses on Feuerbach,* or else to ferret out the *true* philosophy of Marx from the logico-epistemological structure of *Capital* while disregarding those explicitly philosophical statements which can be found in the mature Marx. Althusser opts exclusively for the second alternative, since the first alternative has been consciously eliminated for him by virtue of his exceedingly rigid periodization of Marx's thought.[6] Colletti, who protests against Althusser's *coupures* with a good deal of justification, but also with the risk of jumbling together all the phases of Marx's thought, follows now one path and now the other. In any case, all anti-Engelsian Marxists share the most intense distaste for the single overall (even if

---

[4] It was put forth by Cesare Cases, for example, against the Italian neo-positivists of the fifties, who also were naturally anti-Engelsian; see *Marxismo e neopositivismo,* Turin 1958, p. 65.

[5] *The Concept of Nature in Marx,* p. 207, note 121.

abbreviated) statement the mature Marx has given us of his philosophy: the preface to *A Contribution to the Critique of Political Economy* (1859). For all of them, the best possible development in Marxist philology would be conclusive proof that that preface was written by Engels. With regard to the distinction between structure and superstructure (another 'crudity' which would have to be expunged from Marxism), Colletti reluctantly admits that 'at least part of the blame' for the harmful developments arising from this distinction goes back to the preface of 1859 – although Colletti claims that this distinction 'rarely occurs in Marx and is little more than a metaphor', as opposed to Engels's more frequent and literal use of it.[7] How much more profound and less Engelsian the introduction of 1857 is! It is indeed true that this introduction is not at all simply a rough draft of the preface of 1859, just as the *Grundrisse* as a whole are not a rough draft either for *A Contribution to the Critique of Political Economy* or for *Capital*. Nevertheless, it does, after all, mean something that Marx wrote the preface of '59 later than the introduction of '57 and that, unlike the latter, he published the former.

In counterposition to a retrograde Hegelian Engels, in Colletti's reconstruction, there stands an unconscious Kantian Marx. It makes little difference that Marx's explicit allusions to Kant are exceedingly rare and not very complimentary. Does Marx not say that the 'given' is irreducible to the activity of the thinking subject, and

[6] On this point, see the excellent analysis in Ernest Mandel, *The Formation of the Economic Thought of Karl Marx*, NLB 1971, pp. 158–9, note 15. One cannot help but detect in the rigidity of this periodization the influence of a certain kind of structuralism, according to which history could be reduced to the comparison of different 'states', each of which is self-contained, coherent within itself, and devoid of dynamic impetus. Thus, what could have been (and to a certain degree is) a very important contribution to historicization in the study of Marxism is weakened by this vision of the development 'by spurts' of Marx's thought. Subsequently, Althusser, while following precisely the opposite itinerary to that of the '1844 Marxists' (but one no less absurd and even more paradoxical), was to state that the genuine Marx, freed of all Hegelian influence, was not to be found in the part of *Capital* he published but only in the *Critique of the Gotha Programme* and in the commentary on Wagner. That amounts to saying that almost all of Marx is pre-Marxist, and that the first Marxist is Althusser. The latter's disdain for the 'subject' continues to grow with the one exception of those instances in which the subject is . . . Althusser himself. Grotesque statements of this kind have worn thin the patience of even Luporini (*Dialettica e materialismo*, p. 257, n. 33), who initially had conceded too much to Althusser (indeed still continues to do so, in my opinion).

[7] *From Rousseau to Lenin*, p. 65, note 38.

that 'real existence' is 'something more' than all that is contained in the concept? This, then, is what Marx 'clearly' derives from Kant, 'whether he was aware of it or not, and whatever may have been the process of mediation'.[8]

Colletti is correct when he says that Kant is the 'only classical German philosopher in whom it is possible to detect at least a grain of materialism'.[9] This recognition for Kant is overdue on the part of Marxism, which has too long shared the disdain of Hegel and the young Hegelians for a thinker who had had strong reasons (reasons that were not merely religious and conservative but also scientific and progressive) for not adhering to idealism. It is significant that two Marxists with such diverse backgrounds as Luporini and Colletti should arrive at this recognition by different paths; those pages in which Colletti clarifies his points of agreement and disagreement with Luporini are among the most interesting in *Marxism and Hegel*.[10] But what one cannot understand is why the affirmation of the existence of a reality not reducible to thought (which is a feature shared by all non-idealists) should be regarded in and of itself as specific proof of Kantianism; and why, on the other hand, one should overlook the existence in pre-Kantian English and French thought of philosophers who had very much more than 'a grain' of materialism! On the one hand, Colletti presents himself as a vindicator of Enlightenment motifs within Marxism; and that should mean an opening towards Voltaire, Diderot, La Mettrie, Holbach, and all those thinkers regarded as 'short on speculation' by the spiritualistic tradition in the history of philosophy but reassessed by Marx himself in the famous excursus in the sixth chapter of the *Holy Family*. On the other hand, one has the impression that for Colletti the game has been played out solely within the framework of classical German philosophy, as if the only saint to whom a materialist could have commended himself before Feuerbach and Marx would have been Kant.

For Colletti, Kant's limitation lies in his failure to recognize labour as a practical-knowing activity, by virtue of which the object is not only an 'in itself' but also an 'objectification of the

---

[8] *Marxism and Hegel*, pp. 121–2.
[9] Ibid. p. 105.
[10] See Cesare Luporini, *Spazio e materia in Kant*, Florence 1961 and Colletti, *Marxism and Hegel*, pp. 54ff.

subject'.[11] This is the same criticism made by the young Marx against traditional materialism: its neglect of the 'active side'. It appears that one should conclude that, apart from this lacuna which was bridged only with Marx, Kantianism is already a form of materialism. But if materialism amounted merely to the recognition of a reality external to the subject, then Plato, Saint Thomas, and all their followers would also be materialists. Materialism is not just 'realism'; it is also recognition of the physical nature of the subject, and of the physical nature of his activities traditionally regarded as 'spiritual'. From this standpoint, not only Kant's second and third *Critiques* but even the first are oriented in an anti-materialist direction. The consequence is that even his recognition of a reality external to the subject reduces itself to something exceedingly obscure, always on the verge, on the one hand, of being absorbed within the activity of the subject, and, on the other, of becoming a transcendental reality accessible only to a privileged and supranatural experience. It is not a matter of chance that the anti-idealist Kantians, like Herbart,[12] have less to say to Marxists than the idealists.

Obviously, we do not mean by this that a contemporary materialism can 'leap' from Diderot to Feuerbach and Marx without re-examining the *Critique of Pure Reason* and all of Kant's work. But this re-examination must be accompanied by an awareness that one is dealing with an anti-materialist tradition of thought, different from that to which Marx belongs.

It is precisely Colletti's attitude vis-à-vis Marx's presumed Kantianism that indicates, it seems to me, the rather narrow limits of his materialism. It is an almost exclusively 'methodological' materialism, of the empirio-criticist variety. This accounts, therefore, on the one hand for his particularly intense intolerance for Engels's Hegelian inheritance (in Marx he makes heroic efforts not to see it[13]), on the other hand for his failure to understand Engels's

[11] *Marxism and Hegel*, p. 219.

[12] Johann Friedrich Herbart (1776–1841): German philosopher and educator, who reacted against idealism by returning to the atomistic realism of the Eleatic school of philosophy. (NLB).

[13] With regard to Marx, Colletti has now changed his position somewhat; see 'Political and Philosophical Interview', *New Left Review*, No. 86 (July–August 1974), p. 13, and see also 'Marxism and the Dialectic', *New Left Review*, No. 93 (September–October 1975), pp. 12ff. This essay, because of the serious questions it raises in a lucid and courageous fashion, demands the careful attention of Marxists.

own materialism, which, like every true materialism, is not merely methodological. Rather, to use a word that horrifies the methodologists, it is a *Weltanschauung*, open to all the rectifications which the progress of scientific research and social practice will make necessary, but not so 'open' as to fade into agnosticism.

Colletti, like Schmidt and Fetscher, maintains that Engels ventured into a useless and negative operation when, under the spell of the very vulgar materialism he sought to oppose, he attempted to enlarge Marx's historical materialism into 'cosmic' dimensions. In substance, the argument is the following: Marx's great achievement, at once gnoseological and socio-political, was to have understood that through their labour men enter into social relationships and also into relationships with nature; thus, there is no knowledge that is not a function of man's transformation of nature. Having attained this point of view, so superior to that of all previous philosophy, why should one retrogress back to a philosophy of 'nature in itself'? Why should one patch up a 'philosophic odyssey of matter' to compete with Hegel's and Schelling's philosophy and with the crude generalizations of positivism?

This objection is, in my opinion, mistaken both theoretically and historically. It is the objection of those who, at once, are not materialist enough and fail to take account of the changed philosophic-scientific setting in post-1850 Germany and Europe in comparison with the era in which the young Marx formulated his criticisms of Feuerbach. Although a Moleschott or a Büchner[14] was inferior to Feuerbach from a purely philosophic standpoint, nevertheless their materialism had many more links to the natural sciences than had Feuerbach's so-called materialism (in reality, more of a naturalistic humanism). The former were not satisfied simply with stating the primacy of the sensuous over the conceptual and with turning theology into anthropology. They also searched for an explanation of sensuousness – as well as intelligence and morality – in biological terms. Confronted by a materialism of this kind, the objection raised by Marx against Feuerbach, that the latter overlooked the 'active side', was still valid; but it appeared insufficient and too generic, since the claim of the new materialism

[14] Ludwig Büchner (1824–99): German materialist philosopher and scientist, whose *Kraft und Stoff* (1855) created a sensation with its denial of God and free will and its interpretation of consciousness as a physical state of the brain produced by matter in motion. (NLB).

(as well as of eighteenth-century French materialism) was to explain even this active side in scientific terms, i.e. as a complex of 'material' processes obeying certain laws. And it should be noted that the claim was – *and is* – correct, even if the subsequent execution of the plan was guilty of being quite simplistic and crude. As everyone knows, the simplistic and crude features were the result primarily of two factors: 1. the reduction of man's cultural, moral and political behaviour to biological activities *without any mediation*, and thus a failure to take account of the 'second nature' which labour confers to man within the animal realm, to which man still continues to belong; 2. the assessment of social inequalities and injustices as 'ills' to be cured by science, and thus a disregard for the necessity of the class struggle and an omission of any analysis of the class position (and concomitant non-impartiality) of the scientists themselves. But the reply to these distortions should have been given *within the framework of materialism*, and not with a mere revindication of the subjective element, still conceived in spiritual-istic terms as an unconditioned praxis that finds its limit only in the 'objective (external) conditions' and not also in man's own physical and biological nature.

This became all the more necessary after Darwin's great discovery gave rise to a second wave of materialism, which overtook the old conception of nature as an 'eternal cycle' (still shared, for example, by Moleschott), and which no longer allowed one to regard historicity as a characteristic peculiar to humanity. Here too the danger arose of reducing human history to natural history without any mediations – but to this danger as well one had to reply in materialist terms. Among other things, evolutionism posed again the question of the existence of nature before man, of the origin of mankind and of its future disappearance. To what extent would the 'second nature' established with the appearance of labour and what one might call the 'third nature' developed with the passage to communist society be able to push back the biological limits of man? These were the questions raised by a philosophy which, however crude and reactionary it may have been, at least had the merit of representing itself not just as methodological reflections on science but also as a reflection on man's situation and possibilities as revealed by scientific research. Thus, it represented a powerful claim against anthropocentrism.

On the other hand, contemporaneous with this current of thought in the middle and late nineteenth century, there was a second current, of degenerated empiricism, which tended towards agnosticism and even flirted with religion. The future 'reaction against positivism' was already germinating within positivism itself.

One need only think of this complex situation in order to understand that the so-called cosmological development of Marxism did not represent an impulsive direction undertaken by Engels, but rather an objective necessity. Engels took on this task just as he generally took on all the tasks connected with polemizing with contemporary culture, while Marx concentrated all of his energies on a single great opus, *Capital*. We should note here, *en passant*, that any serious examination of the differences between the two founders of Marxism must begin not with simplistic contrasts between the philosophic profundity of the one and the presumed superficiality of the other, but rather with the division of labour that was established between them. Naturally, this was not a division of labour between two identical men of genius who could just as easily have exchanged parts. The division took place on the basis of the different interests of the two men, and once it had been established it contributed to a further differentiation of the two personalities.[15] In a sense, Engels's lot was the least rewarding, since he, like Lenin in *Materialism and Empirio-Criticism*, had to deal with matters in which he was not a specialist. Moreover, after Marx's death, he could do this only during the odd moments left him by the immense work of editing and publishing *Capital* and by the ever vaster political and organizational tasks which confronted him. The preface to the second edition of *Anti-Dühring* shows that he was aware of the risks, and the fact that he did not complete the *Dialectics of Nature* confirms it. Nevertheless, it was impossible to avoid confronting the natural sciences and the philosophies which had emerged from them.

To regard the writings devoted by Engels to the philosophy of nature as a mere banalized repetition of Hegel's philosophy of

[15] With regard to Engels, one has to take into account both his greater interest in the natural sciences (see the preface to the second edition of *Anti-Dühring*) and his readier receptivity towards new cultural and socio-political facts (see Marx's letter of 4 July 1864: 'You know that 1. I am slow in getting to new things, and 2. that I always follow in your footsteps' [*Werke*, XXX, 418]; this is an obvious allusion to the role of 'precursor' played by Engels in relation to Marx even in the area of political economy – save for the fact that Engels did not precede Marx in going deeper into political economy).

nature (or as a partial capitulation by Engels before vulgar materialism) is to overlook a fundamental feature of these writings: the polemic against the negative sides of positivism. These negative qualities were brought out by Engels with great clarity. *Anti-Dühring*, the notes for the *Dialectics of Nature*, the final part of *Ludwig Feuerbach* and many pages of *The Origin of the Family* are designed to oppose, on the one hand, 'an empiricism which as far as possible itself forbids thought' and precisely for that reason leaves itself open to religious or even superstitious meanderings,[16] and, on the other, the claim of German vulgar materialism to 'apply the nature theory to society and to reform socialism'.[17] With Dühring – an adversary too insignificant in and of himself to merit such a thorough refutation, as Engels himself well knew – Engels argued against the fallacies and the superficial eclecticism typical of a great deal of the positivism of the second half of the nineteenth century.

It is, therefore, too simplistic to say that Engels rejected, in the name of the Hegelian dialectic, 'real materialism, i.e. modern science' as a form of metaphysics. Between Marxism and the science of the second half of the nineteenth century there were the Dührings, i.e. the slipshod and incompetent philosophic interpreters of the great scientific achievements. And at times the scientists and the Dührings were united in the same persons. Among the scientists themselves there was a tendency to dismiss philosophy which resulted in an inability to parallel the great advances of the natural sciences with an equally 'revolutionary' development in the social sciences. This explains Engels's warning that the scientists who 'abuse philosophy most are slaves to precisely the worst vulgarized relics of the worst philosophers'.[18]

Furthermore, Engels saw very well that the vulgar materialism of Moleschott, Vogt,[19] and Büchner himself[20] had arisen as a pre-

[16] Friedrich Engels, *Dialectics of Nature*, New York 1940, p. 84. See also first appendix to *Lugwig Feuerbach*, New York 1941, p. 68: '. . . those numerous scientists who are inexorable materialists within their science but who, outside it, are not only idealists but even pious, nay orthodox, Christians'. See also the essay 'Natural Science and the Spirit World', in *Dialectics of Nature*, pp. 297–310.

[17] *Dialectics of Nature*, p. 153.

[18] Ibid., p. 184.

[19] Karl Vogt (1817–95): German biologist. (NLB)

[20] Büchner is less deserving than the other two of the epithet 'vulgar', although in the socio-political field he shared in their superficiality. [Büchner subscribed to 'Social Darwinism' – NLB.] See V. Somenzi, 'Materialismo e cibernetica', *Nuovi Argomenti*, July–December 1966, pp. 253ff.

Darwinian materialism holding to the theory of the immutability of the species, and that their subsequent adherence to Darwinism (which was not without reservations, particularly on the part of Vogt) had not brought about a total rethinking of their original conception of an ahistorical nature. 'A lease was at once taken out by these gentlemen' on Darwinism, but it was not actually absorbed.[21] This observation is all the more incisive in that the confusion between vulgar materialism (in the strict sense) and Darwinism has persisted, among both idealists and Marxists.

In relation to Darwin's own work, one finds neither an Engels more inclined to unqualified admiration and a Marx more inclined to be cautious and critical, nor an Engels who – in contradistinction to Marx – claimed to 'dialecticize' or to 'Hegelianize' Darwinism. It is a well-known fact that Engels's admiration for the *Origin of Species* was entirely shared by Marx, to the point that he regarded Darwinism as something corresponding in the history of nature to what he was attempting to carry out in political economy.[22] It is also a well-known fact that both of them expressed certain reservations, first with regard to the 'clumsy English methodology' used in Darwin's work,[23] and then, above all, with regard to the aberrant developments of social Darwinism. But it is interesting to see that Engels's objections go somewhat farther than those of Marx.

In his letter of 15 February 1869 to Laura and Paul Lafargue, Marx wrote: 'Recognition of the struggle for existence in English

---

[21] *Dialectics of Nature*, p. 152 (translation modified).

[22] See Lombardo Radice's introduction to the Italian edition of the *Dialectics of Nature*, in which he brings up again the fact that Marx had intended to dedicate the second volume of *Capital* to Darwin. See also Valentino Gerratana, 'Marx and Darwin', *New Left Review*, No. 82 (November–December 1973), pp. 60ff. In some respects, my remarks were anticipated by Gerratana (the essay was first published in Italy in 1959). Gerratana has examined much more deeply than I the relationship between Darwin and Malthus, deflating the scientific claims which have come out of it. Like all of his other writings, the article is completely divorced from any anti-Engelsianism, although it fails, perhaps, to bring out sufficiently the slight – but nonetheless perceptible – difference between Marx and Engels in their attitude towards Darwin's work.

[23] Two themes come together in this criticism: on the one hand, a certain annoyance with that excessive expository detail to which even recent scholars of a non-Marxist background have called attention (see, for example, G. Montalenti's introduction to the Italian edition of the *Origin of Species*, Turin 1959, p. xxxi); on the other hand, that vindication of the great German philosophic tradition as against 'narrow' English empiricism, which represents both a strength and a danger for the Marxist mode of thought (for Marx no less than Engels).

society (the *bellum omnium contra omnes*) led Darwin to discover the struggle for survival as the fundamental law of vegetable and animal life. Darwinism, however, regards this as a decisive reason why human society will never be able to free itself from its feral state.'[24] Of these two analogous movements – from contemporary capitalist society to the biological world and from the biological world to human society *in general* – Marx considered only the second, formulated by 'Darwinism' or the social Darwinists, to be invalid. The first is correct because, as Marx had already noted in a letter to Engels of 18 June 1862, bourgeois society is a 'bestial' society *par excellence* and can thus represent a valid model for the zoologist.

A number of years afterwards, when Engels again took up this Marxist refutation of social Darwinism, he retained Marx's judgment concerning the invalidity of the second movement, but indicated that he was not in complete agreement with the first either. 'The whole Darwinian theory of the struggle for life is simply the transference from society to organic nature of Hobbes's theory of *bellum omnium contra omnes,* and of the bourgeois economic theory of competition, as well as the Malthusian theory of population. When once this feat has been accomplished (the unconditional justification for which, especially as regards the Malthusian theory, is still very questionable), it is very easy to transfer these theories back again from natural history to the history of society, and altogether too naïve to maintain that thereby these assertions have been proved as eternal natural laws of society.'[25]

Thus Marx, although he expressed his reservations over Darwin's use of Malthus, was primarily pleased with the felicitous *polemical* motif represented by the analogy between bourgeois society and the animal world (an analogy which gave full satisfaction to his taste for bringing out the irony inherent in things).[26] Engels, on the other hand, put greater stress on the *scientific* requirement that one not confuse the struggle for life in capitalist society (which

[24] Marx-Engels, *Werke,* Berlin 1965, XXXII, p. 592.

[25] *Dialectics of Nature,* p. 208. An almost identical passage can be found in Engels' letter to Lavrov of 12–17 November 1875.

[26] This polemical motif reappears in Engels, *Dialectics of Nature,* p. 19: 'Darwin did not know what a bitter satire he wrote on mankind, and especially on his countrymen, when he showed that free competition, the struggle for existence, which the economists celebrate as the highest achievement, is the normal state of the *animal kingdom.*'

takes place, as Labriola would have said, on the 'artificial terrain' created by determinate relations of production) with the struggle for life in the animal world (which is a struggle for survival at the most elementary level, conditioned by a natural setting which provides a certain measure of means of subsistence not subject to increase through the efforts of the animals themselves). This distinction – which obviously was also familiar to Marx, but which was not used by him in his polemic against social Darwinism – was developed by Engels with perfect clarity in the latter part of the very note from the *Dialectics of Nature* just cited, where he was polemicizing against those who sought to dissolve the specificity of the class struggle into a generic 'struggle for life'.

Furthermore, the need to disentangle Darwinism as much as possible from Malthusianism – i.e. from an economic theory whose flaws had been brought out by Marxism itself – led Engels to make an even more incisive distinction between the two phenomena: on the one hand, the selection generated by simple animal and vegetable overpopulation; on the other, the selection generated by the necessity of adaptation to a changed environment. He saw only the latter as the mechanism for the formation of new species, viewing the former simply as an accelerating factor, which need not even be present.[27]

Engels always rejected any attempt to represent human institutions as pure extensions of animal 'institutions' (for example, in the particularly effective polemic on monogamy in the second chapter of *The Origin of the Family*). On the other hand, however, he was not satisfied with a mere recognition of the difference between the animal world and the human world. The problem which he regarded as uniquely his own – and which places him in the position at once of ally and critic of contemporary scientific culture – concerns the fusion of the two worlds and two different kinds of historicity. This is the theme of *The Origin of the Family* and of his uncompleted work on 'The Part Played by Labour in the Transition from Ape to Man' in the *Dialectics of Nature*. This was also the reason for his interest in the long period of 'unwritten history' traversed by mankind before its division into classes (one need only think of the note added by him to the first proposition of the *Manifesto* in the English edition of 1888).

[27] *Dialectics of Nature*, pp. 236ff.

There was, of course, the danger of committing the error that was just the opposite of social Darwinism: i.e. of accepting an evolutionary hypothesis not on the basis of its scientific grounding but because it furthered the illusion of a ready fusion between the rhythm of natural history and the rhythm of human history. This accounts, for example, for the favourable judgment which Plekhanov was to pass a little later on Hugo De Vries's theory of evolution 'by leaps', precisely because it appeared to have a more 'dialectical', 'revolutionary', and anti-gradualist character.[28] In more recent times, it also accounts for the neo-Lamarckian and neo-vitalist posturings of Lysenko. In Engels, the most that one could find, if one wished to be pedantic, would be a few remarks indicating an excessive confidence in certain developments in evolutionism brought about by Ernst Haeckel, who took over certain Lamarckian themes with excessive haste and 'systematizing spirit', going so far as to dredge up again the already refuted theory of 'spontaneous generation'.[29] In the final analysis, these tentative remarks are few and far between. The simple-mindedness of Haeckel's 'monism' and his relapse into the mould of the old 'philosophy of nature' despite his ardent professions of materialism did not at all escape Engels's attention. In biology he remained a Darwinian and not a Lamarckian, and his defence of Darwinism against Dühring's misinterpretations and Lamarckian sympathies shows this in the clearest possible way.[30] Thus, the problem of the fusion between the two historicities was formulated by him in the correct terms. On the one hand, he refused to superimpose extraneous evolutionary models on either natural history or human history. On the other hand, he did not close his eyes to the persistence of the 'natural' within the 'human' (and in this respect his teachings were to be followed and developed in an original fashion by Labriola).

[28] Georg Plekhanov, *Fundamental Problems of Marxism*, New York 1969, pp. 46ff.
[29] *Dialectics of Nature*, p. 188; *Anti-Dühring*, London 1939, pp. 80ff; and for Haeckel's ill-famed 'monera', *Dialectics of Nature*, pp. 179–81, 188.
[30] For Engel's critique of Haeckel see *Dialectics of Nature*, pp. 176, 225–6, 319, 320ff; for his defence of Darwinism see *Anti-Dühring*, Part I, Chapter VII, in which, as a polemical reaction against Dühring's anti-Darwinist nonsense, his adherence to Darwinism is more accentuated than in any of the passages from *Dialectics of Nature* cited above. His detachment from Lamarckism and, at the same time, his correct assessment of its great historical importance are expressed well in *Anti-Dühring*, p. 83.

It is true that the Hegelian dialectic – even 'turned on its head' or 'extracted from its mystical shell' – was an inappropriate instrument for correcting the shortcomings of either vulgar materialism or agnostic empiricism. I have already expressed my agreement with Colletti on this point, which still divides Marxists. However, it is completely mistaken, in my opinion, to present this rejection of the Hegelian dialectic in terms of contraposition of a Marx supposed to have formulated a dialectic totally different from the Hegelian one to an Engels supposed to have restated Hegel in a banalized form; or else (as Schmidt tends to maintain) of a Marx who had every right to use the dialectic in the human sciences to an Engels who was so stupid as to attempt to apply it to the natural sciences.

An open-minded analysis of the positions of Marx and Engels in relation to Hegel would show that they were in fundamental agreement.[31] Both were convinced that a materialist reinterpretation of the dialectic would require: 1. that one treat it as a law or body of laws that have an objective existence (and not as laws of thought in relation to which objective reality is only a phenomenal projection); 2. that one establish the existence of these laws in reality through empirical means, without doing violence to reality in order to make it agree with pre-established laws. The difficulties involved in this undertaking, for both Marx and Engels, had to do with the detailed execution of this second task. But the fact that a great deal of work was necessary in order to extract the dialectic from 'things' never lessened their conviction that the dialectic was an instrument which could be used for materialist purposes. The intrinsically idealist character of the dialectic was not clearly recognized by either of them.

If the use of the dialectic appears more insistent in certain well-known pages of the *Anti-Dühring* on the negation of the negation that in any of Marx's texts, this is because the use of logical procedures originating within the historico-human sciences created

[31] On this point, the remarks of V. Gerratana in *Ricerche sulla storia del marxismo,* Rome 1972, pp. 125–30, and those of Lucio Lombardo Radice in his introduction to the Italian edition of *Dialectics of Nature,* (Rome 1967) are quite correct. (Lombardo Radice, however, now tends, it seems to me, to accentuate too much the distinction between Marx and Engels, although still much less so than Colletti.) See also the short article by Gianfranco Di Pietro, 'A proposito dell'interpretazione dialettica del mondo naturale', *Trimestre,* No. I, 1967, pp. 167ff, which states the matter in a way with which I agree.

greater problems when applied to the natural sciences. In so far as the natural sciences were (and still are) more advanced along the path of scientificity, the unsatisfactory character of statements not formulated in quantitative terms is sharpened. But one should remember that Marx himself was not at all hostile to the idea of a dialectics of nature. On the contrary, it is a well-known fact that he gave a small example of it in a note to the chapter on the 'Rate and Amount of Surplus Value' in Book I of *Capital*; and in a letter to Engels he stated he was convinced that 'Hegel's discovery – the law of merely quantitative changes turning into qualitative changes – [holds] good alike in history and natural science'.[32] (A statement such as this rules out the possibility that here Marx was only engaged in a 'flirtation' with the dialectic; do the anti-Engelsians then maintain that he occasionally allowed himself to be led astray by Engels?) Furthermore, and this is the important point, the debate on Marxism and the dialectic cannot confine itself strictly to the question of logic, but must encompass the concepts of supersession, the rationality of history, progress, and the rhythm of historical becoming. It is certainly important to point out, as Colletti does, that the conception of 'contradiction' as a logical and ontological general law of all reality obscures one's understanding of 'oppositions in reality'.[33] But the problem arises also in another form. On the one hand, one can interpret the dialectical rhythm of development in the strict sense of a process of development through successive 'supersessions' (negations-affirmations), and in that case one is forced to admit that it is only *one* of the possible rhythms, even in human history. In point of fact there are also reformist processes, involving a gradual transition as well as destructive, non-dialectical negations. The revolutionary can and certainly must express a preference for the dialectical rhythm of development and must work for its realization. But he must also admit that in many cases it is not realized, because it requires the most favourable of conditions: the oppressed class must be mature enough to be able to distinguish that part of the ruling class's heritage which deserves to be preserved, and at the same time it must maintain an antagonistic consciousness strong enough to resist the temptations

[32] Marx-Engels, *Selected Correspondence*, Moscow 1955, p. 189; the letter dates from 22 June 1867. (NLB).

[33] *Marxism and Hegel*, p. 100; see also on this point 'Marxism and the Dialectic', op. cit.

of reformism. The fact that no revolution corresponding to a 'classical-Marxist' model has yet taken place points up the difficulty of setting in motion a dialectical process in relation to the passage from the capitalist system to the socialist system; but it would be even more difficult to fit the passage, for example, from slave society to feudal society into a dialectical schema.

On the other hand, it is possible to contend that *any and all* historical processes are dialectical, in that they represent a synthesis of being and non-being. Here one interprets the dialectic to mean non-stasis or becoming, and it corresponds to that mode of thinking which rejects rigid schemata, hypostatizations, and supposed 'eternal' and metahistorical concepts. Of course, in that case the dialectic encompasses all of reality. But it remains at an extremely general level, a kind of Heraclitanism which does not do justice to the specificity of Marxism in relation to all other theories which do not deny the historicity of reality.

This ambiguity, which is the primary reason why more precise terms and concepts should be substituted for the dialectic, is also the primary reason for the difficulty which has been and will continue to be encountered in making this substitution. In reality, the dialectic enables one to assert the historicity of all reality and to opt for a particular kind of historicity (movement through negations-affirmations) within the framework of that assertion, avoiding the need to make a clear distinction between the two levels. According to the occasion, it enables one to wage a fight against static and metaphysical conceptions of reality or against a purely gradualist evolutionism; against faith in the absoluteness of certain classifications or against an empiricism that leads to scepticism. It also allows, and this is a point one should emphasize, a kind of elastic (and therefore more resistant) optimism with regard to the struggles which the proletariat must wage against its class enemy. The more the bourgeoisie develops and strengthens itself, the more it develops and strengthens the class which it oppresses. Every victory of the bourgeoisie serves only to lay the basis for an even more sweeping defeat in the future. In the eleventh of his *Flüchtlingsgespräche* (Refugees' Dialogues), Brecht showed great insight in characterizing this vision of the dialectic as a 'sense of humour' that has become second nature in relation to socio-historical events; he brought to light its energizing efficacy and perhaps also the danger (revealed in Ziffel's final quip) that should the decisive crisis be long in coming, the dialectic becomes a form of faith and consolation.[34]

Once one decides, therefore, to do without this concept which is too elusive and overly burdened with a dangerous speculative heritage, one must single out all those things which were justifiably defended by the founders of Marxism and by their followers in the name of the dialectic – so that they can then be reformulated in a scientific manner. To return to Engels, it would be a serious mistake to believe that *Dialectics of Nature* can be reduced completely to verbal games about the negation of the negation or the passage from quantity into quality. As we have seen, those writings also contain the polemic against ahistorical conceptions of nature (a polemic that does not spare Hegel at all and gives due emphasis to Kant's hypothesis on the formation of the solar system[35]); they contain the polemic against social Darwinism; they contain the clear-cut affirmation of the need not to lapse into either vitalism or an overly simplistic mechanism – i.e. of the need to maintain the autonomy, if only relative, of the various 'levels';[36] they contain the polemic against the 'forcibly fixed lines of demarcation and distinctions between classes', and the recognition that 'these antagonisms and distinctions are in fact to be found in nature, but only with relative validity, and that on the other hand their imagined rigidity and absoluteness have been introduced into nature only by our minds'.[37] In short, *Dialectics of Nature* called for a logic of the historical sciences – a call that had become urgent ever since political economy (thanks to Marx) and the natural sciences (thanks to Lyell and Darwin) had incorporated the historical dimension. One should bear in mind that much of twentieth-century epistemology has returned to either subjectivist

[34] Brecht's text reads in part: 'The best school for the Dialectic is emigration. The keenest dialecticians are refugees. They are refugees because of changes and they study nothing other than changes. . . . If their enemies triumph, they calculate how much the victory has cost, and they have a sharp eye for the contradictions. The Dialectic, may it always flourish.' Bertolt Brecht, *Flüchtlingsgespräche*, in *Prosa*, Frankfurt 1965, II, p. 237. (NLB).

[35] See the second preface to *Anti-Dühring*, p. 17: 'In this Hegel fell far behind Kant, whose nebular theory had already indicated the origin of the solar system, and whose discovery of the retardation of the earth's rotation by the tides had already also proclaimed its extinction.'

[36] See the remarks on 'The "Mechanical" Conception of Nature', *Dialectics of Nature*, pp. 319ff.

[37] *Anti-Dühring*, p. 19.

or Platonist conceptions of science, accompanied by a rejection or at least a slighting of the great discovery of the historicity of nature (or else giving it a spiritualistic interpretation as did Bergson); also that contemporary Hegelian Marxism avoids the 'stridency' of the dialectic of nature only because it has again sought refuge in a purely human sphere and has adopted a moralistic-obscurantist attitude in relation to science. Given these circumstances, one has to admit that the salvaging of the worthwhile themes in Engels's philosophy still remains an open question.

Of course, to regard the Hegelian dialectic as philosophy's last gift to science before dissolving into science itself meant that one adopted an altogether too Germanocentric view of philosophy, that one accepted the idea of a world-historical movement of thought tending towards and culminating in Hegel, and that one therefore underestimated a great deal of the most advanced thought of the seventeenth and eighteenth centuries. This mistaken outlook stemmed from an inflexible adoption of that Young Hegelian idea of a division of labour between France, England, and Germany, according to which Germany, while the most backward on the level of economic development and political action, was at the head of the world movement on the level of pure thought.[38] On the other hand, Marx and Engels's Hegelianism gave not undue emphasis to the role often occupied by philosophers as precursors of official science (for example, with regard to evolutionism, which had been a 'phantasy' of thinkers or heretical scientists before it became accepted scientific theory). In *Dialectics of Nature* this emphasis is often excessive. Nonetheless, one must not forget that precisely on this level it once happened that Engels had to restrain Marx's unjustified enthusiasm for Pierre Trémaux's *Origine et transformations des hommes* – an 'ideological' enthusiasm to which Engels counterposes a 'scientific' refutation.[39]

In general, it should be acknowledged that Marx, in his concrete activities as theoretician and historian of political economy in the *Grundrisse* and *Capital,* had actually liberated himself from the Hegelian heritage and 'dialectical' schemata more than Engels.

[38] See Cesare Luporini's introduction to the Italian edition of *The German Ideology* (Rome 1967), p. lvi.
[39] See the correspondence between Marx and Engels from 7 August to 5 October 1866. With regard to this episode (referred to by Lombardo Radice and Gerratana, among the most recent to cite it), the anti-Engelsians remain, of course, silent.

But, first of all, it has to be born in mind that Engels was not a specialist in either the natural sciences or ethnology – whereas both Marx and Engels were specialists in political economy – and that the relationship between 'general ideas' and empirical research presented itself, therefore, in a different way for each of them. One has to take into account also Engels's greater propensity for didactic clarity, his aversion (for better and for worse) towards that hair-splitting and self-diversion with intellectual and verbal games in which Marx indulged at times, and thus also the risk he ran of drifting to the opposite extreme of oversimplification and 'one-sidedness'. Schmidt has stressed the first of these two considerations; but as usual he draws unacceptable conclusions from it, in the sense that authentic Marxism is presumed to have no interest in a 'nature in and for itself'. The second has been stressed by Eric Hobsbawm and Gianni Sofri, whose opinions on the Marx-Engels relationship are among the most perceptive and balanced that I know.[40] Neverthelsss, with regard to the second consideration one should not confuse the difference in mentality (which undoubtedly exists) with the difference in 'literary genre'. A compendium designed essentially to serve a polemical or expository purpose is one thing, a full theoretical treatise is another, and an as yet unfinished work in which the author is exchanging opinions with himself and still keeping open various solutions is a third again. Apart from the author's own propensities, there is necessarily a different degree of 'problematicity' among these three different kinds of writing. When Marx sums up his philosophy in a few propositions, as in the detested preface of 1859, he is just as 'one-sided' and schematic as Engels; indeed, Bernstein based his claim that Marx was more dogmatic than Engels precisely on that preface![41] Today there is a tendency to discover a more modern and problematical Marx – a Marx who is actually able to answer all the problems of working-class struggles in the neo-capitalist countries – on the basis of the unpublished works and exalting, for example, the *Grundrisse* above *Capital*, as does Martin Nicolaus.[42] This is a tendency that leads to a forcing of Marx's thought, and

[40] See Eric Hobsbawm, Introduction to Marx's *Pre-Capitalist Economic Formations*, New York 1965, pp. 50ff; G. Sofri, *Il modo di produzione asiatico*, Turin 1969, pp. 62–4.

[41] Eduard Bernstein, *Evolutionary Socialism*, London 1909, pp. 3–4.

[42] Martin Nicolaus, 'The Unknown Marx', *New Left Review*, No. 48, 1968.

also creates an artificial dichotomy between the 'problematic' Marx and the 'dogmatic' Engels.

As for the former consideration, it should be remembered that there are two sides to every coin. If it is true that the fact that Engels was not himself a naturalist put him at a disadvantage with respect to Marx in the social sciences, it is also true that his closer contact with the natural sciences enabled him to perceive with greater clarity (if only occasionally) the limits of that concept of progress which historical materialism had inherited from Hegel and the entire previous tradition. Already in his notes on Darwinism in *Dialectics of Nature*, Engels stresses that the evolution of the species cannot be regarded unconditionally as 'progress': 'Selection [may result from] greater capacity of adaptation to altered circumstances, where survivors are better suited to these *circumstances*, but where this adaptation as a whole can mean regress just as well as progress (for instance, adaptation to parasitic life is *always* regress). . . . Each advance in organic evolution is at the same time a regression, fixing *one-sided* evolution and excluding evolution along many other directions.'[43] With regard to the course of human history as well, Engels may, on the one hand, vehemently insist on the historical necessity of violence and oppression as against all forms of moralistic recrimination ('without ancient slavery there would not be modern socialism'). But, on the other hand, he calls attention with no less vehemence to the terrible 'regressions' entailed by every advance – one need only think of the conclusion to the third chapter of *The Origin of the Family* and the dramatic tension of *The Peasant War in Germany*.[44] One of the reasons, moreover, why *The Origin of the Family* at first enjoyed success for the wrong reasons and was later even less justifiably discredited is that since it was at first regarded as a kind of paradigm to which all Marxist research in ethnology and prehistory had to conform, it was thought that it could be dispensed with as soon as it showed itself unequal to this task (due in part to the out-dated character of Morgan's studies, which Engels used as his point of

[43] *Dialectics of Nature,* p. 236.
[44] The passage from *The Origin of the Family* reads in part: 'The lowest interests – base greed, brutal sensuality, sordid avarice, selfish plunder of common possessions – usher in the new, civilized society, class society; the most outrageous means – theft, rape, deceit and treachery – undermine and topple the old, class-less, gentile society.' F. Engels, *The Origin of the Family, Private Property and the State,* Moscow 1948, p. 98. (NLB).

departure). In reality, the lasting value of *The Origin of the Family* is based on twin foundations: first, the question we have already mentioned of the fusion between natural history and human history; second, the Rousseauesque and Fourierist spirit which permeates the entire book with its ever-present critique of civilization and its hypocrisies, which extends from the socio-economic level right through to the level of sexual relations and the institution of the family – a level on which Engels was much more open-minded and forward-looking than Marx.[45]

But the cosmic background against which Engels projected his vision of human history put other limits as well on the concept of progress. In all forms of materialism there is a fundamental contrast between an Enlightenment thrust, confident that every emancipation from myth and dogma, every triumph of truth, is in itself a contribution to our greater happiness, and the emergence of pessimistic themes that are the inevitable result of a de-mythologized view of the human condition. As long as a group of intellectuals is organically linked to a class on the rise and is engaged in a struggle against the humiliating and oppressive old prejudices, the former characteristic prevails and materialism is seen as essentially a liberating philosophy. If, however, the struggle bogs down, either as a result of historical 'disillusionment' or simply because of the onset of a phase of relative social stability, the second characteristic comes to the fore, at times completely effacing the former, at times (as in the case of Leopardi) coexisting with it in a delicate balance. The positivist era saw satisfied materialists like Büchner and Moleschott in the bourgeois camp. But it also saw a resurgence of pessimism, which tended towards nostalgic religiosity among the less lucid minds and towards a coherently pessimistic conception of reality among the more lucid (although never so lucid as to be able to overcome their class origins). This coherent pessimism

---

[45] On this last point, see Schmidt's perceptive remarks, *The Concept of Nature in Marx*, pp. 152–3. With regard to the re-emergence of Rousseauesque themes in *The Origin of the Family*, see V. Gerratana, *Ricerche sulla storia del marxismo*, p. 136. I find somewhat unconvincing, however, the reassessment of Morgan and Engels attempted by Emmanuel Terray, *Marxism and 'Primitive' Societies*, New York 1972, on the basis of a structuralist 'reading' of their works (the evolutionist elements contained in them are presumably only incidental dross). The sophistry of this kind of analysis lies in the notion that evolutionism can only be a schematic and one-sided evolutionism, and that structuralism is any kind of typological study. Attempts of this kind do more harm than good to the interpretation of the real Engels and the real Morgan.

represented a single, unchanging vision of the 'human condition' which was inspired by the insurmountable physical-biological limitations of man as well as by historically transient social relations. Carducci and Pascoli[46] on the one hand, and Verga[47] on the other, represent the most obvious examples in Italian literature of the two kinds of pessimistic reaction. But it would be easy enough to confirm the phenomenon on a broader scale, not solely Italian or merely literary. Indeed, among the impulses that gave rise to the idealist resurgence at the end of the nineteenth century, one has to number also this bewilderment produced by a pessimism which was unable to resume and elaborate on the 'struggling' path shown by Leopardi in the *Ginestra* and therefore had to either fall back on some form of religion or else 'flee forward' towards irrationalist activism. In the writings of Croce and Gentile neo-idealism is repeatedly represented as a new religion destined to overcome the dismay caused by positivist materialism. On the other hand, this immanentist religion – which did away with crude myths of transcendence and only called for the capacity to negate one's own 'empirical ego' and experience immortality in so far as one identified with a supraindividual Spirit – appeared in turn to many to be too barren, and was not forceful enough to prevent many relapses into the old mythological religions and many flights of blind activism.

Theoretician and militant of a revolutionary class, endowed with a singularly energetic and dispassionate temperament, Engels certainly did not identify with the inner turmoil of the bourgeoisie of the late nineteenth century. Not only was he devoid of nostalgia for the 'tedious notion of personal immortality',[48] but even the heroic pessimism of a Leopardi, supposing Engels had known it other than superficially, in all likelihood would not have been very congenial to him. One can imagine that at the most Engels would have viewed it as the individual tragedy of an intellect too exalted to belong to the liberal-moderate herd but born too soon and in an

[46] Giovanni Pascoli (1855–1912): Italian poet, whose lyrical, melancholic verse tended to succumb to a pantheistic and nationalistic mysticism. (NLB).

[47] Giovanni Verga (1840–1922): Italian novelist; while his works reflected a melancholic view of life, at the same time they depicted the sufferings of the poor with stark realism (*verismo*). His *I malavoglia* (1881) was the inspiration for Luchino Visconti's famous neo-realist film *La terra trema* (1948). (NLB).

[48] Engels, *Ludwig Feuerbach and the End of Classical German Philosophy*, in Marx-Engels, *Selected Works* in one volume, p. 594.

environment too isolated to know of the new hope of mankind, the working class. But the question of the end of the human race, which weighed so heavily on positivist culture as a whole in the late nineteenth century, did not affect only the 'beloved ego' of the philistine anxious for a place in paradise, but also had an impact on the ultimate prospects of communism.

This question was persistently present in the late Engels. At first, it must have seemed possible to him to incorporate the end of the human race and of the solar system within the framework of the dialectic in a 'left–Hegelian' sense, i.e. by accentuating the critical–negative moment according to which 'all that exists deserves to perish'. In his sketch of the history of socialist theories, Engels remarks that 'Fourier . . . handles dialectics in the same masterly way as his contemporary Hegel', and then goes on to say: 'With the same use of dialectics he brings out the fact, in opposition to the talk about the illimitable perfectibility of man, that each historical phase has its ascending, but also descending curve, and applies this conception also to the future of the whole human race. As Kant introduced into natural science the ultimate destruction of the earth, so Fourier introduced into historical thought the ultimate extinction of humanity.'[49]

But could one really term 'dialectical' a devastation in which the patrimony of knowledge and civilization accumulated by the human race up to its highest stage, communism, would not be passed on and more fully articulated but rather would be scattered to the winds? The more thorough treatment which Engels gave, at about the same time, to this question in his Introduction to *Dialectics of Nature* does indeed begin with the maxim so dear to him, 'all that comes into being deserves to perish'. But he then goes on to give a picture of the future end of our world in which a tragic sense (though it is a serenely tragic sense) about the destiny of mankind predominates. 'Millions of years may elapse, hundreds of thousands of generations be born and die, but inexorably the time will come when the declining warmth of the sun will no longer suffice to melt the ice thrusting itself forward from the poles; when the human race, crowding more and more about the equator, will finally no longer find even there enough heat for life; when gradually even the last trace of organic life will vanish; and the

[49] *Anti-Dühring*, p. 285.

earth, an extinct frozen globe like the moon, will circle in deepest darkness and in an ever narrower orbit about the equally extinct sun, and at last fall into it. Other planets will have preceded it, others will follow it; instead of the bright, warm solar system with its harmonious arrangement of members, only a cold, dead sphere will still pursue its lonely path through universal space. And what will happen to our solar system will happen sooner or later to all the other systems of our island universe; it will happen to all the other innumerable island universes, even to those the light of which will never reach the earth while there is a living human eye to receive it.'[50]

This is a passage which enables us to see how strongly Engels felt about this Lucretian theme of the end of the world. There is a good deal of similarity of expression between one of Engels's sentences and the close of Carducci's ode *Su monte Mario*: '. . . fin che ristretta sotto l'equatore/dietro i richiami del calor fuggente/l'estenuata prole abbia una sola/femina, un uomo . . .' (till man's exhausted progeny/confined beneath the equator/by the call of fleeting warmth/has a single female, one man). This similarity between the two texts is all the more striking in that one cannot imagine two authors more different from one another and there is no possibility that one was derived from the other. It represents further evidence of the wide diffusion of this theme among even the most diverse areas of European culture in the late nineteenth century.

Was this to be the epilogue to not only our own history and that of other galaxies but also to the entire universe? Engels' answer was no. Matter, which possesses movement as its indestructible characteristic, was to give rise to new aggregations and differentiations, to new worlds which would be produced 'even if only after millions and millions of years and more or less by chance but with the necessity that is also inherent in chance'. And conditions favourable to the genesis of organic life would arise again, 'for a short interval' of cosmic history, on one of the planets of these worlds. '. . . We have the certainty that matter remains eternally the same in all its transformations, that none of its attributes can ever be lost, and therefore, also, that with the same iron necessity that it will exterminate on the earth its highest creation,

[50] *Dialectics of Nature*, p. 20.

the thinking mind, it must somewhere else and at another time again produce it.'[51]

Thus, we have the view of an 'eternal cycle', of successive events of cosmic destruction and re-formation, without the transmission of any cultural patrimony from one to the other – a view much more similar to that of certain ancient philosophies (one need only think of the Stoics' concept of a periodic universal holocaust: *ecpyrosis*) than to the modern concept of progress in any of its various forms, including the Rousseauian one of a return to nature. The Introduction to *Dialectics of Nature* concludes paradoxically with a vision which it would be hard to term dialectical, even in the sense of a dialectical materialism. Engels never confronted this problem explicitly, preoccupied as he was with other interests and other tasks within the working-class movement – tasks which were much more urgent and demanding than any meditation on the end of the world!

But that the problem did not altogether escape him can be seen in the remarks he devoted to it some ten years later in the first chapter of *Ludwig Feuerbach,* immediately following upon his demonstration of the possibility of a revolutionary interpretation of the Hegelian dialectic. 'It is not necessary, here, to go into the question of whether this mode of outlook is thoroughly in accord with the present position of natural science which predicts a possible end for the earth, and for its habitability a fairly certain one; which therefore recognizes that for the history of humanity, too, there is not only an ascending but also a descending branch. At any rate we still find ourselves a considerable distance from the turning point at which the historical course of society becomes one of descent, and we cannot expect Hegelian philosophy to be concerned with a subject which natural science, in its time, had not at all placed upon the agenda as yet.'[52] Here the prediction of the end of the human race and of our world is no longer regarded, as it was in the passage cited from *Anti-Dühring,* as an example of revolutionary dialectics, but as a limit – an objection that is probably valid against the dialectical conception. The discussion is postponed to a later date and also is declared less than urgent; but it is not assumed that the question has been resolved.

[51] Ibid. pp. 22, 25.
[52] Marx-Engels, *Selected Works* in one volume, pp. 588–9.

A ready and facile solution was to be provided by the anti-materialist philosophies that sprang up at the beginning of the twentieth century. According to those self-assured thinkers, the external world has as its contents only thought thinking itself. How can thought be slain by its own contents? The end of the human race and the end of the solar system are thus pure and simple nonsense, spectres created by 'naïve realism'. And since, whenever you scratch a twentieth-century Marxist, nine times out of ten he turns out to be a left-idealist, one cannot rule out the possibility that many anti-Engelsian Marxists (not Colletti, but probably Schmidt, Fetscher, Havemann and various others) still agree with the scintillating line of reasoning of those idealists. And although they may replace 'thought' with 'praxis', this does not change very much.[53]

Another consequence of the Hegelian-vulgar-materialist imbroglio into which Engels (and, following his example, Kautsky and Plekhanov) is supposed to have manoeuvred Marxism is, according to Colletti, the acceptance of a fatalistic view of human history. By giving an Hegelian definition of freedom as 'consciousness of necessity', and by constructing a metaphysical materialism vaguely inherited from Spinoza, Engels, Plekhanov, and Kautsky allegedly failed to grasp that connection between causality and finalism which is 'the key to *historical* materialism'. Marx, on the

[53] In the last few decades the prospect of 'atomic suicide' has become an immediate threat to man's survival. But this alone is not reason enough to suppose that the other problem (the 'natural extinction' of mankind) has been overcome. Whether or not this problem can be dealt with in the very distant future through space exploration (assuming that this scientific undertaking, which up to now has served mystifying functions of technocratic ostentation and waste, can one day become useful to mankind), remains for the moment and for much time to come a question which can be discussed only in vague and science-fictional terms. That the question is not 'urgent' does not mean that it is not 'real' since 'it need not be resolved' – as has been suggested by my friend Gerratana, *Ricerche sulla storia del marxismo*, p. 106. The vision of communism as the passage from the realm of necessity to the realm of freedom seems to imply either the eternal existence of the human species or else a disappearance of it which represents not its *extirpation* but its *supersession* – i.e. a supersession in which the values of communism are inherited in some way by another species, and not simply erased so that they have to be attained again *ex novo* beginning with a new feral state, a new slave society, etc. It is interesting to note that the prospect of the 'end of the world' as a limit to the vision of mankind's perpetual progress reappears in Trotsky, as an obvious result of Engels' influence. Here, however, it appears in a substantially 'optimistic' context; cf. Leon Trotsky, *The Revolution Betrayed*, New York 1965, p. 45.

other hand, had made very clear in a famous passage of *Capital* that the distinctive characteristic of man in relation to animals is his capacity to set a goal for himself and to subordinate means to that end, thereby overturning the cause and effect relationship.[54]

However, a closer reading, not confined to the chapter of *Anti-Dühring* on 'Freedom and Necessity' and to a few isolated passages from Plekhanov and Kautsky, shows that the capacity to order means to ends as a characteristic peculiar to human action was well recognized by Engels and his much more limited followers. In his essay on the process of humanization of the ape, Engels states that 'the further men become removed from animals, . . . the more their effect on nature assumes the character of a premeditated, planned action directed towards definite ends known in advance'. He then emphasizes the point further: 'In short, the animal merely *uses* external nature . . .; man by his changes makes it serve his ends, *masters* it. This is the final, essential distinction between man and other animals, and once again it is labour that brings about this distinction.'[55] The same distinction is taken up again in chapter IV of *Ludwig Feuerbach* and significant elaborations were made by Kautsky in *Ethics and the Materialist Conception of History*.[56] Kautsky notes that the development of the brain turns this organ into a centre for the collection and elaboration (and not just the mere passive reception) of sense impressions. Whereas in the lower animal there is an unmediated succession of *stimuli* and *responses*, in the higher animal these two elements are mediated precisely by the brain's elaborative function, which in man takes on an altogether new importance with the emergence of language and the possibility of forming 'abstract concepts and scientific notions and beliefs'. This enables man to master nature in part, and gives human history a character and rhythm different from the preceding history of nature.

But in addition to this recognition of human action as finalistic

[54] Colletti, *From Rousseau to Lenin*, pp. 66–72; *Marxism and Hegel*, ch. XI.
[55] *Dialectics of Nature*, pp. 290–91.
[56] It is obvious that this short work is anything but a masterpiece, and that it does not at all provide a definitive basis for a Marxist ethics. But the half page devoted to it by Colletti (*From Rousseau to Lenin*, p. 73) gives a distorted picture of it. It is not at all true that Kautsky 'reduces Marx to Darwin'. The two final chapters ('The Ethics of Darwinism' and 'The Ethics of Marxism') are designed to show that a naturalistic ethics, while it suffices to bring spiritualism into crisis, is not, however, in a position to explain moral conduct in all of its complexity.

action (which is perfectly consistent with the passage from *Capital* referred to by Colletti), Engels and later Kautsky and Plekhanov go on to make certain essential distinctions, without which one runs the risk of lapsing back into the old mythological conception of 'free will', as the Austro-Marxists did and as much of subsequent Marxism has done. To begin with, Engels remarks, there exists a gap between the goal and the result of our actions that becomes wider and wider as distant results are taken into account ('once and twice removed') and when the effects arising from the combination of many individual wills are considered.[57] This observation shocks Althusser, who needs only hear mention of a distinction between individual wills and their results before he accuses Engels of having forgotten Marx's polemic against the 'robinsonades' of classical bourgeois philosophy and economics.[58] Althusser's anti-humanism thus arrives at a denial of the individual as a *relatively* independent psycho-physical entity – which is no better, despite the scientistic pomposity with which it is declaimed, than the old denial of the empirical ego on the part of idealism. Nor does it make any sense to object that the individual wills are determined in turn by the general socio-economic situation. Engels knew this very well, but he also knew that the reflections of a socio-economic situation at the level of consciousness and the changes in this situation which individuals seek to realize through their various plans of action are infinitely varied even within the same social class as a result of the infinite diversification in cultural background, physical temperament, etc. For this reason alone – not to mention other factors such as the unpredictability of the reactions of the opposing class and of the many strata and individuals who are insufficiently politicized, etc. – the results are greatly different from the plans. Engels probably thought primarily in terms of the historical experience of the French Revolution. We have our own confirmation in the experience of the October Revolution. More accurate are Althusser's observations with regard to the less than perfect consistency, in the letter to Bloch, between this question of the relationship between individual intentions and collective outcome and the other question of the relationship between structure and superstructure. Here we can be helped by the observation that those remarks did not have

---

[57] See *Dialectics of Nature*, pp. 19–20 292ff, and the letter to Bloch of 21 September 1890.
[58] Louis Althusser, *For Marx*, London 1969, pp. 117ff.

their origin in the letter to Bloch, but were carried over from preceding writings (*Dialectics of Nature*, pp. 19–20, 292 and the fourth chapter of *Ludwig Feuerbach*) without Engels's having felt the need to recapitulate the entire line of argument. But a comparison with those earlier formulations also shows how foreign to Engels was the 'optimistic' belief ascribed to him by Althusser, according to which the fusion of individual wills would produce a 'general' effect as the result of a kind of miracle or pre-established harmony.[59] On the contrary, Engels views the great gap between intentions and results as proof that mankind has only emerged in part from its 'natural' phase and has yet to 'leap' into the realm freedom. The two passages cited from *Dialectics of Nature* state this very clearly.

Secondly, and as we mentioned above, men's wills are not an unconditioned *primum*, but are themselves the product of a sum of biological, social, cultural, etc. causes. Engels rightly notes that the inconsistency 'does not lie in the fact that *ideal* driving forces are recognized, but in the investigation not being carried further back behind these into their motive causes'.[60] And Plekhanov, polemicizing with Stammler, notes that not only is the choice of a means necessarily determined by its relationship to the end (if I wish to obtain this end, I must make use of this means), but *even the choice of the end* is necessarily determined by all of the preceding history of the individual.[61] It is not true, as Colletti seems to believe, that this argument renders nugatory what was said above about the causality-finalism nexus. The capacity to make plans and to order means in relation to ends is still within man's powers, as a consequence of an intellectual development engendered essentially by labour. It is shown, however, to be illusory to claim that the determination of the end is *not caused*, or that at a certain point there develops in man, a product of nature, a process whereby he is totally released from the bondage of nature, at least with regard to his 'will'. The formula of *umwälzende Praxis* – quite suggestive precisely because of its various possible meanings – can be given a miraculist meaning which does not lead to a mature Marxism but to Dewey and all the forms of pragmatism that make no attempt to give a scientific explanation of *praxis* itself. And mature Marxism –

[59] Ibid. p. 125.
[60] *Ludwig Feuerbach*, in Marx-Engels, *Selected Works* in one volume, p. 613.

not just that of Engels but also that of Marx's embarrassing preface of 1859 – explicitly rejects that meaning, and talks instead about 'indispensable relations independent of their will' which men enter into in the process of production.

From what we have said, it can also be seen how deceptive it is to identify freedom with the so-called 'subjective conditions' of our action and necessity with the so-called 'objective conditions'. In relation to extreme forms of voluntarist subjectivism, an appeal to objective conditions is already a step forward. Nonetheless, the element of 'necessity' does not refer solely to the existence or non-existence of the means suited to a given end; rather it is also inherent in the subjective factor, i.e. in the determination of the end and in the possession of a will that is energetic and perservering enough to pursue that end. In fact, all the work related to education, propaganda and agitation is directed towards the transformation and orientation of the 'subjective conditions' (i.e. men's wills) in a particular direction. To the extent that this work meets with success, the wills of those who have been eduated are determined by this work itself (and by all the biological, social, etc. circumstances without the existence of which no education or propaganda campaign can succeed). To the extent that it does not meet with success, the wills of those who have been educated are determined but are caused by all the other antecedent circumstances. There is, of course, a difference between an authoritarian education (or a dogmatic and sectarian form of propaganda) and an education which attempts to shape 'responsible' and 'free' individuals. But in the scientific and non-mythological meaning of the term, responsible and free mean that a person is aware of the means best-suited to attain the greatest possible happiness and that he is aware of the social, non-individualistic, character of this objective and of the means for attaining it. Thus, Colletti's statement that man is both causality *and* finalism, cause *and* effect, does not go far enough. The finalism exists entirely within the causality – it is not a kind of 'reverse side' to causality, as it is with Kantian man, who is phenomenon inserted within a causal chain and noumenon endowed with a metaphysical freedom. The *something more* that man possesses in relation to animals is a greater capacity to foresee and order means in relation to an end and a greater understanding in the determination of the end, but it is not a greater measure of 'free will' in choosing between various ends.

Of course, both Colletti and Havemann are correct in expressing their dissatisfaction with the Spinozist and Hegelian formulation of freedom as 'consciousness of necessity' which Engels adopts in *Anti-Dühring*. But why is this formulation unsatisfactory? Not because of its anti-voluntarism, but because of its anti-hedonism; because it denies the importance of the meaning of freedom as the absence of painful constraints and the presence of all those conditions which ensure the happiness of the individual; and because it insists that man not only recognize necessity but also glory and efface himself in it. Thus, it is part of that conception of philosophy as asceticism and self-repression (in short, a kind of religion for educated persons) which Marxism utterly rejects.

On this point Marxism is obviously anti-Spinozist, and therefore an unqualified appeal to Spinoza (with whom Marxism has fundamental points of contact on other matters) would be an error. It is necessary to add, however, that Engels, in the chapter in *Anti-Dühring* on 'Freedom and Necessity' (a chapter which is part of the more general treatment of 'Morality and Law', and which devotes only a few pages to the problem that actually interests us), articulates that formulation not so much in the Spinozist sense of an acquiescence in and apotheosis of reality, as in the Baconian sense that nature obeys us only if we obey it. 'Freedom does not consist in the dream of independence of natural laws, but in the knowledge of these laws, *and in the possibility this gives of systematically making them work towards definite ends.*'[62] The final clause, which we have italicized, introduces an essential distinction because it does away with the old concept of 'inner freedom'; and the subsequent part of the argument as well shows clearly that for Engels freedom will be fully realized only with the advent of communist society and with complete mastery over the forces of nature. It still remains slightly unclear what is meant by complete mastery over nature and up to what point this is possible (as we have seen, Engels did not hold to a limitlessly optimistic outlook with regard to the distant future of the human race). Also unsettled is the question of the extent to which certain 'apolitical' (as opposed to generically 'egotistical') tendencies on the part of the great majority of men are themselves a part of a 'human nature' which is not readily altered – leaving aside those moments of exceptional social tension when the majority becomes politicized – and therefore represent an obstacle to the realization and maintenance of a communist society which is 'classless' in the broadest sense of the term.[63]

One idea deeply rooted in the Marxism of the twentieth century is that the denial of free will leads to fatalism also at the political level, i.e. to that notorious waiting for the 'spontaneous collapse' of capitalism. I think that the reply to this objection which is given by Plekhanov in his essay on 'The Role of the Individual in History' is still valid, even though it is far from definitive. Plekhanov noted, in the first place, that history gives us many examples of people who denied free will and yet exerted themselves with great forcefulness, such as the Moslems at the time of their great conquests, or Calvin, or Cromwell. In the second place, he pointed out that if an individual regards his actions as indispensable in order to obtain an objective (i.e. if he believes that among those events 'governed by necessity' are numbered not only the actions of others but also his own actions), the denial of free will then comes to mean for him a 'complete inability to remain inactive'.[64]

As I said, this reply is not definitive because, in seeking to refute the proponents of a rigouristic, Kantian type of ethics (Plekhanov's actual adversaries in this essay), it situates itself too much on their terrain. In other words, it merely attempts to show that the very kind of 'heroic' conduct which, according to a Kantian, is made possible only by the doctrine of moral freedom and the categorical imperative can be elicited just as easily from the Spinozist-Hegelian theory of freedom as the recognition of necessity. This moreover, is a danger to which those who seek to theorize materialist ethics often succumb. Limiting themselves to giving a materialist grounding to traditional moral precepts and modes of conduct, they fail to call into question the content of these. Their materialist fervour even leads them to attempt to show that there is no man more *moral* than the materialist – in the sense that no one is more radically altruistic and detached from his own immediate interests. This tendency, which is present even in the great Epicurus, can be found

[63] My attention has been called to this point particularly by Luciano Della Mea. When dealing elsewhere with the question of man's biological limitations, I have always emphasized man's physical 'frailty' and precariousness, rather than his lack of political educability. See Della Mea's remarks in *Eppure si muove*, Milan 1970, pp. 15, 259–62.

[64] Plekhanov, 'The Role of the Individual in History' in *Fundamental Problems of Marxism*, p. 141.

in its most conventional and conservative form in many works of nineteenth-century positivism, for example in Ardigò's *Morale dei positivisti*.[65] Obviously, Plekhanov's case is different; while he was still free from social-patriotic involutions, he was well aware of the difference in content between 'our morals and theirs' (as Trotsky would have said). Nonetheless, even 'our' morals presented themselves to him in a rigouristic guise. Thus, in his analysis of the motives underlying moral conduct, Plekhanov was led to over-generalization and oversimplification. It is rare that someone who sacrifices his own immediate interests and fights for a higher principle does so because he considers his own contribution to be irreplaceable. More commonly, he does so – at least initially – in response to a number of 'external' pressures, such as fear of the low esteem of others or fear of no longer being able to belong to a group into which he has by now become integrated and on the basis of whose 'scale of values' he has become accustomed to judging himself and others, etc. Moral codes based on pure inward-ness, on duty for duty's sake, or on the unmediated identity of knowledge of the good and moral action, all take as their 'principle' what if anything should be a destination – a destination which runs the risk in turn of degenerating into a dreary exaltation of sacrifice as an end in itself and of forgetting that the ultimate aim of human action is after all man's happiness. The statement that morality is a social fact should not be understood simply in the sense that every society and every class has its moral code, but also in the sense that the impulse to sacrifice oneself for *others* would not arise (except perhaps in some instances related in origin to animal instincts: love for one's children, etc.) if others did not bring pressure to bear, in one form and degree of intensity or another, on each individual for that purpose, and if each individual had not already compro-mised himself by soliciting and assessing positively such forms of altruistic behaviour. Certainly, in the conflict between immediate hedonistic impulses and the impulse to fight for more general, broadly gauged interests, the dominance of one over the other has nothing to do with 'freedom' in the spiritualistic sense.

Nor can it be said that the de-mythologizing of 'free will' and 'praxis' leads to 'historical justificationism'. This point has a certain importance because historical justificationism has played an

[65] Roberto Ardigò (1828–1920): Italy's greatest positivist philosopher. (NLB).

important, though always secondary, role in the crisis of Gramscism since 1956 and in the fact that historical studies in Italy have once again been moving towards the right (or, which amounts to the same thing, towards an insipid apoliticization) – while the new generation of Marxists is no longer made up primarily of historians like its predecessor, but is instead made up of philosophers, with all the advantages and disadvantages implied by that.

Historical justification can have an openly idealist version, according to which it is assumed that history is entirely 'rational', entirely progressive, entirely at one with the very development of the Spirit. It is needless to point out to what degree this conception stands opposed to historical materialism. Here once again one finds the deceptive character of the concept of freedom as 'consciousness of necessity'. It tends to lead to a confusion of causal necessity (which does not imply any glorification of *faits accomplis,* since the 'necessary' event may be entirely unjust and retrogressive, entirely inconsistent with the happiness of great masses of men) with a finalistic or even providential necessity.

But historical justificationism assumes also another and more insidious function. On the one hand, it supposes that there is an objective situation so absolutely binding that only a single course of action is possible and all other solutions are condemned in advance to failure. On the other hand, it assumes the existence of a political subject (whether individual or group) totally free from corporative limitations and sectoral interests, totally capable of discerning that single obligatory choice with perfect lucidity. When stated in these terms, all the negative effects of a political choice (the starvation of southern peasants in post-unification Italy, the suppression of any possibility of discussion and initiative from below in Stalinist Russia, etc.) can then be regarded as the 'necessary price' of the step forward that was being undertaken at that particular historical moment. And any criticism of the action taken by the Italian Right or the Stalinist bureaucracy comes to be regarded as moralistic, utopian, antihistorical, etc.

This conception is mistaken both in its way of characterizing the objective conditions – which obviously have a very great determining force, but not such as to foreclose the possibility of arriving at different solutions – and in its way of characterizing the political subject – which may commit errors in the execution of a particular policy and even opt for a mistaken policy, precisely because the solutions are not completely binding. A political elite is undoubtedly the expression of a given social class; but that elite may give expression to the *immediate* aspirations of its class (including features that may be premature or outdated), or it may tend to express the class's more fundamental, long-range needs; it may focus on one or another stratum or social group within the class; it may draw the lines of the relationship between the class that it represents and the subaltern or hegemonized classes and strata in a number of different ways – either more authoritarian or more inclined to attempt at least a partial consensus. Whether it is oriented towards one or the other of these various options depends on its cultural-political background in a broad sense that encompasses both the *immediate* socio-economic situation in which the choice among the various options presents itself and the entire 'past' of that ruling group and each of its members – a past that includes the effects of the previous practical experiences and currents of thought they have been exposed to, the political and cultural education they have received, and finally, with regard to single individuals, their psycho-physical constitution and their familial and local milieu.[66]

The failure of revolution in Western Europe and the need to build socialism in a backward and besieged country set insurmountable limits to the actions of any communist leader, even the most internationalist with the greatest trust in democracy from below. This is confirmed by the fact that both Lenin in his last years and Trotsky before he entered the opposition were themselves 'Stalinists' to a certain degree. But in *Stalin's Stalinism* (and in the Stalinism of the bureaucratic group led by him and personified by him) there was also an *extra measure* of brutal authoritarianism, denial of any possibility of dissent, manipulation of the entire world communist movement, falsification of Marxism in order to adapt it to all the contingent shifts in Russian state policy. And this *extra measure*, this extra price that the working class of the USSR

---

[66] A preliminary analysis which moves in the direction of the remarks made here can be found in Marx's preface to *The 18th Brumaire of Louis Napoleon*, where he criticizes opposing conceptions of Victor Hugo and Proudhon. With regard to the possibility that members of the ruling group may commit mistakes, see the remarks of Antonio Gramsci, *Selections from the Prison Notebooks*, London 1972, pp. 407–8. In extreme cases, it may happen (and does happen) that a ruling group is attracted to *another class* and used by that class for its own purposes, or that it forms itself into a caste and defends its privileges against the class which it originally represented.

and of the entire world was made to pay, was a result of the fact that the Stalinist ruling group was itself in many ways a product of Russian backwardness, of an ill-assimilated Marxism, of a formation that was too narrowly national, etc. Stalin did not commit the errors and crimes he did as the result of a 'free choice'; being what he had become, he could not have acted any differently. But this impossibility of acting differently was not the consequence solely of the objective situation, as the historical rationalizers maintain, but also of subjective shortcomings. Different men would also have had to implement policies that were largely authoritarian and, in many respects, non-socialist (assuming that they were unsuccessful in setting off a new revolutionary tide in the West). But the degree of authoritarianism would have been very different, and thus the right-wing involution undergone by the USSR and the people's democracies during the post-Stalinist era would also have been less disastrous.

As I have mentioned, historical justificationism has had an important role in the vicissitudes of Italian left-wing culture during this second post-war period. Till 1956 a justificationist attitude prevailed among Italian communist or philo-communist intellectuals in relation to Stalinism. This represented a mélange of a tradition of revolutionary thought which took as its model the French Revolution (necessity and historical justification of the Terror) and an anti-democratic and anti-humanist Crocean culture (with its view of politics as the expression of force rather than of justice, with its facile references to Machiavelli and perhaps even to Marx but its substantial adherence to Treitschke, Bismarck and the 'Prussian' conception of politics). In reality, these two component elements were quite heterogeneous with respect to one another. The former accepted violence as a painful but transitory price to be paid for the construction of a society without violence. The latter viewed violence as a permanent element in the history of mankind, and ridiculed all egalitarian, libertarian and pacifist programmes. But in the minds of most Italian Marxists, by origin historicists and Croceans, the difference was not altogether clear. And one of the reasons for the great cultural-political success enjoyed by Palmiro Togliatti for a good fifteen years was the fact that he personified this confusion and typified with undeniable culture and skill the historicist Stalinist (as opposed to the fanatical and sectarian Stalinist).

At the same time, however, anti-justificationist stirrings inspired by Gramsci's notes on the *Risorgimento* and by Emilio Sereni's *Capitalismo nelle campagne* (which had an impact before Gramsci's notes were even known) ran through historical studies on the *Risorgimento*, which were the main object of attention of left-wing intellectuals who went through their intellectual tutelage during the years immediately following the Resistance. The nineteenth-century Italian bourgeoisie was accused of not having fully carried out *its own* revolution for fear of possible Jacobin developments; it was accused of having failed to carry out its 'national' mission. The political struggle waged by the Italian Communist Party during the Resistance and after was seen as a resumption and consummation on the part of the proletariat of that national-popular revolution *manqué*. This is not the place to discuss Gramsci's conception of the *Risorgimento*, nor to examine the degree to which it was faithfully interpreted by the Togliattian cultural-political group. (In my opinion, the question remains open, and certain hasty dismissals of Gramsci's political and historiographic thought are altogether unacceptable.) I merely wish to point out here that the fact that the *Risorgimento* was regarded in a certain sense as a historical phase that *had not yet been concluded*, made the contrast less striking between justificationist historicism, to which the Crocean-Togliattians generally adhered, and the 'revisionism' in *Risorgimento* studies which they claimed a right to carry out in that specific case. It made the contrast less striking, but on the theoretical level it did not actually resolve matters.

When the twentieth congress of the CPSU brought Stalinism into crisis in Italy as well, the lack of clarity with regard to this basic problem came to light. Bourgeois and social-democratic critics did not fail to take advantage of it. On the one hand, they had a great time of it turning around against the USSR the argument about the objective situation being absolutely binding. The indictment of Stalinism was not enough; it had to be extended to Leninism, which had engendered Stalinism as an inevitable consequence, and to all forms of revolutionary communism, which would always be destined to end in Stalinism. Thus, either social democracy or Stalinist tyranny in all of its aspects. On the other hand, it was held that the moment had arrived to launch an attack on 'revisionism' in *Risorgimento* studies. A second-rate 'Stalinist of capitalism', Rosario Romeo, took on the task of defending the position that all the suffering endured by the peasant masses in the aftermath of Italy's unification, all the corporative narrow-mindedness and all the authoritarianism of the regime established by the *Right,* represented the price that had to be paid for the sake of primitive accumulation, without which there could have been no capitalist development of Italy. This kind of economistic caricature of Marxism – according to which all problems related to cultural development, broadening of popular consensus, etc. counted for absolutely nothing in the calculations of the post-*Risorgimento* ruling class – achieved an astonishing success. This was due in part to the fact that the predominately humanistic training and limited familiarity with economic history of many Italian Marxists left them nonplussed when faced with some tables and some comparative data on economic development in backward countries, and in part to the fact that these same Italian Marxists were unarmed before a theory of historical justificationism.[67] A revival of Marxist histiography will, in my opinion, have to take place on the basis of a refutation of justificationism that places itself firmly on a materialist and anti-voluntarist grounding. Such is the orientation of the cursory and incomplete remarks expressed above.

If one wants to distinguish, as we have attempted to do, the cultural-political background of the groups and individuals who operate in history from the immediate socio-economic situation in which they have to act, one has to reassert the need to articulate more fully the relationship between structure and superstructure. As is well-known, this relationship is still largely an open question within Marxism. Precisely for this reason, there is a strong tendency to 'dissolve' the problem rather than to resolve it. As we have already pointed out, the distinction between structure and super-structure is, according to Colletti, more Engelsian than Marxist (Marx is presumed to have weakened only in that unfortunate preface of 1859). The distinction leads, presumably, to a notion of the structure as a purely ' "*technical*-economic" domain, not includ-

---

[67] Among the few exceptions to this school of thought is Aurelio Macchioro, 'Risorgimento, capitalismo e metodo storico' in *Studi di storia del pensiero economico e altri saggi,* Milan 1970, pp. 673ff. See also the remarks by Ernesto Ragionieri, 'L'Unità d'Italia' (Florence: speech given 27 March 1961), pp. 16–26; and Stefano Merli, 'La filantropia del sistema di fabbrica: dal dott. Ure al prof. Romeo', *Classe,* No. I, 1969, pp. 227ff. [The work by Rosario Romeo referred to is his *Risorgimento e capitalismo,* Bari 1959. NLB]

ing social relations and hence inter-subjective communication'.[68] Colletti suggests that both terms should therefore be grouped under the concept of 'social relations of production'.

This is a suggestion that calls to mind only too many other 'solutions' of a Crocean and Gentilian variety, in which all problems of the relationship of A to B were splendidly evaded by identifying A with B (after having first demonstrated that it was impossible to give an absolutely rigorous and 'separate' definition of each of the two terms). This is a retrograde form of dialectic which should not be to the liking of the anti-dialectical Colletti.

In the concept of social relations of production as delineated by Colletti, there does not appear to be any hierarchy in the priority and conditioning power of, on the one hand, the actual socio-economic sphere and, on the other, juridical-political forms and cultural phenomena. Consequently, there is not even a preference for explaining cultural or political facts by *beginning with* the socio-economic facts, as opposed to the opposite procedure (or to the view that society is a system in which all the elements are conditioned and conditioning to an equal degree). This would place us outside not only the positivist contaminations of Marxism but also the Marxism of Marx himself.

I do not agree with the idea that the difficulties inherent in the relationship of structure and superstructure can be resolved, as the professional philosopher inevitably tends to do, with operations to increase 'conceptual rigour' which – after many twists and turns – end by identifying the two terms or by stating in general terms that there is a dialectical or reciprocal relationship between the two of them. Rather, they can only be resolved by specifying, through a series of empirical observations, what is meant by the relative autonomy of the superstructure. The first person to consider this question was Engels, in his well-known letters to J. Bloch and C. Schmidt. The fact that he did not come to a definitive solution to the problem was underscored by Engels himself on numerous occasions. It is not true, however, that he did no more than rattle off the two formulae of 'reciprocal action' and of the structure as the decisive element 'in the final analysis'. In those same letters can be found very important remarks which make it possible to give content to those two formulae.

---

[68] *From Rousseau to Lenin*, p. 65.

In the letter to Conrad Schmidt of 27 October 1890 we find the following: '. . . As a definite sphere in the division of labour the philosophy of every epoch presupposes certain definite thought material handed down to it by its predecessors, from which it takes its start. And that is why economically backward countries can still play first fiddle in philosophy: France in the eighteenth century as compared with England, on whose philosophy the French based themselves, and later Germany as compared with both. But in France as well as Germany philosophy and the general blossoming of literature at that time were the result of a rising economic development. I consider the ultimate supremacy of economic development established in these spheres, too, but it comes to pass within the limitation imposed by the particular sphere itself: in philosophy, for instance, by the operation of economic influences . . . upon the existing philosophic material handed down by predecessors. Here economy creates nothing anew, but it determines the way in which the thought material found in existence is altered and further developed, and that, too, for the most part indirectly, for it is the political, legal, and moral reflexes which exert the greatest influence on philosophy.'[69]

Apart from the question of the relationship between the different superstructural levels (the juridical-political, the philosophic, etc.), this passage clearly brings out that culture is determined both by the structure of the society in which it develops and by antecedent culture – and we might add, by the contemporaneous culture of countries with *different* social structures. The assertion that ideas do not arise by parthenogenesis from other ideas remains correct in the sense that this is never the fundamental source of the truly important ideas of an era, and that therefore there does not exist a history of ideas (or of artistic expressions, or of other so-called spiritual phenomena) which can be conceived as a continuum independent of socio-economic facts. Nonetheless, ever since there have been traditions, i.e. the transmission of cultural products, it is beyond question that ideas have been influenced also by other ideas. Such is the case in those elementary processes of 'immediate transmission' as represented in its simplest forms by family, religious and state forms of education. But the phenomena become much more complex as a result of the possibility of giving a

[69] Marx-Engels, *Selected Works* in one volume, p. 688.

permanent and lasting form to cultural products (writing, artistic representation, etc.) and of transmitting them over a long distance in time and space. With regard to the influence that Greco-Roman antiquity had on European culture of the Renaissance, one naturally has to ask the question: what *contemporary* needs were being met by that apparent return to the ancients? Thus, we are led back to the socio-economic facts that determined the end of the Middle Ages. It is, however, also true that the influence of ancient thought and art was far from inconsequential in giving Renaissance culture its particular characteristics. In short, there exist 'archival sources' in all cultural movements, sources which may at times influence things in a traditionalist direction (a group of intellectuals may be so attached to a fossilized cultural tradition that they lag behind contemporary socio-economic reality) or in an anticipatory or even utopian direction (such is the effect of the culture of socially and politically advanced countries on contemporary countries which are more backward; sometimes, however, the culture of more backward settings, which are nevertheless at least in certain areas more democratic and egalitarian, such as the Greek *polis* and other much more primitive civilizations, may apply pressure on the culture of countries in which 'progress' has created more alienation and inequality). Does all of this mean that one is letting back through the window the idealism that was thrown out of the door? Not at all, since one always finds a 'material' moving force behind all ideas. There are, however, certain disjunctures between the structure of a given society and its cultural phenomena, precisely because culture can be transmitted far beyond the socio-economic situation which generated it.

In the same letter to Conrad Schmidt, Engels makes the following remarks with regard to the relative autonomy of the juridical level from the economic level. 'In a modern state law must not only correspond to the general economic condition and be its expression, but must also be an *internally coherent* expression which does not, owing to inner contradictions, reduce itself to nought. And in order to achieve this the faithful reflection of economic conditions suffers increasingly. . . . Thus to a great extent the course of the "development of right" consists only, first, in the attempt to do away with the contradictions arising from the direct translation of economic relations into legal principles, and to establish a harmonious system of law, and then in the repeated breaches made in this system by the influence and compulsion of further economic development, which involves it in further contradictions.'[70]

These are remarks which can be extended also to other institutions and cultural forms. Their autonomy (always relative) from the structure results not only from the character of cultural traditions but also from a process of increasing internal coherence, i.e. from a tendency towards 'systematicity' – a systematicity which, as Engels hastens to point out, is always subject to crisis as a result of the successive transformations of the structure. Here Engels accords to synchrony and diachrony (i.e. to the system and to the forces which continually tend to throw the system out of balance) what is due to them. Furthermore, it should be pointed out that this process of increasing internal coherence can at times operate in a conservative direction and at other times in a progressive direction, just like the effects of cultures which are different in time and space. As a conservative force, the internal coherence and relative autonomy of a juridical system puts up greater resistance to innovations precisely because it appears to be universally valid and independent of the socio-economic situation. It may operate also as a progressive force in that the capacity to carry out mental operations of generalization and extension by analogy, while not allowing a society ever to overcome its own class limits, may, however, allow particular individuals and avant-garde groups to 'reason beyond' these limits. Such groups and individuals may be led to claim, for example, during a period of flourishing slavery that slavery should not exist because slaves are not inferior by nature to freemen; or they may be led to put forward a number of criticisms of the capitalist system on the basis of a logical extension of those principles of freedom and equality which the bourgeoisie must confine to the political-juridical sphere in the very act of proclaiming them. It is by virtue of processes of this kind that one can deduce that capacity of the superstructure to 'act back upon the structure' which is often represented in somewhat miraculistic terms as the obscure effect of a dialecticity inherent in all reality.

Finally, Engels brought out the fact that in a class society (and even in a socialist society which has not yet reached the higher phase of communism), the problem of the relationship between structure and superstructure cannot be separated from the problem

[70] Ibid., pp. 686–7.

of the division of labour and the particular post occupied by various groups of intellectuals as workers specifically *assigned to superstructural activities*. This accounts, on the one hand, for their recurrent illusion and claim to be not just relatively but absolutely autonomous from the socio-economic base, and to incarnate the eternal values of the spirit. On the other hand, it also accounts for their greater capacity (once they have rejected the idea that they are a caste unto themselves and have switched to the side of the oppressed class) to commit themselves unwaveringly to long-term objectives and to resist, as Lenin pointed out in *What is to be Done?*, the immediate allurements of reformism and anarchism, to which the non-intellectual comrade is more vulnerable. The Leninist conception of a party which infuses the working class with a revolutionary consciousness 'from the outside' does not derive from a presumed philosophical or political voluntarism on Lenin's part (from *Materialism and Empirio-Criticism* through to *'Left-Wing' Communism* Lenin always remained a rigorous materialist and always maintained that no revolution was possible without an economic crisis). Rather, it derives from a recognition of that diversification in the 'way of becoming revolutionary' which distinguishes intellectuals from proletarians. Today we can see even more clearly the grave dangers entailed by this dualism: a permanent delegation of authority from the base to the leadership, a gradual degeneration of the ruling group itself with alternating phases of sectarianism and opportunism and with a final involution in the direction of a conservative-bureaucratic authoritarianism. It is correct, therefore, to study and put into effect all possible countermeasures, while still holding to the assumption that the only radical countermeasure would be a *de facto* supersession of the distinction between intellectual and non-intellectual revolutionaries, and that the proletarianization of intellectuals which is taking place today represents only a beginning, as yet insufficient, in overcoming the distinction. It is not merely a matter of chance that the problem of direct democracy still remains the one farthest away from solution for all proletarian movements, whether in a pre-revolutionary stage or in an accomplished socialist revolution.

One cannot help but recognize also that there are *non-superstructural* elements in cultural activities and institutions. I have attempted to show above how this admission does not in any way undercut materialism, but rather calls forth a closer consideration of that biological nature of man which Marxism, and particularly contemporary Marxism, tends to disregard. The binomial of structure-superstructure still remains fundamental – despite all the attempts to discredit and dissolve it on the part of Marxism's opponents – for it points to the preponderant part played by the economic structure in determining the major transformations of juridical-political institutions, cultural milieux and forms of collective psychology. Thus, it represents a discovery of immense significance, both as a criterion for explaining social reality and as a guide for transforming it. It becomes inadequate, however, when it is taken as an exhaustive classification of reality, as if there were nothing that existed which was not either structure or superstructure.

Colletti repeatedly uses the formula 'Marxism of the Second International' in his introduction to Bernstein in order to characterize the banalization and distortion of Marxism which, according to him, was begun by Engels and carried forward by Kautsky and Plekhanov. The formula is designed to underscore the link between vulgar materialism (with its Hegelian origins) and social-democratic revisionism. The accounts do not balance out so easily, however. Revisionism is indeed bolstered by a contribution from the vulgar evolutionists (among whom Engels does not number, nor even the early Kautsky in all respects); but it soon began to develop through the efforts of neo-Kantians, empirio-criticists and semi-idealists of various kinds. Precisely because it reflected the hegemony of the bourgeoisie, revisionism followed the bourgeoisie in its passage from positivism to idealism. On the other hand, the greatest revolutionary Marxist of the early twentieth century, Lenin, took a clear-cut position against the shift towards empirio-criticism of the late nineteenth century and later against western European vanguard revolutionism based on subjectivism and voluntarism; equally anti-voluntarist, particularly in her disagreement with Lenin over the conception of the relationship between party and class, was Rosa Luxemburg. There is a way to define the Marxism of the Second International which, paradoxically, leads to the inclusion of Lenin and to the notion that Karl Korsch or Piero Gobetti,[71] or even Sorel, represent the most authentic third

[71] Piero Gobetti (1901–26): liberal anti-fascist and journalist, who characterized the working class as the foremost modern-day force for the advancement of human freedom, writing in his journal *Rivoluzione Liberale* (1922). (NLB).

internationalists.

It is necessary, therefore, to develop a line of argument that is more articulated and, at the same time, more political. The real limitation of the Marxism of the Second International did not consist in a lack of voluntarism, but rather in a schematic and tenaciously Eurocentric 'philosophy of history', in a non-Marxist conception of the State, in an inadequate understanding of the imperialist phase of capitalism, and in a persistent illusion that the bourgeoisie was already and would become increasingly a peace-loving and 'contented' bourgeoisie, precisely at a time when it was getting ready for more ambitious militarist and reactionary adventures. Furthermore, one should not forget that in all political movements theoretical degeneration comes after an opportunist *practice* has already taken root – an opportunist practice that remains disguised by the solemn reaffirmation of sacred principles which are believed in less and less. Rereading Bernstein, one has the impression that he is right on one point alone: in reproaching the leaders of his party with conducting themselves in their everyday practice according to those criteria of collaboration with the bourgeoisie and repudiation of any revolutionary perspective which they still did not allow to be proclaimed with any openness.[72]

Is it possible that the rise of revisionism was abetted by Engels' famous introduction to *The Class Struggles in France*, in which he expressed, shortly before his death, a pessimistic judgment on the possibility of armed insurrection in the cities, and ascribed a positive value to the electoral victories of the German Social-Democratic Party? One has to admit that Colletti expresses himself cautiously in this regard. He recognizes that to go from Engels's introduction to revisionism strictly speaking, one still has to take a big step – i.e., the transformation into a strategy of what Engels had simply presented as a tactic.[73] Nevertheless, even here Colletti's exposition contains an anti-Engelsian tendentiousness, which comes out above all in the fact that strangely enough he does not mention even in passing that Engels's introduction had to be censored at various

[72] Bernstein, op. cit., especially pp. 196–9; see also Colletti, *From Rousseau to Lenin*, p. 49. The two above-mentioned phases of the process of social-democratization (first, practical repudiation of the principles, then, theoretical revisionism) were often effectively brought out by Lelio Basso in the polemics which accompanied the involution of the Italian Socialist Party from 1956 onwards.

[73] *From Rousseau to Lenin*, pp. 49, 105.

points in order to meet with the approval of the German social-democratic leaders (and Engels regarded those passages as essential to his argument, as can be seen in his letter to Lafargue on 3 April 1895).[74] In point of fact, that introduction does not at all assign to the proletariat the goal of a peaceful conquest of power by electoral means. Rather, the objective is the growth of the party under legal circumstances, so that it is then able to confront from a position of strength the inevitable final showdown, which comes when the bourgeoisie itself abandons the field of peaceful competition. Moreover, in more general terms, the introduction raises the question of a 'majoritarian revolution', in which the entire working class, and not just a restricted vanguard, would be in a position to conquer and utilize power. The solution put forth by Engels can only appear simplistic today, given the experience we have had (and which Engels did not have) of the enormous capacity for absorption and 'peaceful' neutralization which advanced capitalism possesses in relation to the working class. But the question remains open for anyone convinced that the Leninist model of the relationship between party and class and 'minority revolution' cannot be realized in just those terms in the countries of advanced capitalism, and that, in any case, it does not resolve the question of the direct management of power on the part of the proletariat after the revolution.

In *Marxism and Hegel* the notion of 'Marxism of the Second International' recedes into the background, since here Colletti tends to merge together into a single indictment dialectical materialism and so-called western Marxism, Engels and Bergson (see chapter X), the early and late Lukács, Lenin and his revolutionary-subjectivist opponents. But what escapes Colletti in both writings – and, for that matter, escapes almost all contemporary Marxism – is the significance of the shift in bourgeois culture between the end of the nineteenth century and the beginning of this century: i.e. the shift from positivism to idealism. Unless one makes an assessment (not just philosophical, but also political-cultural) of this shift, one remains, despite all good intentions, entrapped in the

[74] The letter reads in part: 'Liebknecht has just played me a fine trick. He has taken from my introduction to Marx's articles on France 1848–50 everything that could serve his purpose in support of peaceful and anti-violent tactics at any price. . . . But I preach those tactics only for the *Germany of today* and even then *with many reservations*.' Friedrich Engels-Paul and Laura Lafargue, *Correspondence*, Moscow n.d., III, p. 373. (NLB).

anti-materialism which pervades all of contemporary western culture, and the critique of positivism (*de rigueur* for a Marxist) becomes laden with anti-materialist themes.

Obviously, this was not a shift caused by the advent to power of a new class, since positivism and idealism are both expressions of bourgeois culture. And it is also true that there is a certain continuity between the two movements of thought, for within positivism and rigorously materialist positions were always those of a minority. Nevertheless, such a profound change of the cultural climate with such lasting effects (comparable in certain respects to the shift from the Enlightenment to Romanticism which took place a century earlier) cannot be regarded as one of those 'purely superstructural' transformations for which it would be senseless to search for a socio-political origin. Nor can one explain everything, as Colletti attempts to do, with the theory of one extreme calling forth the opposite extreme ('Iron necessity thus evokes its abstract opposite, Freedom; determinism absolute indeterminacy', etc., etc.[75]). It still remains to be explained, however, why the two 'extremes' followed one another in precisely that order, and to what needs of the bourgeoisie and of that part of the proletariat under the hegemony of the bourgeoisie they corresponded.

The most conspicuous characteristic of the shift at the end of the last century is an increasingly radical anti-objectivism. Generally, its point of departure are real and serious problems in the epistemology of the sciences, related to the need for a re-examination of the very foundations of scientific knowledge. But this epistemological crisis is quickly used in order to reassert an absolute, mythological creativity and freedom belonging to man, and in order to be able to disregard both the real conditioning to which man is subject and the way to overcome it. It then becomes possible to proclaim a completely rhetorical and mystifying subjectivism-voluntarism.

Both are forms of bourgeois philosophy; but the 'respect for reality' is not the same in both. During the positivist phase the belief was widespread that myth, the irrational and obscurantism were arms which served not the bourgeoisie in its most progressive form but rather the old feudal-absolutist forces, against which the bourgeoisie had waged recent struggles. The dissemination of scientific truth was also seen to coincide with the general interests

[75] *From Rousseau to Lenin*, p. 73.

of the bourgeoisie in the shorter or longer run, and it was even deemed possible that scientific truth would gradually be able to overcome the antagonism between bourgeoisie and proletariat. Significant groups of intellectuals in both the literary and the scientific field claimed for themselves a particular, relatively autonomous function (different, however, from the old 'humanistic' autonomy) in this process of disseminating a lay knowledge and of elevating the proletariat socially and culturally – at the same time that they continued to be organically linked to the bourgeoisie.

That this expectation was illusory and that the 'scientific truth' of the positivists was permeated with retrograde ideologies (racism in relation to underdeveloped peoples and reformism in relation to the industrial proletariat) are, of course, well-known facts. However, to the extent that the nineteenth-century bourgeoisie still had *enemies on the right* and not just on the left, there still existed a real area of overlap between the interests of the bourgeoisie and scientific truth. Of course, the spectre of communism had already been haunting Europe for some time; and Lukács is right to emphasize that the years 1848–9 represented a watershed after which the anti-proletarian consciousness of the bourgeoisie became evident. But just as the bourgeoisie had often oscillated between an anti-feudal struggle and an anti-proletarian struggle before those years, similarly in the period following them there were times when it felt things were sufficiently calm on its left to be able to afford that partial revival of the Enlightenment which was represented, with all its limitations, by positivism.[76]

Nor did the experience of the Paris Commune extinguish once

---

[76] A balanced assessment of nineteenth-century positivism has yet to be made. It should take into account not just the philosophic works in the strict sense (which are generally mediocre), but also the historiography, the linguistics, the scientific activity and the literature of that period. While the distinction between a 'romanticist' positivism and an 'Enlightenment' positivism is useful in many respects, it too runs the risk of lumping together with the 'romanticist' current all of the positivists who had a materialist *Weltanschauung,* and of limiting the authentic heirs of the Enlightenment to only those positivists of an empirio-critical and agnostic tendency – i.e. to the precursors of neo-positivism. Among other things, this leads to a very narrow conception of the eighteenth-century Enlightenment, almost as if La Mettrie, Diderot, Helvétius, and Holbach did not belong to it. I am particularly in agreement with the assessment of positivism which is implicit (and also explicit in a number of places) in the book by C. A. Madrignani, *Capuana e il naturalismo,* Bari 1970 – a book whose significance goes much beyond its specific subject matter. See also, by the same author, *Ideologia e narrativa dopo l'Unificazione,* Rome 1974.

and for all the lay features and universalistic claims of bourgeois culture. It was only with the development of imperialism that the bourgeoisie's reactionary calling became absolutely predominant (although it was always present from the beginning, in that there never was a bourgeoisie without a proletariat to exploit, oppress and deceive ideologically). There then arose an intellectual adventurism tending to portray the very attempt to attain objective truth as a kind of naïveté (just as materialism is invariably prefixed by the epithet 'vulgar' in the writings of idealists and semi-idealists, similarly realism is constantly qualified as 'naïve'). The polemic against positivist mediocrity and quietism and the reassertion of voluntarism which pervaded the early twentieth century may have assumed a revolutionary guise (often initially in good faith). But with startling speed the 'revolutionaries' of this kind became the standard-bearers for imperialist adventures during the years leading up to the first world war. An objective analysis of Italian culture during the early twentieth century (the phenomenon is far from being limited just to Italy, however) could not help but show that, above and beyond the differences in moral temperament, there was an ideological matrix common both to fascism and to a certain anti-fascism which was also a product of the interventionism of World War I – an anti-fascism which still competes with fascism in laying claim to being the authentic representative of 'the Italy of Vittorio Veneto'.[77] Nor is it enough to isolate the most blatant forms of irrationalism as being pre-fascist, for that overlooks the fact that in a more fundamental sense all of the neo-idealist culture of the early twentieth century is irrationalist.

Within Marxism itself there were those who deluded themselves into thinking that the 'idealist renaissance' could serve as a tonic against the gradualism and parliamentarism of the Second International. This illusion was shared, with a great deal of moral fervour, by Korsch, by the early Lukács,[78] even by the early Gramsci in certain respects, as well as by certain fellow travellers of Marxism, such as Piero Gobetti and many of the forces which

[77] Vittorio Veneto was the site of the Italian army's successful assault on Austrian lines on 29 October 1918, which led eventually to the defeat of the Austrian army. (NLB).

[78] See M. Vacatello, *Lukács*, Florence 1968, particularly the first two chapters.

later were drawn into the *Partito d'Azione*.[79] It was a great merit on the part of Lenin not to have assented. For the present-day vanguards of the extreme left in the West, the danger of lapsing back into idealism is an objective possibility precisely because of their character as intellectual vanguards.

As long as it had not given up the idea of itself as a representative of scientific truth and a class capable of elevating and absorbing within itself the proletariat, the bourgeoisie had need for a fusion of the culture of the intellectuals with that of the masses. This need, which manifested itself in nineteenth-century science as well as in literature and music, was satisfied in a variety of forms, ranging from the narrowly paternalistic to the more or less broadly democratic. It is entirely correct to point out the inter-class ambiguity of even the most progressive forms of this relationship between intellectuals and masses. In particular, it is necessary to point out the mystifying function always carried out by patriotism, even in its least chauvinist versions, in the creation of this relationship. Above all, one must reject any anachronistic attempt to return to that situation, any nostalgia for the 'healthy' bourgeoisie of the last century. But one must realize also that the great realist art of that century (with its 'verist' developments, which were not altogether a step backward) and the great science contemporary to it, with its Enlightenment and humanitarian impetus, were not a mere 'fraud'. Rather, they possessed a positive force precisely because of the continued existence within the nineteenth-century bourgeoisie of motifs related to the struggle *against the right,* and, at the same time, because of the continued existence of a measure of autonomy among progressive intellectuals in relation to the immediate class interests of the bourgeoisie.

With the crisis of positivist culture and the emergence of various forms of neo-idealism in philosophy and of decadentism in art, this relationship between intellectuals and masses changed drastically. All attempts to unite culturally the educated class and the masses were abandoned, and in their stead a policy of cultural division was pursued. On the one hand, there developed a 'high culture' with distinct characteristics of spiritual aristocracy and

[79] *Partito d'Azione* (Action Party): a left-wing, non-communist party which was formed during the Resistance, but dissolved in 1946; composed primarily of intellectuals, its leader, Feruccio Parri, nevertheless became President of the Council of Ministers for a short time. (NLB).

disdain for the proletariat. On the other hand, there developed a second-rate semi-culture assigned the task of maintaining the proletariat in a state of submission, sometimes by redirecting its revolutionary potential towards aims of imperialist plunder, at other times by instilling in it petty-bourgeois ideals of moralism and maudlin sentimentalism (and for this purpose making increasing use of the once-despised churches). Despite the positive effects of the concept of 'populism' (as introduced by Asor Rosa[80]) in the polemic against the cultural politics of the Italian Left during the last twenty-five years, its widespread use has, in my opinion, led to a blurring of the distinction between these two different kinds of relationship between intellectuals and masses. Even worse, it has led to a legitimation of the unqualified admiration of Asor Rosa (a revolutionary in politics – at least till 1970 – but a decadentist in literature) for 'high bourgeois' art, leaving out of account the fact that the latter can only exist by virtue of a division of labour between great intellectuals, who disregard the masses, and populists who have a syrupy love for them and 'keep them quiet'. (If the efforts of the latter should not suffice, the former also are ready, however, to sound the patriotic and moralistic trumpets, as frequently happened during crucial moments of World War I and during the first and second post-war periods.)

By referring to the anti-objectivist tendency in twentieth-century bourgeois culture, we do not mean to infer that there existed a hostility towards science in general. Of course, within the reaction against positivism there were expressly anti-scientific currents of thought, especially in Italy (Croce and Gentile). But it is not conceivable – and, in fact, it did not happen – that during a period of extraordinary technical-scientific development the bourgeoisie of the most advanced countries could for any length of time adopt an ideology which liquidated the sciences. Thus it was possible, in a country as relatively backward as Italy in the early years of this century, for the neo-idealism of the absolute Subject, which denied all cognitive value to the sciences, to predominate through the efforts of thinkers belonging to the southern

---

[80] Timpanaro's reference is to Alberto Asor Rosa's *Scrittori e popolo*, Rome 1965; the book's central thesis was that reformism is the inevitable consequence of the attempt to base a movement for social reconstruction on the traditions (folklore, popular literature, etc.) of the nation; a revolutionary consciousness can be the product only of a radical break with those traditions. (NLB).

agrarian bourgeoisie (while outlooks more closely linked to the industrial North, such as the critical positivism of Giovanni Vailati,[81] remained in a minority, and attempts – some of them extremely intelligent – at an upgrading of the sciences within the context of idealism, undertaken by left-wing followers of Gentile, were not followed up). However, in countries in which the bourgeoisie was more advanced, the reaction against positivism developed primarily within the field of science itself. The empirio-criticism of Avenarius and Mach, the conventionalism of Poincaré, the contingentism of Boutroux with its Bergsonian developments, all of these rejected the idea (which, in substance, was accepted by Croce and Gentile) that science had an irreparably materialist nature, and that, therefore, the only refuge from materialism lay in denying science itself. Rather, these thinkers sought to show that materialism is the product of pre-scientific 'common sense', and that study of the foundations of the sciences represents the best possible refutation of materialism.

The textbooks in the history of philosophy which were used in Italian schools at the time of Croce and Gentile's hegemony treated the above-mentioned currents of thought with a restrained benevolence, as the anti-positivist reaction's first sallies, which remained enmeshed in large part in the very fallacies they sought to refute. Only with Italian neo-idealism (Croce's or Gentile's, depending on the preferences of the textbook's author) was the naturalistic dross finally eliminated! Italian idealism's claim to greater internal coherence was not, admittedly, entirely unjustified; and justified as well were the polemical retorts against relapses into transcendentalism, such as took place, for example, with Blondel and the late Bergson. Although the masters of Italian idealism were much more outmoded in their cultural background and were always ready to align themselves with the Church in political matters (and perhaps even to aid it in defeating modernism within its ranks), they maintained unswerving devotion to the belief that educated men could live without the false comfort of transcendental illusions. (As is well-known, this is the principal reason for that residuum of admiration which Gramsci had for Croce up to the very end.) Nevertheless, in the long run the other currents of anti-objectivist thought, from which neo-positivism and structuralism arose, have

[81] Giovanni Vailati (1863–1920): Italian student of the theory of science, who developed a late interest in a pragmatist theory of language. (NLB).

shown much greater vitality than Italian humanistic idealism, precisely because they corresponded to the need to accept and promote technical-scientific progress – although they stripped it of that charge of combative secularism and destruction of all spiritualistic myths which science had possessed during the eighteenth century and again during the nineteenth after the Romantic interlude.

These new modes of thought do, of course, propose, in their own way, to win over the masses to 'science'. It may appear, and to a certain extent it is true, that they have taken up again the programme of the old positivist culture. In reality, however, the relationship between intellectuals and masses is conceived in a very different way. No attempt is made at a cultural unification and popularization of science in an anti-religious and humanitarian vein, as was the case, for better or for worse, during the nineteenth century. Instead, maintaining and heightening the rupture between experts and non-experts, the aim is to *épater* the non-experts with the wonders of technology and reduce them increasingly to being mere passive consumers of that technology.

The danger which threatens Marxism today is that of dichotomizing its position in this regard: on the one hand, a purely moralistic rejection of this technological fetishism which expands into an absurd negation of science itself; on the other, a hastily conceived conciliation of Marxism with the most recent philosophic-scientific orientations (psychoanalysis, neo-positivism, structuralism), without undertaking the work necessary to separate what is scientific from what is ideological in these orientations. It is not enough, as is often done, to ask the positivists, structuralists and Freudians to pay greater attention to social factors, as if the question of the compatibility of these philosophies with Marxism could be settled merely by supplying them with an increased social dimension rather than by subjecting their theoretical bases to analysis. It is necessary to bring out the idealist features which those tendencies of thought carry with themselves right from their very origin – i.e. from the anti-materialist reaction of the late nineteenth century. The struggle against historicist and humanistic interpretations of Marxism is correct, but it is a rear-guard action. Nowadays it is no longer a question of combating an idealism that denies science, but rather of combating the idealism *within modern science*. This struggle entails: upholding a materialist epistemology as against either Platonist-theoreticist or empiricist-agnostic conceptions of science prevailing today; rejecting the antithesis science-history (something not done with sufficient clarity by the anti-historicists), and placing the historical sciences of nature and their consolidation with the human sciences at the centre of the discussion; and, finally, elaborating on the link between materialism and hedonism, with all the consequences it has for the model of the socialist society we envisage for ourselves.

Anti-Engelsism represents a rejection of this outlook. It is, therefore, symptomatic of a lingering idealism, even if it prides itself on its polemic against *one* form of idealism, the Hegelian form. Engels offers no ready-made solutions to any of the problems we have mentioned. But Engels must be the point of departure for confronting them once again.[82]

---

[82] Since the first publication of this essay there has appeared an article by Christine Glucksmann, 'Hegel et le marxisme', *La Nouvelle Critique*, April 1970, pp. 25–35, with which I find myself in substantial agreement. It discusses Colletti's position, and spells out with a great deal of insight the limits of Lenin's supposed 'return to Hegel' in his *Philosophical Notebooks*. I continue, however, to maintain (and on this point I am not in complete agreement with Glucksmann) that Hegel has had certain negative effects on the thought of Marx and Engels which cannot be brushed aside, and that attempts to salvage a materialist dialectic are of rather doubtful utility in relation to the tasks facing Marxists today. Other important contributions to the discussion on Engels have recently been made by N. Badaloni, 'La rivolta contro Hegel e il ritorno di Engels', *Rinascita*, 16 January 1970, pp. 16ff; 'Scienza e filosofia in Engels e Lenin', *Critica Marxista*, No. 4, 1970, pp. 80ff; and by E. Ragionieri, 'Il "vecchio" Engels e la storicità del marxismo', *Nuova Rivista Internazionale*, 1970, pp. 1454ff. With regard to the cultural-political policies of Togliatti and the strategy pursued by the Italian Communist Party during the past twenty-five years, there remains, of course, a difference of judgment between these two friends and myself. [Badaloni and Ragionieri both belong to the P.C.I. – NLB]. But Badaloni brings into sharp focus certain Engelsian themes developed by Lenin (especially with regard to the fusion of natural history with the social history of mankind and with regard to a non-voluntaristic way of conceiving of man's active intervention in history), and he makes justified criticisms of Althusser's 'anti-Engelsian Leninism'. And Ragionieri, drawing on his previous studies on the relationships between German social-democracy and the European socialist parties of the late nineteenth century, puts together a synthesis and also a broad plan for future work on the activities of the late Engels as a leader of the international workers movement. In the meanwhile, anti-Engelism continues to appear in ever more exasperated forms; see especially the essay (completely unacceptable, in my opinion) by L. Kolakowski, 'Le marxisme de Marx, le marxisme d'Engels', in *Contemporary Philosophy*, Florence 1970, Vol. IV, pp. 405ff; and the volume by Carlo Cicerchia et al., *Leninismo e rivoluzione socialista*, Bari 1970, pp. 93, 159–65.

POSTCRIPT 1974

Since the first publication of this book, the reassessment of Engels, with all its highs and lows, has made decided advances. In the first place, one has to mention the work by Geymonat and some of his students – most of which in fact predates my own essay, though it was published later as a result of editorial delays. I shall confine my citations to the following: Geymonat (ed.), *Storia del pensiero filosofico e scientifico,* Milan 1971, the chapters devoted to the background of the early Engels (Vol. IV by E. Rambaldi, pp. 517ff.) and to the mature Engels and his present-day 'relevance' (Vol. V by Geymonat himself, pp. 322ff.); the articles by Geymonat himself, his students and other Marxist scholars published in *Critica Marxista* No. 6, 1972 (*Sul marxismo e le scienze*). Although none of these writings is devoted entirely to the study of Engels's thought, Engelsian themes and developments run through almost all of them. The same can be said for the recent volume by E. Bellone, L. Geymonat, G. Giorello, and S. Tagliagambe, *Attualità del materialismo dialettico,* Rome 1974; also for Eleonora Fiorani, *Friedrich Engels e il materialismo dialettico,* Milan 1971. I must register a certain amount of disagreement with these works as far as the validity of the materialist use of the dialectic in Engels and Marx is concerned; nevertheless, my agreement far outweighs my disagreement, as I have attempted to make clear in a review of Geymonat's *Storia* published in *Belfagor,* XXVIII (1973), pp. 371–8.

With regard to the relationship between the natural sciences and the human sciences in Engels's thought, and with regard to certain present-day theoretical developments brought to light by recent epistemological developments, see the particularly interesting work by G. Prestipino, *Natura e società: per una nuova lettura di Engels,*

Rome, 1973.

Engels's early background and his political activity prior to 1849 have been illuminated by new translations into Italian of texts, accompanied by important introductory essays: Engels, *Anti-Schelling,* ed. E. Fiorani, Bari 1972; E. Fiorani and F. Vidoni, *Il giovane Engels: cultura, classe e materialismo dialettico,* Milan 1974; *Friedrich Engels viandante e soldato della rivoluzione,* ed. B. Maffi, Florence 1972. Engels's studies of German antiquity (in the area of socio-political history, institutions and language) have only recently disclosed their unsuspected value. They link up with that field of interests which had its most complete expression in his *The Origin of the Family.* However, on a number of points in the linguistic field they anticipate results arrived at only much later by 'professional' linguistics. In this regard, see the works of V. M. Schirmunski, *Deutsche Mundartkunde,* Berlin 1962, and G. Dolfini, 'Engels filologo', *Il Corpo,* 1 (1965), pp. 65ff.; and, more recently, see in particular the introductory essay by Paolo Ramat to Engels, *Storia e lingua dei Germani,* Rome 1974.

In Lucio Colletti's 'Political and Philosophical Interview' (cited above), he refers to a change in his ideas with regard to the Marx-Engels relationship (pp. 13–14). But this shift tends more towards a 'de-sacralizing' of Marx (itself perfectly legitimate, since it has nothing to do with bourgeois or reformist revisionism) than towards a positive reassessment of Engels. As Colletti puts it, 'The facts, after all, speak for themselves. Everyone knows that Marx spent a large part of his life studying in the British Museum, while Engels was working in a cotton-business in Manchester.' This *boutade* certainly fails to explain the extraordinary competence which Engels displayed in the most diverse fields (military art, natural sciences, ethnography, socio-political history), without ever lapsing into a desultory encyclopedism or losing sight of the basic objective underlying all his investigations. The fact that he assisted Marx not only financially and in the political-organizational activities of the workers' movement, but also by pointing out books to him and discussing problems with him, is well-known by all and acknowledged by Marx himself on numerous occasions. That certain 'anti-Engelsian' letters by Marx existed, and that they were destroyed by Marx's family after his death, are indisputable facts (as Colletti reminds us); and we certainly must deplore the misguided zeal of those who, perhaps with the best of human and political intentions, destroyed them. We are unable, however, to assess the significance of the fact that Marx wrote such letters. Did theoretical disputes prevail in them (and even in this case, Marx was not necessarily always right – see above, note 39), or were they disagreements over contingent political matters? Or, alternatively, was the predominant feature of the letters the kind of passing irritability which is more than understandable in a man who was largely dependent financially on his friend, and who, despite the strong and sincere affection for his family, was more or less a prisoner (unlike Engels) of a 'Victorian' morality. (With regard to the inevitable alternations between self-repression, occasional transgression, and the need for deception which accompany this morality, see Pierre Durand. *La vie amoureuse de Karl Marx,* Paris 1970, Ch. VI and *passim.*) The lack of understanding shown by Marx for the sorrow Engels experienced on the death of his friend, the worker Mary Burns (cf. the correspondence between Marx and Engels during January 1863), probably had its roots not just in purely contingent circumstances but also in that 'Victorianism' of Marx, according to which love not properly legalized was regarded, more or less unconsciously, as something less serious than conjugal love. Nevertheless, the fundamental agreement between the two men – which does not at all mean that they were 'twin souls', but rather that they complemented one another – remains an undeniable fact. It is no matter of chance that those who have embarked on a 'Marxism without Engels' have arrived, coherently enough, at a 'Marxism without Marx'. Nor do I think it fair to make a comparison (as Colletti does) between the Marx of *Theories of Surplus Value,* the *Grundrisse* and *Capital* and the Engels of *Dialectics of Nature.* One should not forget that the first impulse to deal with questions of political economy came to Marx via Engels; *The Condition of the Working-Class in England* and *Outlines of a Critique of Political Economy* were two essential premises of the later great works of Marx. Nor should one neglect, from among Engels's major works, a book as open to the future as *The Origin of the Family*; in this case, the first impulse came to Engels via Marx, but the critique of bourgeois customs, of bourgeois sexual and familial morality, bears unmistakeably the mark of Engels. Furthermore, I do not believe at all that the Hegelian residues in *Dialectics of Nature,* in the much maligned *Anti-Dühring,* and in *Ludwig Feuerbach* are sufficient to negate their materialism and to cancel out the importance of the attempt at a union of the 'natural' and the 'social'.

A more subtle, but no more persuasive, form of anti-Engelsianism appears in Luporini's 'Marx secondo Marx' (now in *Dialettica e materialismo*, pp. 252ff.). To formulate an indictment against Engels on the grounds that he misinterpreted Marx's method in a historicist (and therefore reformist) direction, basing one's claim simply on Engels's incomplete and probably reluctant review of *A Contribution to the Critique of Political Economy*, seems to me to be a highly debatable procedure. With regard to this essay by Luporini I simply wish to note that although Luporini has succeeded in recent years in clarifying his points of disagreement with structuralism and Althusser's structuralist Marxism, he still seems to equate the 'primacy of synchrony' with a revolutionary point of view, and that of diachrony with a reformist-historicist point of view. If this is the way things really stood, then we would have to choose Linnaeus and Cuvier over Darwin, Smith and his epigones over Marx. It seems to me also that Luporini ascribes an exaggerated importance, within the framework of Marxist methodology, to the old Aristotelian problem of what is 'first according to nature' and what is 'first with respect to us'. Both of these methodological itineraries have their dangers, not just the former. One need only recall that Gentile's *attualismo* (and, to a less self-consistent degree, all forms of idealism) is precisely an affirmation of the absolute and sole reality of the 'first with respect to us'.

The worst kind of anti-Engelsism and crude anti-Leninism, based on a pragmatist interpretation of Marxism which gives it the illusion of being revolutionary, can be found in the essay by Helmut Fleischer, 'Lenin e la filosofia', in *Storia del marxismo contemporaneo*, Milan 1974, pp. 779ff. In this history, which is inevitably somewhat eclectic but on the whole praiseworthy for its objectivity and balance, the essay by Fleischer represents a real eyesore.

# 4

# Structuralism and its Successors

The summary negative reference to structuralism at the end of my 'Considerations on Materialism' has elicited the legitimate reservations of two friends particularly qualified to discuss these questions: Giulio Lepschy and Tullio de Mauro.

In a long letter, which deserves to be printed in its entirety and which draws on themes he has developed in his writings on structuralist linguistics, Lepschy calls my attention to the fact that structuralism does not exist 'as a relatively unitary movement' to which one can attribute the characteristics indicated by me. The concept of an ahistorical, Cuvierian[1] 'closed system', which I consider inherent in structuralism, is, in Lepschy's words, 'something of a polemical phantasy'. At the most, it may correspond (and not without stretching matters) to Hjelmslev's conceptions. It certainly does not correspond to the resolution of the split between synchrony and diachrony put forward by the Prague school and, in particular, by Jakobson. Nor does it correspond to any of the quite different positions in American structuralist linguistics (one need only think of the materialism of Bloomfield and its links with the tradition of the neo-grammarians[2]; of the broad ethnographic and cultural-linguistic interests of Sapir; and of Chomsky's emphasis on the element of creativity in linguistic activity).

Tullio de Mauro ('Strutturalismo idealista' in *La Cultura*, No. 5, 1967, pp. 113ff.) remarks that in Saussure, particularly in the

---

[1] Reference is to Georges Cuvier (1769–1832), the French zoologist whose research in comparative anatomy led him to postulate the principle of the 'correlation of parts', according to which the anatomical structure of all the organs in an animal's body are functionally related to one another; as a corollary to this principle, Cuvier maintained that no species had changed since Creation, for each was already endowed with a perfect structural-functional coordination of its parts. (NLB).

authentic Saussure brought to light during the last fifteen years through the efforts of Godel and Engler, there is no lack of interest whatsoever in the 'genesis from below' of the linguistic system and in the relationship between language and social reality. To this Saussure, 'quite different from the lifeless image which is bandied about Europe by many anti-Saussurians and even by many Saussurians', de Mauro feels intimately related, through an interest which is not simply cultural-historical but also theoretical and contemporary, as anyone knows who has read his *Introduzione alla semantica* and the other writings in which he has articulated and developed his ideas.[3] For de Mauro, therefore, the question is not one of passing from outside a judgment which accepts or rejects structuralism, but rather of taking up a position within structuralism against excessively formalistic conceptions, on the one hand, and also against a crude realism which overlooks the fact that reality is not comprised solely of 'things' but also of relationships and functions.

I shall attempt below to clarify in what sense and within what limits that summary anti-structuralist statement of mine still seems to me to be valid. For the time being, let me say that Lepschy's and de Mauro's remarks (which derive from points of view and tendencies within structuralist linguistics which partially differ from one another) are valid not only with regard to their specific content, but also because they call for studies which have yet to be carried out with any thoroughness: 1. a characterization of the different ideologies which have influenced the various tendencies in structuralism and have been influenced by it; 2. a focusing of the

---

[2] Leonard Bloomfield (1887–1949): American linguist whose major work, *Language* (1933), emphasized the need for a behaviourist study of language. Such an approach was to establish necessary relationships between aural stimuli and verbal responses, thereby dispensing with the need to account for 'meaning' in terms of mental or conceptual categories. The 'neo-grammarians' (also known as the *Junggrammatiker*) were a group of German scholars who, in the eighteen seventies, propounded a new set of fundamental principles for linguistic science: 1. that all changes in the sound system of a language are subject to the operation of sound laws with no exceptions to them; 2. that the origin of sound changes is traceable to individuals and can be explained on the basis of the science of psychology; 3. that the study of living languages is essential to the reconstruction of prehistoric languages. (NLB).

[3] See especially 'Eliminaire il senso?', *Lingua e stile*, II (1967), pp. 131ff., and the 'Saggio di teoria formalizzata del noema lessicale' in appendix to the third edition of *Introduzione alla semantica*, Bari 1970. See also de Mauro's commentary to Saussure's *Cours de linguistique générale*.

relationship between science and ideology, not within structuralism taken as a bloc but within the various historical phases and developments which the structuralist movement has gone through.

There has, of course, been no lack of articles and debates on the question of 'structuralism and Marxism'. In France especially there has been a veritable inflation of them, and in Italy too the question has received some noteworthy contributions.[4] But among the Marxists, there has been a tendency either to arrive at too hasty a conciliation of the two orientations (at times creating structuralist parodies of Marxism which approach the grotesque), or to push for a voluntaristic, and even anti-scientific, Marxism in opposition to a structuralism which is regarded as modern-day science *tout court*. There has almost never been a reaffirmation, let alone an original development, of the materialist side of Marxism. Thus, the debate has ended once more with the Marxists forced to assume a subordinate position with respect to both of the *two* forms of idealism which today are rivals in the field of western culture: historicist-humanistic idealism and scientistic idealism (in its Platonist and empirio-critical variants).

This has taken place also because a particular contemporary structuralism (primarily the structuralist anthropology of Lévi-Strauss) has been taken into account almost exclusively, without analyzing the passage from linguistic structuralism to extra-linguistic structuralisms, and without making any attempt to situate the historical genesis of structuralism within the movement of anti-materialist reaction which had its beginning in the late nineteenth century and is still in progress.[5] To situate structuralism within this historical context certainly does not amount to a denial of the scientific gains it represents (the same can be said for many

---

[4] This is not the proper place for long bibliographical references. Throughout the essay I shall refer only to those contributions which seem to me the most important.

[5] Historical research of this kind has been rightly called for by Lucien Sève, in M. Godelier and L. Sève, *Marxismo e strutturalismo,* Turin 1970, pp. 93ff. But the very brief sketch given by Sève is inadequate. In an effort to show that dialectical thought is more 'modern' than structuralism, he maintains that the former began 'to have a sizeable audience only around 1930'. It is not altogether clear what precise meaning that date has for him, and which thinkers he regards as representing the 'dialectical conception of evolution' which *during that period* is presumed to have 'entered into the modern sphere of Marxism'. With regard to certain interesting features of Sève's thought, see the concluding part of this essay.

other tendencies in modern science, from psychoanalysis to quantum mechanics). But it will help to identify with greater clarity certain ideological extrapolations, however cloaked in scientific rigour and objectivity they may be.

I do not propose to carry out here a work of this kind, which would require a broader competence than I have. I should only like to set forth some preliminary observations which, perhaps, will be useful for future research and discussion.

The point of departure for an investigation of this kind should obviously be Saussure. Great advances have been made in the last few years in the reconstruction of the great linguist's cultural background. I am referring, in particular, to Tullio de Mauro's annotated edition of the *Cours de linguistique générale*, which takes into account and discusses also the contributions of previous scholars. There remain, however, certain aspects of the relationship between Saussure and antecedent linguistics which should be studied in greater depth. I am not thinking so much of the 'precursors' of Saussure himself, about whom much has been clarified, as of the *opposing* tendencies with respect to which Saussure's ideas represent a polemical reaction.

Historical accounts of nineteenth-century linguistics generally indicate a line of development which, from Rask and Bopp to Schleicher,[6] and from Schleicher to the neo-grammarians, asserts ever more forcefully the unconscious character of so-called phonetic laws and their freedom from exceptions. The peremptory assertions by Brugmann and Osthoff, Delbrück, and Paul about the 'blind' and 'necessary' workings of these laws appear as the extreme formulation of what had already been proclaimed and practised – although not without some hesitation and inconsistency – by previous linguists oriented in a more or less decidedly naturalistic

---

[6] Rasmus Rask (1787–1832): Danish philologist whose work, anticipating that of Grimm on the law of regular consonant sound changes, led him to conclude that Greek, Latin, the Germanic and the Baltic-Slavic languages were all inter-related. Franz Bopp (1791–1867): German philologist whose work on the comparison of verb morphology in Sanskrit, Greek, Latin, Persian and German launched comparative linguistics as a systematic field of study. August Schleicher (1821–68): German philologist whose studies in comparative linguistics were underpinned by the application of a Hegelianized Darwinism to the study of language; language was seen as an 'organism' exhibiting the features of a natural life cycle. (NLB).

direction.[7]

This summary historiographic synchronization requires some further remarks with regard to the place of the neo-grammarians. To begin with, the reaction against 'naturalism' had already begun before the neo-grammarians, within Schleicher's own school – i.e. within the school which had been most forthright in its assertion that linguistics is a natural science. Students of Schleicher such as Johannes Schmidt and Hugo Schuchardt contraposed more articulated and refined models to Schleicher's model of the 'genealogical tree' (i.e. the notion of the descent of a number of well-defined daughter-languages from one mother-language through a branching-out process).[8] Schmidt's writing on the affinity of Indo-European languages dates from 1872. Schuchardt's first objections to an overly rigid classificationism within the field of the Romance languages can already be found in his great work on the vowel system of Vulgar Latin,[9] almost a decade before the movement of the neo-grammarians took precise shape. Similar ideas about the impossibility of making rigourous demarcations of one language from another were held by Paul Meyer and Gaston Paris during the eighteen-seventies in France.[10] Even then the reaction against genealogical and classificatory schematism was accompanied by the polemic against the assimilation of linguistics to the natural sciences. On this point, Schuchardt found himself

[7] Karl Brugmann (1849–1919) and Hermann Osthoff (1847–1909): German philologists who were early proponents of the neo-grammarian school of thought. Berthold Delbrück (1842–1922): German student of the comparative syntax of Indo-European languages and collaborator with Brugmann. Hermann Paul (1846–1921): German philologist whose *Prinzipien der Sprachgeschichte* (1880) stressed that the evolution of language was intelligible only in terms of regular sound laws operating through the reciprocal influence of individual speakers. (NLB).

[8] Johannes Schmidt (1843–1901): German philologist who proposed as an alternative to the 'family-tree' theory a 'dialect-wave' theory, according to which the various languages of the Indo-European family do not constitute sharply demarcated branches (as implied by the family-tree theory), but rather are the product of the diffusion of dialectal peculiarities emanating from diverse centres. Hugo Schuchardt (1842–1927): German philologist who insisted on the limited validity in time and space of 'sound laws', and traced the origin of sound changes to psychical factors. (NLB).

[9] H. Schuchardt, *Der Vokalismus des Vulgärlateins*, Leipzig 1866–8. Cf. the work by the same author *Ueber die Klassifikation der romanischen Mundarten*, written in 1870, but published much later, Graz 1900.

[10] Paul Meyer (1840–1917) and Gaston Paris (1839–1903): French students of medieval French and Provençal languages. (NLB).

in agreement with older linguists with a philological and historical-ethnological background, such as Georg Curtius and Heymann Steinthal, who had never accepted the separation of linguistics from the historical disciplines, as Schleicher had theorized it.[11]

The movement of the neo-grammarians, which had its official consecration with the preface by Brugmann and Osthoff to *Morphologische Untersuchungen* (1878), does not represent, therefore, the culmination of a one-sided evolution in linguistics. Rather, in certain respects it represents a reaction against disintegrative tendencies which had *already* called into question the 'scientificity' of linguistics. The claim that phonetics is governed by exception-less laws – which created such a sensation at the time – is indeed a consequence of the confidence inspired by the great success of studies in Indo-European phonetics during the eighteen-seventies, as a result of which previously inexplicable 'exceptions' were shown to display a deeper, underlying regularity.[12] But it represents also a polemical stiffening vis-à-vis 'historicist' stirrings already in progress, such as those which were beginning to emerge among Schleicher's students and in French linguistics. On two key points at least the neo-grammarians themselves proved not unaffected by such stirrings. Linguistics, they claimed, is an historical science with a psychological foundation, not a natural science. The phonetic laws are indeed without exceptions once they have been demonstrated, but the *beginning* of phonetic change is to be ascribed to an (unconscious) innovation on the part of a single speaker or small number of speakers, which is then generalized through imitation.[13] Phonetic innovation is not something which is *collective from its very beginning,* dependent on a transformation of the phonetic organs or of the physical or social environment, or on a kind of evolutionary force inherent in language itself, as if the latter were an 'organism' independent of its speakers and endowed with its

[11] George Curtius (1820–85) German philologist. On Steinthal see p. 49, note 20. (NLB).

[12] Cf. H. Pedersen, *Linguistic Science in the Nineteenth Century*, Cambridge, Mass. 1931, pp. 277ff.

[13] On this point (the beginning of innovation on the part of a single individual or of a small group of individuals), the early neo-grammarians already showed differences and fluctuations; see, for example, the passages which I cited in my *Classicismo e illuminismo nell'Ottocento italiano,* Pisa 1969 (2nd ed.), p. 322; on the position of Ascoli and Schuchardt towards the neo-grammarians, see ibid., pp. 318–28.

own life. Benvenuto Terracini is, therefore, not altogether mistaken when, from his idealist point of view, he perceives in these
ideas of the neo-grammarians 'an initial movement towards a
return to the interpretation of language and its vicissitudes in
terms of man's creative spirit'.[14]

The opposition to the neo-grammarians was two-fold from the
very beginning. On the one hand, Schuchardt thought that the
new school was too mechanistic, for although he was far from
conclusions of a Crocean type, he still leaned more and more
towards a conception of phonetic laws as mere 'tendencies' and
stressed the cultural side to linguistic facts. On the other hand,
Graziadio Ascoli found too much psychology and too little
naturalism in it; for it seemed to him that by ascribing an individual
origin to phonetic transformations one detracted from their
character as phenomena governed by universality-necessity. This
is not to imply that the alliance established between Ascoli and
Schuchardt against the neo-grammarians was the result of mere
polemical contingencies. Both scholars had a strong sense of the
inter-connectedness of the various aspects of reality, and they
displayed, therefore, an equal degree of annoyance with the claim
put forward by the new school that linguistics was an 'autonomous'
science. The fact remains, however, that the kind of inter-
disciplinarity Ascoli had in mind was primarily a union of linguistics with biology and with an anthropology conceived in
naturalistic and evolutionistic terms – whereas the kind Schuchardt
had in mind was a union of linguistics with the historical-philologi-
cal sciences, with a tendency to emphasize the cultural facts of
language as opposed to unconscious mechanisms.

While the conception of linguistics as a 'Darwinian' science lost
more and more ground after the eighteen-eighties (Ascoli remained
in this and other respects an isolated figure), neo-grammarians and
followers of Schmidt and Schuchardt divided up the field. The
great syntheses of Romance and Indo-European comparative
grammar carried out according to neo-grammatical principles by
Brugmann and Meyer-Lübke were counter-balanced by the work
of Kretschmer in the Indo-European field and by that of Gilliéron

[14] *Archivio glottologico italiano*, XLI (1956), p. 91. See also Croce's not altogether
unfavourable remarks (even if accompanied by certain reservations) concerning
Paul in *Aesthetic,* New York 1953 (revised ed.), pp. 403 and 419, and *Problemi
di estetica,* Bari 1940 (3rd ed.), p. 470.

and Schuchardt in the Romance field – works which displayed a tendency towards an anti-classificatory and individualist historicism, which was later to become openly idealistic with Vossler and the Crocean linguists.[15]

It is this crisis situation in the linguistics of the late nineteenth century which, in my opinion, has to be considered in order to understand certain features of Saussure's theory, beginning with its antinomic framework (*langue-parole*, synchrony-diachrony) and the insistence with which Saussure stressed the need to keep the polar terms absolutely distinct, free from all contaminating influences. This determination to make rigorous distinctions (which are, admittedly, distinctions between 'points of view' and not between 'things themselves', but which are not for that presented as any less irreconcilable) serves what I would call a 'defensive' function in relation to those tendencies which appeared to be designed to bring about the dissolution of linguistics as a science.

At a time when the scientificity of linguistics was threatened by a one-sided and ever greater insistence on the subjective side to linguistic facts, Saussure maintained that this scientificity could be saved only by a rigorous separatism. In other words, the reality of both aspects of language (the *langue* as a collective institution and the *parole* as an individual embodiment of the system),[16] must be acknowledged, but they must not in any way be brought into contact with one another or tested against each other in the treatment of linguistic problems. Rather, they must be regarded as two spheres of study completely independent of one another. In this way, the conception of *langue* as a system cannot be blurred by the consideration of phenomena dealing with individuals, since

[15] Wilhelm Meyer-Lübke (1861–1936): German student of Romance philology. Paul Kretschmer (1866–1956):German student of ancient Greek. Jules Gilliéron (1854–1926): Swiss linguist concerned with the geographical distribution of Romance dialects. Karl Vossler (1872–1949) and Crocean linguistics took as their starting point Croce's dictum that language was a form of poetry; language was seen, therefore, as the expression of a creative artistic act. (NLB).

[16] Saussure's own terms, *langue* and *parole*, have been retained throughout (as is the case also in Timpanaro's text), in preference to Baskin's rendering of them as 'language' and 'speech'. Perhaps the most accurate rendering, not adopted here for stylistic reasons, would be 'language system' and 'language behaviour', as suggested by John Lyons. (NLB).

*by definition* the latter are extraneous to *langue*. It is no longer necessary to become embroiled, as a follower of Ascoli or a neo-
grammarian would have done, in an endless debate with the
followers of Schuchardt or Gilliéron as to whether the collective
or the individual aspect is the most essential in language viewed as
a unitary fact. It now becomes a matter of delimiting from the
outset the object of 'the linguistics of *langue*', in such a way that
the facts of *parole* are declared not non-existent but simply irrelevant.

After he has observed that the object of linguistics runs the risk
of slipping through the hands of the linguist and being divided up
among a variety of disciplines, Saussure goes on to state the
following. 'As I see it there is only one solution to all of the fore-
going difficulties: *from the very outset we must take langue as our
point of departure and use langue as the norm of all other manifestations
of language*. . . . Taken as a whole, language (*langage*) is many-sided
and heterogeneous; straddling several areas simultaneously –
physical, physiological, and psychological – it belongs both to the
individual and to society; we cannot put it into any category of
human facts, for we cannot discover its unity. *Langue,* on the
contrary, is a self-contained whole and a principle of classification.
As soon as we give *langue* first place among the facts of language,
we introduce a natural order into a mass that lends itself to no
other classification.'[17] To devote oneself to the linguistics of *langue*
means, therefore, to latch onto the single feature of language which
is susceptible to scientific study and (what for Saussure amounts
to the same thing) to *autonomous* study, thereby preventing the
absorption of linguistics within the other disciplines.

Furthermore, the very way in which Saussure conceives of
*parole* has a polemical character to it. Although Saussure's *parole* is
not reducible to phonation alone, but also encompasses the capacity
to combine individual signs into sentences, there can be no doubt
that Saussure stresses that *parole* is primarily a material manifestation
of *langue,* and that such outward manifestations (which necessarily
vary from case to case) are irrelevant to the study of language as a
system of signs.[18] Thus, there is a common anti-materialist

[17] Ferdinand de Saussure, *Course in General Linguistics,* London 1966, p. 9
(translation modified). In the French text (hereinafter indicated in parentheses),
the reference is to p. 25 of the edition published under the supervision of Charles
Bally and Albert Sechehaye, Paris 1968.

[18] *Course in General Linguistics,* pp. 9–13 (pp. 25–9).

orientation shared by Saussurianism – with the subsequent advances made by the Prague School and the Danes – on the one hand, and the more or less idealist and individualist linguistics which runs from Schuchardt to Vossler and the Italian Croceans, on the other. The value schemes of the two anti-materialist orientations are, however, the opposite of one another. For an idealist-historicist, the spirituality of language stems precisely from the absolute individuality, the unrepeatability of individual expression, whereas any view of language as a 'general schema' or institution is seen as 'naturalistic' in that it would limit the freedom of the expressive act. For Saussure and even more for his followers, the stain of materialism afflicts a linguistics which gives primacy to the individual act of *parole,* which is a *material* manifestation (and therefore inevitably changing, approximate and irreducible to a rigorous science) of that system of 'ideal' signs represented by *langue.* Here we are witness to a kind of 'anti-materialist back-scratching' on the part of an intuitionist and subjectivist idealism – which sees the positive in the creative act and the negative in its hypostatization – and on the part of a mathematical-Platonist idealism – which sees the positive in the system of abstract concepts and the negative in their changing empirical manifestations. With Saussure, this 'Platonic' stance is still embryonic. Although oriented towards an upgrading of the 'abstract', he still concurs in and feels the negative connotation of this term (as de Mauro has perceptively pointed out),[19] and therefore asserts the 'concreteness' of *langue.* It is, however, unquestionably with Saussure, in linguistics, that we have the beginning of that *Querelle* over the abstract and the concrete which is destined to develop in a great variety of fields through the whole course of twentieth-century culture: historical concreteness versus naturalistic abstractness, according to the idealist-historicists; abstractness as the essential character of scientific knowledge versus an intuitionist and vulgarly empirical pseudo-knowledge, according to the structuralists and the followers of other epistemological orientations with a mathematical foundation.

The other Saussurian dichotomy, synchrony versus diachrony, can also be traced back to the same 'defensive' exigency. Even the neo-grammarians, together with an entire antecedent tradition of the nineteenth century, regarded the diachronic study of language

[19] See de Mauro's comments in his critical edition of the *Cours,* Paris 1972, p. 393, note 70.

as what distinguished scientific from merely descriptive linguistics. Hermann Paul, writing in his *Prinzipien der Sprachgeschichte*, stated: 'From the moment we go beyond the mere ascertainment of individual facts and attempt to grasp their connection, we then enter into the field of history, even if we are not aware of it'.[20] But we have already seen how the neo-grammarians, by ascribing the origin of linguistic changes to individuals, had played a part in undermining, in a certain sense, faith in the scientificity of diachronic linguistics, and how the linguists influenced by neo-idealism went even farther in this direction. It was precisely in order to redeem the absolute necessity and generality of phonetic changes as against the neo-grammarians that Ascoli upgraded the theory of the substratum to the point where he made it the distinctive feature of his school.[21]

Saussure made no attempt at a 'salvaging operation' of this kind. He acknowledged without further ado that diachrony is not amenable to rigorously scientific study in that it is the realm of fortuitous and asystematic phenomena. 'Changes never affect the system as a whole but rather one or another of its elements.' 'Diachronic facts are then particular . . . [events which] are isolated and form no system among themselves.'[22] If the linguist 'takes the diachronic perspective, he no longer observes *langue* but rather a series of events that modify it'.[23] This is exactly the opposite of what Paul stated in the passage we just quoted. The diachronic perspective, far from being a guarantee of scientificity, makes it inevitable, according to Saussure, that language is regarded as a mélange of facts 'without any connection' between them. This cannot, therefore, be the basis for establishing linguistics as a science. Rather, it is on the basis of synchrony that the systematic nature of language reveals itself. Naturally, for Saussure, the findings of historical-comparative linguistics have not been completely useless. They have helped to free linguistics from a naïve finalism and from the

[20] Hermann Paul, *Prinzipien der Sprachgeschichte*, Halle 1909 (4th ed.), p. 20.

[21] For Ascoli, every ethnic community possesses a certain number of 'oral habits'. Whenever such a community is forced to learn a new language (by reason of conquest, colonization, etc.), it carries over these 'oral habits', which become the 'substratum' of the new language; thus, the phonetic changes brought about in the new language are collective in nature from the very beginning, and Ascoli believed this essential to establishing phonetic laws on a less psychological and more naturalistic basis. (NLB).

[22] *Course in General Linguistics*, pp. 87, 95.

[23] Ibid., p. 90.

identification of language with logic.[24] '. . . But this only goes to prove clearly that diachronic linguistics is not an end in itself. What is said of journalism applies to diachrony: it leads everywhere provided you get out of it.'[25]

It is not simply a hypothesis of ours that the crisis in late nineteenth-century historical linguistics had an effect on Saussure's negative assessment of the possibility of a scientific diachronic linguistics. For confirmation one need only look at the way in which Saussure resolves the questions debated by the neo-grammarians and the followers of Schuchardt and of 'linguistic geography'.

In agreement with the neo-grammarians, Saussure maintains that linguistic innovation is initially a fact of *parole*, which only later, after it has been adopted by the mass of speakers, becomes a part of *langue*. 'It is in *parole* that the germ of all change is found. Each change is launched by a certain number of individuals before it is accepted for general use.'[26] From a certain number of individuals or from a single individual in a single act of *parole*? The notes of his students show variations in this regard: 'Forms, grammar, have only a social existence, but changes begin with an individual'; 'every kind of change is undertaken *by a group of individuals*' (variations: '. . . by a certain number of individuals'; 'by an individual').[27] We have seen that a similar wavering can be found in the formulations of the neo-grammarians. Godel is probably mistaken, therefore, in maintaining that the 'individualistic' formulation does not correspond to Saussure's thought. The equivocation must have been in the lectures of the master himself, and not in the misinterpretations of his students.[28]

Saussure agrees with the neo-grammarians also in stipulating that, despite the beginning of linguistic change in individuals, so-called phonetic laws have no exceptions: 'This regularity, which has at times been disputed, is apparently firmly established; obvious exceptions do not lessen the inevitability of such changes, for they can be explained either by more special phonetic laws . . . or by the interference of facts of another class (analogy, etc.).'[29] This

[24] Ibid., pp. 85 and 90ff.; see also R. Godel, *Les sources manuscrites du Cours de linguistique générale de F. de Saussure*, Geneva-Paris 1957, p. 186.

[25] *Course in General Linguistics*, p. 90 (translation modified).

[26] Ibid., p. 135.

[27] *Cours de linguistique générale*, ed. R. Engler, Wiesbaden 1968, I, p. 223; Godel, op. cit., p. 156.

is exactly what the neo-grammarians maintained against the old and new proponents of genuine 'exceptions'. But Saussure immediately adds that to call these sound changes 'laws' is completely mistaken, for they deal only with *individual events*. A sound change does not affect *all* words. Rather, it is only a *single* sound which changes under particular conditions completely independently of the words in which it is found. To use the terminology which will be introduced later by Martinet, phonetic changes concern only the 'secondary articulation' of language. 'No law exists if one cannot point to a number of individual facts which are connected together. . . . It is absurd to say that *one* element is governed by a law.'[30] Thus, conceding that sound changes have no exceptions, Saussure immediately strips the statement of that scientificity which the neo-grammarians were so proud to ascribe to it – and does so in a far more radical way than by admitting certain exceptions. Saussure can thus conclude that 'in spite of certain appearances to the contrary, diachronic events are always accidental and particular. . . . [They] force themselves upon *langue* but are in no way general.'[31]

If on this point Saussure is, despite everything, still closer to the neo-grammarians than to Schuchardt and to Gilliéron, on other points (the non-existence of clear-cut boundaries between linguistic areas, the origins of linguistic differentiation) he has clearly absorbed to a great degree the ideas of Schuchardt, Johannes Schmidt, Paul Meyer and Gilliéron. To convince oneself of this, one need only read the chapters of the *Cours* on the 'Causes of Geographical Diversity' and on the 'Spread of Linguistic Waves'. The notes from his 1891 lectures already show this orientation

---

[28] Cf. Godel, op. cit., p. 156, n. 90. The proposition concerning the individual origin of linguistic innovation can certainly be debated and rejected; but it does not seem to me that Lepschy, in his *La linguistica strutturale,* Turin 1966, p. 34 [a revised and abridged version of this work has been published in English under the title *A Survey of Structuralist Linguistics,* London 1970 – NLB], is correct in presenting it ironically as a proposition of an Italian-idealist stamp, as an anti-scientific declaration of faith in the 'creativity of the spirit'. Rather, it represents a proposition which is supported by some neo-grammarians (see note 13), by Otto Jespersen, *Mankind, Nation and Individual from a Linguistic Point of View,* London 1946, pp. 27ff., and perhaps, as we have seen, by Saussure himself. It does not imply any adherence to the Crocean concept of a linguistic creativity identified with artistic creativity.

[29] *Course in General Linguistics,* p. 94.

[30] Engler, op. cit., p. 210 and cf. p. 208.

[31] *Course in General Linguistics,* pp. 93, 95.

clearly: no permanent features in languages, the impossibility of defining a dialect which covers any considerable area – e.g. the Savoyard dialectic – since each of the features which could be regarded as distinctive extends beyond the confines of Savoy.[32] This is not the place to ask whether these concessions to linguistic geography do not ultimately have the effect of undermining the very concept of a synchronic linguistic system, which presupposes a relatively homogeneous and well-defined community of speakers. Rather, what is important to point out here is that in diachronic linguistics Saussure is Schmidtian and Schuchardtian to a considerable degree; and to the extent that he is a neo-grammarian, he gives an interpretation of neo-grammatical theory which seeks to deny or to limit the scientificity of diachrony. The diachronic dimension is surrendered to the enemy, so to speak. The retrieval of linguistics as a science is to be sought elsewhere, on synchronic ground, which is accorded pre-eminence by Saussure. The synchronic aspect 'predominates' over the diachronic, both from the standpoint of the speaker, who perceives synchrony as 'the true and only reality', and from the standpoint of the linguistic scholar, who can give a rigorous definition to the object of his science and engage in linguistics strictly speaking (and not in physiology, philology, or some other discipline) only if he takes the synchronic aspect as his point of departure.[33]

But it is not just the crisis in historical linguistics which inclines Saussure to opt for synchrony. It is the entire intellectual climate in general. Saussure himself refers to the so-called 'debate over methodology' which unfolded during the late nineteenth century between the followers of the 'historical' school and those of the 'theoretical' school in the economic sciences.[34] But this debate was, in turn, an episode in a broader debate on the scientificity of historiography, which involved, on the one hand, Marxism (which had brought about an historicization of economics in a much more profound way than had the 'historical' school of Gustav von Schmoller)[35] and, on the other hand, the natural sciences. The

[32] Godel, op. cit., pp. 39, 185.

[33] *Course in General Linguistics,* p. 90.

[34] Ibid., p. 79; cf. note 165 to de Mauro's critical edition of the *Cours,* Paris 1972. See also Charles Gide and Charles Rist, *Histoire des doctrines économiques* (7th ed.), Paris 1947, II, pp. 436–68.

[35] Gustav von Schmoller (1838–1917); German proponent of the 'younger historical school' of economics, which rejected the universal validity of the laws

great achievement of geological and biological evolutionism had been the demonstration of the historicity of nature, and thereby the supersession of the old antithesis between a static (or cyclical) nature and a progressing history presumed to be the exclusive privilege of the Spirit. Between 1850 and 1880 the historical sciences of nature had become the avant-garde sciences of European culture, with all of the advantages (the historicization of nature, the defeat of spiritualism) and the dangers (blurring of the distinction between the two different historical rates of development, the biological and the human-social) which that entailed. At the end of the nineteenth century there re-emerged, however, a split between the 'human' and the 'natural', and correspondingly, between the 'historical' and the 'scientific'. The new historicism went back to Hegel in its claim that the only real history is that of the Spirit, but it now stressed the particularistic features of the historical event which make it unrepeatable. Thus, it became heavily laden with irrationalism and intuitionism. In scientific culture, on the other hand, the place of biology receded dramatically in favour of the physico-mathematical sciences, which focussed on epistemological models of either an empirio-pragmatist (experiments as the production of phenomena) or a Platonist nature (dissociation of 'theory' from experiments). In biology itself, evolutionism went through a period of crisis as a consequence of the rediscovery of Mendel's laws and the rise of genetics, which initially appeared destined to refute rather than support Darwinian theory.

Historicists and new epistemologists were in agreement in declaring 'Down with materialism'. But the former said, 'Down with science, which is materialistic', the latter 'Long live science, which is the best refutation of materialism'. Similarly, these orientations developed opposing viewpoints with regard to history, even though they had a common starting ground in their anti-materialism.

In this general atmosphere one can understand very well the origins of the two fundamental tendencies in twentieth-century linguistics: one which takes Schuchardt (although also in polemic with him) as its point of departure and moves towards increasingly

---

formulated by classical economics and favoured descriptive research into the historically and nationally determinate details of economic life. (NLB).

idealistic positions; the other which moves from Saussure towards structuralism. The first orientation accepts an individualizing historicism, and later makes heroic attempts to salvage a minimum of 'objectivity' and 'collectivity' in the linguistic fact, so that linguistics cannot be simply dissolved into aesthetics, as Croce would have liked. For Saussure's part, there is an abandonment of any attempt to incorporate the diachronic dimension into science. He is largely in agreement with the 'historicists' in regarding such attempts as entirely futile. He is not, however, in agreement with them when it comes to abandoning science. Thus, he accepts a dualistic conception of the linguistic fact: the pole *parole*-'diachrony' belongs to the world of becoming, the accidental and the atomistic, a world (as Plato would have said) which is not amenable to science but only to 'opinion'; the pole *langue*-synchrony belongs to the realm of being, and it is only in relation to such a world that true science is possible.[36]

Given our argument to this point, should we rush to the conclusion that Saussurianism is a scientistic-Platonist ideology? This would be a grave mistake. To begin with, the fact that the distinctions made by Saussure carry the mark of the cultural climate in which they arose does not detract at all from their scientific side, which is ideologically neutral and acceptable even to someone who follows a completely different philosophico-political orientation. It remains true that, given the slowness with which language changes, its evolution generally goes unnoticed by the speaker (or is noticed only in the form of stylistic differences), and that only this slowness makes it possible to use language as a means of communication. It remains true that although language evolves diachronically, it functions synchronically, as Coseriu says.[37] Secondly, it has to be acknowledged that in speaking of the

---

[36] From what we have already observed it may be concluded that, although it is highly likely that a man of Saussure's cultural stature possessed a knowledge of Hegel's thought, nevertheless the belief of R. Jakobson (see 'La Scuola linguistica di Praga' in *Selected Writings*, The Hague 1971, II, pp. 543ff.) and of other scholars that Hegelianism had a genuine influence on Saussure's thought should be treated with caution. I shall limit myself to these cursory observations: a) Saussure's antinomies do not give rise to a 'synthesis', but rather Saussure insists on their irreconcilability and paradoxicality; b) for Saussure there is no 'rationality in history', but rather diachrony is, at least in the linguistic domain, the realm of the accidental and the fortuitous; and pre-eminence belongs to the static moment, which for Hegel is 'abstract' in a pejorative sense.

[37] Eugenio Coseriu: contemporary Spanish linguist. (NLB).

Platonism, anti-materialism, etc. in Saussure's thought I have to some extent forced the argument. In other words, I have brought out the *seeds* of tendencies which in the authentic Saussure are still neutralized to a considerable degree by what has been called (applaudingly or reproachfully, depending on one's point of view) his positivism. The 'psychological' which Saussure counterposes to the 'physiological' is not yet the 'spiritual' (and furthermore, as we know, the claim that linguistics was a psychological and not a physiological science had been put forth by the neo-grammarians against Schleicher and Ascoli). He takes pains to emphasize that the seat of *langue* is 'in the brain' of speakers.[38] *Langue* is supra-individual in a 'social' sense, obviously not in the sense of the idealist-Romantic Ego or in a strictly Platonist sense. The waverings in Saussure's thought and the dissatisfaction which prevented him from formulating his theory in a fully perfected form stem *also* from his reluctance to give up a realistic viewpoint in the study of language.

It is this reluctance which puts such strain on Saussure's thoughts on the arbitrariness of signs, on value and signification, and on the concept of signs itself. On the one hand, there is the tendency to detach signs from any relationship with extra-linguistic reality and to define them only in relation to other signs. Language is then no longer a means for communicating experiences or volition, but simply a system closed unto itself and basking in its own internal coherence, 'like a game of chess'.[39] The fear of falling into naïve realism, into the conception of language as nomenclature, and the need to go beyond the simplistic conventionalism of Whitney[40] often lead Saussure to over-react by slighting the instrumental value of language; at the same time, he is led to underestimate the communicative imperfections present in all languages, which require a particular context to make them intelligible. (This point is, however, brought out by the Saussurian Bally and by other more recent scholars – though not by the more formalistic currents of structuralism.[41])

One should add, however, that in Saussure the relationship

[38] *Course in General Linguistics*, pp. 13–14.
[39] Ibid., p. 88.
[40] William Dwight Whitney (1827–94): American philologist who insisted on the purely conventional character of language and linguistic signs as a means of communication. (NLB).

between language and what language serves to communicate is never completely lost from sight. 'But here is the paradox: on the one hand, the concept seems to be the counterpart of the sound-image within the sign; and on the other hand, the sign itself (i.e. the relationship which links its two elements together) is also and to an equal degree the counterpart of the other signs of the *langue*. . . . Even outside the *langue* all values are apparently governed by the same paradoxical principle. They are always composed: 1. of a *dissimilar* thing that can be *exchanged* for the thing of which the value is to be determined; and 2. of *similar* things that can be *compared* with the thing of which the value is to be determined. . . . Thus, to determine what a five-franc piece is worth one must know: 1. that it can be exchanged for a fixed quantity of a different thing, e.g. bread; and 2. that it can be compared with a similar value of the same system, e.g. a one-franc piece, or with coins of another system (a dollar, etc.). In the same way, a word can be exchanged for something dissimilar, an idea; besides, it can be compared with something of the same nature, another word.'[42]

If in this instance Saussure talks only of paradox, in certain hand-written notes stronger expressions can be found: this two-fold character of linguistic value 'va jusqu'à désespérer l'esprit'.[43] The temptation to resolve the paradox in favour of simply the second characteristic (i.e. to define signs merely in relation to the other signs which form a system with them) is undoubtedly very strong in Saussure. It is the emphasis he has given to the second characteristic which he regards as his most original contribution and the reason why he has advanced beyond Whitney. Nevertheless, he usually insists on both characteristics: 'What is indisputable is that value moves between these two axes, that it is determined concurrently along these two axes.'[44] One could say that the

---

[41] Cf. Charles Bally, *Linguistique générale et linguistique française*, Bern 1965, pp. 40–45, 210ff.; Giacomo Devoto, *I fondamenti della storia linguistica*, Florence 1951, pp. 16ff. and *passim* (with the important distinction between 'representation' and 'evocation'); and more recently, Mario Wandruszka, 'Der Ertrag des Strukturalismus', *Zeitschrift für romanische Philologie*, LXXXIV (1968), pp. 106ff.

[42] *Course in General Linguistics*, pp. 114–15 (translation modified).

[43] Engler, op. cit., p. 259.

[44] Ibid. See also, in Godel, pp. 245–7, two passages which are cited and discussed, in the first of which the relationship between one sign and the others is considered 'primary', and in the second primacy is given to the relationship between the concept and the acoustic image within each sign. It is always possible to interpret this 'primacy' in two different senses and therefore to maintain, as

similarity between *langue* and the monetary system (the notion of an *exchange between dissimilars* and of a relationship of correspondence, but not of identification, between words and concepts) has served as a fortunate counterbalance to the similarity between *langue* and a game of chess (with all of the formalistic perils which that implied).

This realistic dimension re-emerges in Saussure's remarks on the arbitrariness of signs. 'The idea of "sister" is not linked by any inner relationship to the succession of sounds *s-ö-r* which serves as its signifier in French; that it could be represented equally by just any other sequence is proved by differences among languages: the signified "ox" has as its signifier *b-ö-f* on one side of the border and *o-k-s* (*Ochs*) on the other side.'[45]

Ever since Benveniste,[46] this explanation of arbitrariness has been regarded as a regrettable relapse on Saussure's part into the conception of language as a naming-process which he had himself so effectively opposed. This 'ox in itself', which is called by two different names in France and Germany even though it is the same, was not at all to the liking of those who maintain that there is no reality outside language. When confronted with an animal characterized by such unwelcome and crude objectivity, no recent linguist appears to be prepared to say, 'T'amo, o pio bove'.[47] And even a scholar oriented in so vigorously an anti-formalist direction as de Mauro shares this negative judgment at least in part, and is at most prepared to attribute a didactic value to the example of *boeuf-Ochs*.[48] A look at the hand-written sources, however, makes it impossible this time to ascribe the 'crudeness' to the editors of the *Cours*, or to perceive any evolution in Saussure's thought on

Godel does, that there is no contradiction. Nevertheless, one cannot help but wonder whether such reconciliatory interpretations do not arbitrarily gloss over the tormented and problematic side to Saussure's thought.

[45] *Course in General Linguistics*, pp. 67–8.

[46] Reference is to Émile Benveniste (1902–76) and his work *L'origine de la formation des mots*, Paris 1935. (NLB).

[47] Reference is to the opening lines of Giosue Carducci's poem *Il bove*; literally, the line reads, 'I love you, o godly ox'. (NLB).

[48] See de Mauro's commentary to Saussure, op. cit., pp. 394 note 74, 413, 415, with the bibliography. Cf. Mario Lucidi, *Saggi linguistici*, Naples 1966, p. 60. and note 20 (although he remains within the framework of a polemic with Benveniste's general interpretation); Godel, op. cit., p. 196; G. Lepschy, 'Ancora su "l'arbitraire du signe",' *Annali della Scuola Normale Superiore di Pisa* (1962), p. 89 (this study by Lepschy on the problem of the arbitrariness of signs remains fundamental).

this point.[49] It seems to me that this explanation of arbitrariness is essential, and can be integrated with – *but not replaced by* – other, more subtle explanations. That language is not *reducible* to a naming-process is perfectly true, both in the sense that the continuum of experience is divided up by the different languages in different ways so that there is no biunivocal correspondence between objects and words, and in the sense that language is not made up of labels but of phrases, which take on very different logico-syntactic forms in the different languages. If, however, one wishes to maintain that language *has no nomenclatural features at all*, i.e. that it does not refer back to any sensory-conceptual experience which is distinguishable from language itself (even though incapable of developing without the aid of language as a tool) and represents a common point of reference for those who speak different languages,[50] then one arrives at two possible conclusions, both equally unacceptable: either language becomes a *système pour le système* which has no meaning and serves no purpose, or else it is asserted that there are as many conceptions of the world as there are languages. In the latter case, one lapses into a degenerate form of the Romantic conception of a *Volksgeist,* according to which there is presumed to be an absolute (and not merely a relative and partial) intranslatability between languages, so that, for example, Lenin's thought is presumed to resemble more closely that of Tsar Nicholas II, by virtue of the common language, than it does that of Marx and Engels. As de Mauro points out, Saussure is far from taking this point of view.[51] Such is the case, however, precisely because he does not entirely reject Whitney's conventionalism, but rather elaborates on it and incorporates it within his theory. The much deprecated example of *boeuf-Ochs* is elementary – and as such far from definitive – but it is not at all erroneous. To reject it one would have to believe that there is a 'French way of

[49] Engler, op. cit., p. 152.

[50] The question which interests us most directly here concerns the distinction between language and 'experience'. But it is clear that for a materialist the inter-subjectivity of experience is, in turn, founded on the objectivity of the external world and on the biological nature (as well as the social nature) of sense and cognitive processes. In addition to the well-known works of a neo-positivist orientation dealing with this question, one should give attention to L. O. Reznikov, *Semiotica e marxismo,* Milan 1967, a book of no great genius, perhaps, but one which clearly brings out certain undeniable 'realist' exigencies.

[51] See de Mauro's commentary to Saussure, op. cit., pp. 439–40; see also Lepschy, 'Ancora . . .', note 17 on p. 93.

conceiving ox' which is completely different from a 'German way' of conceiving it – or one would have to claim that the equation *boeuf* = *Ochs* is just as absurd as, shall we say, the equation *boeuf* = *Himmel*.

Our acknowledgement that the continuum of experience is divided up in different ways by different languages should always be kept in mind, but it should not be inflated out of proportion. Obviously, to reiterate the examples which are passed on from textbook to textbook, the French *bois*, the Danish *trae* and the Italian *bosco* do not completely coincide with one another, since *bois* encompasses the signifieds 'woods' and 'wood' and *trae* those of 'wood' and 'tree' – and there exist countless other examples of such non-coincidences. But this does not mean that each language sets the values of the individual words in a completely unpredictable way, grouping together the most disparate concepts. There is a limit to the arbitrariness of the classifications which each language imposes on experience, and this limit is set by man's very psychophysical structure, by his needs, by his responses to particular stimuli and by his cognitive-practical activities, which are not absolutely different from one people to another, nor even from the present to the remotest of times. The arbitrariness in the classification of reality is, therefore, much less than the arbitrariness involved in the naming of the individual 'segments of reality'. Even when their mode of classification is the same, languages distinguish themselves from one another by the different names they give to the segments. This is what was brought out by the example of *boeuf-Ochs*. Furthermore, as a result of the possibility which languages have of expressing all things with different means, the translatability of one language into another is much greater at the level of phrases than at the level of individual words. Saussure was cognizant of all of this (although not without some wavering). It is for this reason that he states that the conception of language as a naming-process is 'simplistic', but not totally mistaken. It 'can bring us near the truth by showing us that the linguistic unit is a double entity, one formed by the associating of two terms'.[52]

'Association' or 'combination' or 'totality'? All these various terms are used by Saussure and indicate that his wavering between the conceptions of language as a tool for communicating something

[52] *Course in General Linguistics*, p. 65.

and language as a self-sufficient system finds its way into the concept of 'signs'. At times this latter term indicates an association of signifier and signified in which the two terms retain a relative autonomy; thus, the need to make a distinction between language and what language has to communicate is salvaged, but there reappears the spectre of the naming-process, Whitney's conception, which Saussure regards as inadequate. At other times the term indicates an inseparable synthesis, in which case the difficulties connected with the blurring of the two levels re-emerge. Saussure's well-known dissatisfaction with the choice of the two terms 'signifier' and 'signified' and with the term for the totality ('sign') goes beyond a merely terminological dissatisfaction. With the terms signifier and signified 'we have yet to arrive at the word which we still need and which should designate, without any possibility of equivocation, their union together. Whatever term is chosen – "sign", "term", "word", etc. – it will shift over to one side and runs the risk of designating only one of the parts. Probably there could not even be a suitable term. As soon as a term is applied to a notion of value, it is difficult for it not to fall off to one side or the other.'[53] In point of fact, the term (and very concept) 'sign' almost always manages to 'fall off to one side or the other'. Either it again becomes a synonym for 'signifier', as often happens in Saussure,[54] or else it ends by swallowing up the signified (indeed in the very choice of the term 'sign' to indicate the union of what is commonly meant by this word together with the *signifié,* there is already a certain anti-objectivist propensity, an alliance between the two elements which is established not on an equal footing but to the detriment of reality, which tends to be absorbed within language).

Saussure's distance from a subsequent form of structuralism which goes beyond linguistics can be assessed by noting the insistence with which he emphasizes the differences between language and the other human institutions and activities. It is true that he foresees a future science of signs, semiology, of which linguistics will represent only one part.[55] He states that the boundaries of this new science have yet to be determined: 'Why will semiology come

[53] Godel, op. cit., p. 192.
[54] See the passages indicated by de Mauro, note 155.
[55] *Course in General Linguistics,* pp. 16–17.

to a halt? It is hard to say in advance.'[56] But it is clear from all his remarks that only systems of signs in the strict sense belong to semiology: 'writing, the alphabet of deaf-mutes, symbolic rites, forms of politeness, military signals, etc.'. Even rites and forms of politeness – which, together with the 'customs' mentioned a little later, would appear to justify an extension of semiology to cultural anthropology – fall into the category only to the extent that they have something conventional and 'unexplained' (*immotivé*) about them. The less arbitrary they are, the less they can be regarded as typically semiological. Saussure rejects the notion and term of 'symbol' (which will later be so successful with Cassirer) for the linguistic sign, precisely because the symbol 'is never wholly arbitrary. . . . The symbol of justice, a pair of scales, could not be replaced by just any other symbol, such as a chariot'.[57] Even further removed from language (because even less 'arbitrary') are familial institutions, such as monogamy or polygamy.[58] Similarly, laws and even customs, which had initially been grouped under semiology, are subsequently distinguished from language in a clear-cut fashion.[59] Saussure even takes Whitney to task for not having made the distinction sufficiently clear.[60] Even economics, which Saussure had used as a model to clarify the twofold nature of linguistic 'value', is dissociated from language because economic value 'is rooted in things and in their natural relations'.[61] It can be concluded, therefore, that according to Saussure various other branches of knowledge will enter *in part and by approximation* into the future semiological science, but that only linguistics, accompanied at most by the study of writing and sign systems in the strict sense, has a full claim to belong to it. In general, the emphasis is not on the analogy between language and other institutions, but on the singularity of the former, which 'is a human institution, but of such a kind that all the other human institutions, with the exception of writing, can only lead us astray as to its real essence if we trust in their analogy'. And even more decisively: 'We are convinced that whoever sets foot on the ground of language is

---

[56] Engler, op cit., p. 46.
[57] *Course in General Linguistics*, pp. 68, 72ff.
[58] Ibid., p. 73.
[59] Ibid., p. 75.
[60] Ibid., pp. 75–6; cf. de Mauro's note 157.
[61] Ibid., p. 80.

bereft of all the analogies of heaven and earth.'[62]

Saussure is thus very far from using the conventional and 'systematic' character of language as a model which can be freely applied to all the other sciences. He is very far from attempting a reduction of all reality to language, or to a 'system' in a formalistic sense. Rather, he senses very strongly the non-conventionality (i.e. the lesser conventionality) of everything in life and human society which is not language. In his general vision of reality, to the degree that it appears in the interstices of his reflections on linguistics, he is even more of a realist than in his conception of language.

★     ★     ★

A good deal of twentieth-century structuralism can be regarded as a one-sided development of those tendentially Platonist-idealist features noted in Saussure, detached from the realist counter-tendencies which keep Saussure's thought in a precarious equilibrium. Naturally, this is not a development which proceeds by parthenogenesis from Saussure's theory alone; it emerges instead under the pressure of an entire cultural-political situation quite different in its openly anti-materialist climate from that in which Saussure grew up. Although the theories of the Copenhagen and Prague schools represent important gains, they immediately show themselves to be much more 'ideologized' than Saussure's theory. One need only read Brøndal's introductory article to *Acta linguistica* (1939)[63] in order to see that it is no longer necessary, as in Saussure's case, to look for 'inklings' or 'seeds' of anti-materialism and to run the risk of indicting the author's intentions. Here the intentions are explicit, the Platonism is completely unshrouded, and it takes on the shape of a global antithesis between the thought of the nineteenth century (at first historicist and Romantic, later

---

[62] See the passages of *Notes inédites* published by Godel and cited by de Mauro, pp. 324 and 328. There Saussure stresses the fact that 'the other institutions are all founded, in varying degrees, on the *natural* relationships of things. . . . For example, a nation's legislation, or its political system, or even the whimsical fashion which sets our mode of dress: the latter cannot overlook even for a moment the given proportions of the human body'. As far as concerns the distinction between language and social institutions, and the salvaging of it by Stalin as against the school of N. J. Marr, cf. 'A proposito del parallelismo tra lingua e diritto', in *Belfagor*, XVIII (1963), pp. 1ff.

[63] Reference is to the Danish linguist Viggo Brøndal (1887–1942); the article, 'Linguistique structurale', can be found in his *Essais de linguistique générale*, Copenhagen 1947. (NLB).

historicist and positivist) and that of the twentieth (ahistorical-scientistic, anti-evolutionary, anti-empiricist and intent on discovering the unchanging structures of reality). From an ideological and epistemological standpoint this article is a mishmash,[64] for in his anti-evolutionary zeal Brøndal takes as allies a Lalande and a Meyerson[65] without realizing the important differences between their metaphysics and structuralism, and lumps together as opponents of slow and gradual evolution a great achievement of modern science like quantum mechanics with a biological theory of limited value at best like Hugo De Vries's 'mutations by leaps'. And all of this confusion serves, in a certain sense, only to highlight the meaning of the *prise de position*. The conception of language as a system has already become obsession and systematic mysticism. Given the Cuverian conception of a system (and Brøndal does not hesitate to exalt 'Cuvier's ingenious and profound ideas' as against Darwin), the movements from one state to another can be explained only with sudden and miraculistic leaps, just like Cuvier's 'catastrophes'. This does not prevent Brøndal, a little later, from admitting with a certain unconscious humour that 'one has to acknowledge after all that time – this great impediment to any rationality – makes itself felt within the synchrony. . .'. It is an admission made necessary not only by the self-evident facts of reality, but also by the fact that the Prague school, to which Brøndal refers back on numerous occasions in his essay, fails him as a possible ally on this point. But it remains an inconsistent admission in the midst of that hymn to ahistoricity represented by his preamble to *Acta linguistica*.

Obviously, Brøndal cannot be reduced to this and other unfortunate articles of a general nature. And one should hasten to point out that the Copenhagen school has had a much greater representative (because more scientific and endowed with much greater internal coherence, if only in an ideological sense) in Louis Hjelmslev. But the internal coherence of Hjelmslev is that of someone

---

[64] There is worse than this to be found in Brøndal's production; see, for example, the passages cited by Lepschy in 'Aspetti teorici di alcune correnti della glottologia contemporanea', *Annali della Scuola Normale Superiore di Pisa* (1961), p. 223, and the incisive critical comments by Lepschy himself.

[65] André Lalande (1867–1964): French philosopher who opposed to the idea of progressive evolution the notion of an homogenizing involution which, in human affairs, expresses itself in an expansion of the realm of universal reason. Emile Meyerson (1859–1933): French philosopher of science who insisted that causality is a form of logical identity, in that the effect is already present in the cause. (NLB).

who, as Martinet says, 'makes explicit in the most intrepid fashion all of the consequences of an irrealism latent in his predecessors', and makes use of a linguistics 'whose science of the expression is not a phonetics and whose science of the content is not a semantics': 'an algebra of language, operating with unnamed entities'.[66] We should make clear that the right to abstraction is not at issue. At issue is the usefulness of such a high level of abstraction for the purpose of studying languages and the possibility of linking up such an ethereal theoretical element with the empirical element – something which has already been amply debated within structuralism itself. As a result, the requirement formulated by Hjelmslev himself that theory be 'appropriate' (i.e. capable of explaining reality) goes unsatisfied.

Some parenthetical remarks are in order here on the use made by structuralism – not only Danish but also even to some degree that of Prague – of the notion of 'relevance', which is also used to develop some of Saussure's hints in a particular direction. Every science which does not wish to be a collection of observations made from the most diverse points of view must, unquestionably, raise the problem of what is relevant to it and what is not, and together with this the problem of how it is distinct and autonomous in relation to the other sciences. But for a great deal of twentieth-century linguistics the question of relevance has served the purpose of an ever increasing 'purging' of the science of language of everything which might appear naturalistic. Already in Saussure, but even more among his successors, this entailed on the side of the 'signifier' a flight from *sound,* the materiality of which implied a dangerous commingling of linguistics with physiology or acoustics; and on the side of the 'signified', a flight from the *things* denoted, which in their turn led back to a materialist or at least a realist philosophy. The second operation led to that expunging of semantics from linguistics which has been criticized so effectively by de Mauro.[67] The first operation led to the distinction between phonetics and phonology (in the Prague meaning of these terms). It is a distinction which unquestionably has a scientific side to it

[66] André Martinet, *Économie des changements phonétiques,* Bern 1955, p. 33 (see also the reservations expressed by Lepschy, 'Aspetti teorici . . .', p. 247 and *La linguistica strutturale,* p. 89); Louis Hjelmslev, *Prolegomena to a Theory of Language,* Madison, Wis. 1963, p. 79.

[67] See above, note 3; see also C. Tullio Altan, 'Linguistica e antropologia culturale', *Rivista di sociologia* v (September–December 1967), pp. 25ff.

which is destined to remain a permanent achievement. But it was formulated by Trubetzkoy with a rigourism and a separatism which were so absolute as to make it untenable. In this extreme position, in this *noli me tangere* which Trubetzkoy proclaims in relation to phonetics, it is impossible not to see an ideological concern – the concern to 'de-materialize' phonology as much as possible. This same concern led Trubetzkoy to group phonology exclusively with *langue* and phonetics with *parole,* i.e. to attempt to establish here too a clear-cut distinction between the ideational system of language and its material and accidental manifestations.[68]

During Saussure's time, it appeared that anti-materialist purposes were sufficiently served by setting the 'psychic' off against the 'physiological' (as Steinthal and the neo-grammarians had already done against Schleicher). Later, for very different reasons, although within the framework of a common struggle against the residues of positivism, everything that had a connection with psychology fell under the suspicion of both Crocean idealists and Platonistic idealists. Similarly, the links between language and socio-cultural history were dissolved on the grounds that they were irrelevant. Hjelmslev remarks that one of the shortcomings of Saussure's *Cours* is that general linguistics is still conceptualized 'on an essentially sociological and psychological basis'. But he goes on to add that in reality Saussurianism 'can only be understood as a science of pure form'.[69] Thus, while the links between linguistics and everything that has an empirical and naturalistic quality about it are being severed, an equal concern is not shown for maintaining the distinction between linguistics, on the one hand, and logic or, in more general terms, formalistic epistemology based on *a priori* models, on the other. We are witness, therefore, to a *one-sided use* of the criterion of relevancy which forces linguistics to higher and higher levels of abstraction, to the point that the very term 'linguistics', contaminated by 'an unsuccessful study of language proceeding from transcendent and irrelevant points of view', is abandoned in favour of another term, 'glossematics'.[70] But is this

---

[68] In this regard see Martinet's objections, op. cit., pp. 18–19 and note 12.

[69] Hjelmslev, op. cit., p. 108.

[70] Ibid., p. 80. Obviously, they are 'transcendent' with respect to the absolute autonomy of the 'algebra of language'. The accusation of 'transcendence', like that of 'metaphysics', is generally directed in the philosophical debates of our century against those who in reality advocate an *immanent* and *physical* point of view.

merely a repudiation of previous *linguistics*, or is it also a rejection of *languages*, concretely given and poorly adjustable to Hjelmslev's algebra?

On the other hand, once the criterion of relevancy has carried out its anti-naturalist function, the reverse process begins: the *winning over to a formalist viewpoint* of all those sciences which had been so carefully distinguished from the science of language. Glossematics, just like bourgeois States, no sooner concludes its struggle for independence than it immediately displays a desire to take away the independence of others and pass over into its imperialist phase. After he has consigned 'substance' to physics and social anthropology, while reserving 'form' for linguistics, Hjelmslev discovers that everything is form and that everything is part of semiology. 'Thus all those entities which in the first instance, with the pure consideration of the schema of the object semiotic, had to be provisionally eliminated as non-semiotic elements, are reintroduced as necessary components into semiotic structures of a higher order. Accordingly, we find no non-semiotics that are not components of semiotics, and, in the final instance, no object that is not illuminated from the key position of linguistic theory.'[71] It is easy to see how far removed this semiological expansionism is from the care with which Saussure had sketched the initial outlines of the new science.

It is true that the conclusion to *Prolegomena to a Theory of Language* unexpectedly rings humanistic. Hjelmslev tells us of a sudden that all that effort at abstraction from 'life and concrete physical and phenomenological reality' was necessary only for the purpose of founding a new science which would encompass 'man and human society behind language, and all man's sphere of knowledge through language'. The book ends with the sonorous Latin motto, *humanitas et universitas*. But this 'bit of humanism' stuck on at the end of the treatise fails to satisfy anyone who does not wish to be catapulted from mathematical logic into an absolutely vague, and therefore idealist, recovery of the 'human', skipping over all the problems related to man's biological constitution and class position.[72]

---

[71] Hjelmslev, op. cit., pp. 77–8 and 127.

[72] While saying this, I wish in no way to belittle the seriousness of Hjelmslev's humanistic commitment, which has been brought out very well by A. L. Prosdocimi in his 'Ricordo di Louis Hjelmslev', *Lingua e stile*, 1 (1965), pp. 107ff.

The Prague school has had the merit of sensing much more concretely the need for interdisciplinarity and putting forward anew the need for an interpenetration of synchrony and diachrony. But this is an interdisciplinarity and a re-historicization which take place under the standard of spiritualist philosophies. A link is established with literary criticism, and this is something important; but it is. with a literary criticism that is excessively formalistic.[73] Diachrony is upgraded, but it is a diachrony which is linked to a teleological conception of the evolution of language. Sharp objections have been raised within linguistics itself against this conception, most recently by de Mauro.[74] It is perhaps opportune to add that the Prague school, and in particular the early Jakobson, drew inspiration from anti-Darwinian evolutionary theories, propounding so-called 'evolution through internal causes', such as Lev Berg's *Nomogenesis*[75] and the theories of Czechoslovak biologists cited by Jakobson himself.[76]

In this regard, one should bear in mind that there are two fundamental attitudes towards evolutionism in the spiritualistic culture of the twentieth century: on the one hand, an out and out repudiation of it (although with various justifications, ranging from a subjectivism which denies the sciences, as in Croce and Gentile, to a Platonistic-mathematical idealism); on the other hand, a spiritualist and finalist 'interpretation' which is in fact a misrepresentation. This second orientation has its principal philosophic spokesman in Bergson and its technical exegetes among the biologists cited by Jakobson (to whom others could be added, such as the Italian Daniele Rosa with his theory of hologenesis). In linguistics, the

---

I wish only to express a certain perplexity with regard to this direct juxtaposition of humanism and mathematical scientism, which is typical, moreover, of not a few scientists.

[73] The complex questions of the relationship between Russian formalism and structuralism go beyond my area of competence and the limits of this essay.

[74] See de Mauro's commentary, op. cit., pp. 427ff.

[75] Reference is to Lev S. Berg, *Nomogenesis; or Evolution Determined by Law*, Cambridge, Mass. 1969. (NLB).

[76] See the works cited by Jakobson in N. Trubetzkoy, *Principes de phonologie*, Paris 1949, p. 352 and in 'La scuola linguistica di Praga', in *Selected Works*, II, 544, where particular importance is given to *Teleology as a Form of Scientific Knowledge* by the Czech scientist Karel Engliš, Prague 1930. Many of these works are, unfortunately, inaccessible to me; but as for the general orientation which they represent, see, for example, Emanuele Padoa, *Storia della vita sulla terra*, Milan 1959, pp. 275–80 and Giuseppe Montalenti, *L'evoluzione*, Turin 1965, pp. 98–100.

first orientation is reflected in the undervaluation of diachrony, hinted at by Saussure and made altogether explicit by the Copenhagen school (or else, in the subjectivist and intuitionist variant, Croce or Vossler's theory, according to which every new linguistic expression is an unconditioned creation). The second orientation is reflected in that particular kind of upgrading of diachrony which was carried out by the Prague school.

In this latter perspective, diachrony, which was the realm of isolated and accidental facts for Saussure, is readmitted to its place of honour in science – but on the condition that every change is made to appear as an expression of the system's need to adapt more fully to its function as a system of signs, and of such proportions as to bring about a reordering of the entire system. Or, at least, a strong *a priori* preference is given to *this* type of change, whereas pre-Saussurian linguistics is accused not only of having neglected synchrony (a charge levelled by Saussure himself), but also of having considered diachrony from an 'atomistic' standpoint (as if, to give a macroscopic example, the *Lautverschiebung* in Germanic languages had to wait for structuralism in order to be discovered).[77] Thus, instead of debunking the synchronic 'closed system' in which *tout se tient,* the same systemic obsession is extended to diachrony.

The linguists of the Prague Circle were firmly convinced that finalistic and vitalist biology, to which they adhered, had already won a definitive victory over Darwinism. As Jakobson wrote at the time, 'Linguistics runs the risk of becoming more naturalistic than the natural sciences themselves.'[78] That belief has shown itself to be unfounded. The various theories of evolution by internal causes are altogether discredited today, vitalism appears less and less tenable and neo-Darwinism (shored up by genetics, and not contradicted by it, as had appeared the case at the beginning of the twentieth century) is not readily subject to confutation. Of course, a teleological conception of evolution, misconceived in biology, could be correct in linguistics. But diachronic structuralism has borne relatively little fruit; the results have not been proportional

---

[77] The *Lautverschiebung* was a linguistic discovery made by Jacob Grimm (1785–1863); he found that certain basic 'sound shifts' had occurred in the prehistory of Germanic, and that once these were taken into account one could establish a systematic correspondence between particular sounds of Germanic, Greek, Latin, and Sanskrit. (NLB).

[78] In Trubetzkoy, op. cit., note 33.

to the theoretical pretensions; no Ascoli, no Brugmann, no Meillet has been produced by the Prague Theses. In place of an interaction between theory and experience, there has been a kind of super-fœtation of theory – linguistics has been reduced almost exclusively to 'philosophizing about itself'. Furthermore, the argument has been directed to a great degree against the neo-grammarians, leaving out of account an entire orientation in linguistic-philological studies, represented on the linguistic side most prominently by Jacob Wackernagel,[79] and on the philological side by scholars such as Wilamowitz, Leo, Pasquali and Eduard Fraenkel.[80] Although they did not trouble themselves to formulate an appropriate theory, these thinkers overcame *de facto* certain limitations of the neo-grammarians; they dealt with questions of syntax and semantics in an extraordinarily productive way and, while not opposing 'historicism' in general, they argued against its degraded Crocean and Vosslerian forms. The fact that Wackernagel's name does not appear even once in Maurice Leroy's *Main Trends in Modern Linguistics* and in Bertil Malmberg's *Nouvelles tendances de la linguistique* (at least not in their indexes), i.e. in two works which do not deal exclusively with structural linguistics but cover all the currents in modern linguistics, is an egregious lacuna. It is not the result of a simple oversight, but corresponds to a theoreticism which is altogether self-absorbed and unable to learn adequately from the great historical-empirical linguists.

Even the linguist with a Prague background who has been most successful in freeing himself from the ideological deadwood of his school, André Martinet, remains more important as a theoretician than as a historian of language. In reading *Économie des changements phonétiques* one cannot help but be struck by the poverty of the second part (devoted to theoretical 'applications') in relation to the first part. Nonetheless, Martinet, precisely because he has a greater aptitude for historical research, has argued more than the others against the excesses of structuralism's abstract rigour. He has championed the claims of 'realism' against 'formalism'; he has cautioned on a number of occasions against making too clear-cut

---

[79] Jacob Wackernagel (1853–1938): Swiss philologist known for his historical studies of ancient Greek and 'old Indic' grammar. (NLB).

[80] Ulrich von Wilamowitz-Moellendorff (1848–1931), Friedrich Leo (1851–1914), Eduard Fraenkel (1888–1970): German classicists. Giorgio Pasquali (1885–1952): Italian classicist. (NLB).

a separation between phonetics and phonology; he has given a 'functionalist' interpretation of the Prague school's teleologism which frees it from a great deal of poor philosophy; he has given due acknowledgment to the roles of 'inertia' and the 'asymmetry of vocal organs' in the evolution of language; he has argued against the presumed 'inevitable incompatibilities and congruities' within a given phonological system. The pages of this structuralist are filled with polemical comments against the European structuralists: against Brøndal, Hjelmslev, Trubetzkoy, Jakobson.[81] Despite all that, it is still legitimate for us to harbour the suspicion that there remain traces of the original teleological approach of the Prague school – just as it is legitimate, in my opinion, to express reservations, as I have done, about the relative paucity of concrete results. But none of this alters the fact that the work Martinet has done to 'de-ideologize' European structuralism remains exceedingly important.

It is more difficult to pass judgement on the figure of Roman Jakobson. Is there a coherent theoretical position which corresponds to the great wealth of interests and extraordinary versatility of this scholar? Apparently not. In Jakobson there are, on the one hand, anti-formalist, realist propensities which move in the opposite direction of that restrictive and tendentious use of the criterion of relevance alluded to above. (*Linguista sum, linguistici nihil a me alienum puto*, Jakobson rightly says against these tendencies.) In his studies on aphasia and child language there is a fruitful opening towards psycho-physiology, the value of which would remain even if particular findings proved to be incorrect or too hurried. On the other hand, there is the teleologism referred to above, there are the significant residues of an anti-realist conception in his treatment of the question of the signified,[82] there is a probably illusory ambi-

[81] Realism vs. formalism: *Economie des changements phonétiques*, pp. 33ff.; phonetics and phonology: p. 11 and *passim*; limits to the concept of finality in linguistics: pp. 18ff., 66, 88ff.; 'inevitable incompatibilities and congruities': pp. 147ff. Whereas Martinet has a tendency to gloss over certain points with regard to Trubetzkoy's teleologism, in relation to Jakobson his argument is more clear-cut; see especially pp. 11, 67, n. 8, 73–5, and 125ff. as against binary theory and the attempts at establishing 'linguistic universals'. See also in his *A Functional View of Language*, Oxford 1962, p. 4, his stance against a certain structuralism which has degraded itself to 'irresponsible juggling'; see also in *Économie* (p. 233) the reference to the 'medievalistic formalism which threatens to sterilize linguistic research'.

[82] See, for example, *Fundamentals of Language*, The Hague 1956, pp. 60–62,

tion to establish universal laws of language – an ambition which has had such a harmful effect on Lévi-Strauss. One has the impression that one is dealing with a scholar precariously poised between great genius and charlatanry. In this sense, Jakobson is the structuralist linguist who more than all others resembles non-structuralist linguists, and it is not a matter of chance that he has met with the greatest success among them. The very preference for inter-disciplinary studies which distinguishes him and is undoubtedly one of the primary reasons for the prestige he enjoys, appears to be based more on his unusual capacity to assimilate all the latest developments in western culture rather than on a theoretical point of view which is genuinely unitary and unifying. His is the inter-disciplinarity of UNESCO congresses, which runs the risk of reducing itself to a clever mimesis of the languages of the other sciences (with the resulting ability to *épater* the poor specialist in a single science), rather than a genuine unification of the sciences.

Quite different is the panorama presented us by American structuralism. For one thing, here one finds a scholar who is openly materialist, an opponent of all forms of intellectual foppery and prestidigitation, deeply serious and lucid: Leonard Bloomfield. Before referring to the 'shortcomings' of Bloomfield's materialism, we should state our admiration for the forcefulness, the concrete-ness, and the anti-methodologism which flow from it. This *forma mentis,* so profoundly different from that of almost all the European structuralists, is also reflected in his very different attitude towards nineteenth-century linguistics. Bloomfield never believed himself an opponent of the neo-grammarians. Rather, he saw himself as their continuer even though he claimed to have surpassed them in essential respects and to have benefited from Saussure's teachings. Moreover, it is known that despite his non-Marxist background he had more than a passing sympathy for Marxism.[83]

Bloomfield's limitation lies in his identification of materialism with behaviourism and in his contention that the enemy was not

---

and the objections of C. Tullio Altan, 'Linguistica . . .', p. 68. Nevertheless, the follow-up of that essay by Jakobson, 'On Linguistic Aspects of Translation', in *On Translation,* ed. R. A. Brower, Cambridge, Mass. 1959, pp. 232–9, makes greater concessions to the realist point of view than is apparent from a reading of the first pages.

[83] See the remarks by Zellig S. Harris, 'Sapir's *Selected Writings', Language,* XXVII (1951), p. 296; see also, for example, the 'philo-proletarian' statement in Bloomfield, *Language,* London 1933, p. 499.

idealism (in *all* the variety of forms which it has taken in our century, which have penetrated linguistics from various directions and at different levels), but simply 'mentalism'. Bloomfield's argument does not begin with a critical analysis of the conceptions of language engendered by the anti-materialist crisis of the late nineteenth century, together with their connections with the different anti-materialist and anti-Marxist philosophies. Rather, it confines itself to an attack on a spiritualist way of conceptualizing mental activity as such. And even within the framework of this argument it does not attempt a *materialist explanation of thought*, but instead a kind of *negation of thought*, a reduction of (so-called) thought to an extremely simplified mechanism of stimulus and response. Thus, the question of the relation between thought and language – which must be examined materialistically, but still remains a problem even for a materialist – is also suppressed. For Bloomfield, language becomes a mere surrogate for practical action, and the entire function of mediation and elaboration carried out by the brain of social man is skipped over or at least disposed of in a very summary fashion.

On the other hand, connected to this over-simplification is a kind of ultra-rigourism, according to which the linguist should deal only with what is amenable to exact science. Thus, for the moment (a moment which could last indefinitely) entire fields of research are declared to be outside scientific linguistics. The most sensational and well-known case is represented by Bloomfield's rejection of semantics, on the grounds that a scientific semantics would imply a rigorous description of all reality. This is a linguistics whose excessive rigour leads it to withdraw from the field. Bloomfield underestimates the importance of the inexact sciences and the usefulness of a 'tendentially materialist' treatment even in those fields of knowledge which are still not reducible to an exact science.[84] Thus, for example, it happens that in his exclusion of semantics from linguistics Bloomfield finds himself in an uncom-

[84] Cf. Lepschy, *La Linguistica Strutturale*, p. 109 (see p. 88 of the English text): 'What is of greatest interest today are the concrete conditions under which linguistic analysis is possible, the specification of the highest degree of rigour with which it can actually be carried out; of little interest are those abstractly conceived ideals of scientificity in relation to which linguistic studies (together with many other fields of study, including those in the natural sciences) fall far short.' On Bloomfield's repudiation of semantics, cf. de Mauro's *Introduzione alla semantica*, the new appendix.

fortable alliance with an entire sector of modern linguistic thought which de-values or rejects semantics for reasons stemming from its subjectivism or exaggerated formalism.

Precisely because it is both too simplistic and too rigorous, Bloomfield's materialism ends by giving ample breathing-space and legitimacy to Sapir. Lepschy is perfectly right in remarking that 'Sapir's work has served to recall the existence and importance of problems which certain tendencies in structural linguistics tended irresponsibly (as a result of a misunderstood sense of the responsibility imposed by scientific methodology) to dismiss without having resolved them.'[85] Furthermore, one has to admit that Sapir cannot be dismissed simply by defining him as a mentalist. Despite his weakness for Croce and his lack of understanding of Darwinism and Marxism,[86] the wealth of cultural and linguistic-ethnographic interests which he demonstrates makes him in many ways resemble Carlo Cattaneo, and his insistence on maintaining contact with empirical reality clearly distinguishes him from the Platonizing structuralists of Europe.

What has already been said, despite its summary nature, has I think made it relatively clear that there exists a great ideological distance between Marxism and structural linguistics. This is primarily a consequence of the origin of European structural linguistics in the general anti-materialist and anti-Marxist movement of the late nineteenth century, and also a consequence of the subsequent influence which spiritualistic ideologies (founded on mathematical Platonism or finalistic biology) have had on particular currents of structuralism itself. When Cassirer, in a famous lecture given in 1945 shortly before his death, hailed the advent of structural linguistics as a victory of the 'friends of Ideas' over the

[85] Lepschy, *La Linguistica Strutturale,* p. 104 (see pp. 77–8 of the English text).
[86] Cf. Paolo Valesio's introduction to the Italian edition of Sapir's *Language,* Turin 1969, pp. xxviff. and xxxiff. Remarks against evolutionism are on pp. 130–31 of the English text, New York 1939. As for his 'philo-Croceanism' (stated in the preface to *Language* and again on pp. 237 and 239), Valesio is correct in remarking that it should not be overestimated, and that 'Sapir's view of language as a collective creation is not only distinctly different from Croce's conception but is the very opposite of it' (p. xxvii). But while this is true, it is also true that when Sapir states that 'among contemporary writers of influence on liberal thought Croce is one of the very few who have gained an understanding of the fundamental significance of language' (p. iii), he showed that he failed to understand the consequences of Croce's identification of linguistics with aesthetics.

'supporters of matter' (referring to a famous passage in Plato's *Sophist*),[87] he was too familiar with both modern philosophy and linguistics to be mistaken. This shows how superficial and ill-conceived are certain 'ideological unifications' of Marxism and structural linguistics which are apparently taking place in the Soviet Union.[88] On the other hand, however, structural linguistics, like many other scientific approaches born of the 'crisis of fundamentals' of the late nineteenth century, can lay claim to scientific achievements which it would be absurd to reject in a Zhdanovist spirit. For example, it would be absurd to deny the importance of synchronic descriptions of linguistic states, or the utility of the notion of a phoneme (once it has been purged of the subjectivist and anti-naturalistic strains with which it first emerged). Furthermore, with regard to the ideological features as well, we have seen that it is necessary to make some important distinctions. We have to distinguish the authentic Saussure from a later schematized and idealized Saussurianism, without however making any claim to have 'annexed' Saussure and wrested him away from the intellectual climate in which his thought took shape. We have to give greater importance to the impulses towards concreteness and anti-formalism which led Martinet to become an incisive critic of much of structuralism's bad ideology, despite his adherence to structural linguistics. Above all, we have to make a separate argument with regard to American structuralism, which differs considerably from European structuralism even in its cultural-historical genesis; moreover, as we have seen above, this separate argument would pertain not just to the materialist Bloomfield but, to a considerable degree, also to the 'mentalist' Sapir. Taken as a whole, structural linguistics thus contains strong self-critical stimuli, strong reactions to the most openly formalistic and anti-historical tendencies.

\*     \*     \*

The picture changes considerably when we move from linguistic

[87] Ernst Cassirer, 'Structuralism in Modern Linguistics', *Word*, I (August 1945), p. 112. In the same lecture there are interesting parallels between linguistics and spiritualistic biology, accompanied by a favourable reassessment of Cuvier (cf. the passage from Brøndal cited above) and by an attempt to show that, despite the disagreements between Cuvier and Geoffroy Saint-Hilaire and Goethe's seconding of the latter's evolutionist propositions, the real opposition is between these three on the one hand and Darwin on the other (pp. 105–9).

[88] Cf. G. Lepschy, 'Note sullo strutturalismo e sulla linguistica sovietica recente', *Studi e saggi linguistici*, VII (1967), pp. 1ff.

structuralism to that mélange of linguistics, ethnology and psycho-analysis which began to take shape in French culture during the nineteen fifties and sixties, and which has increasingly shown, in the works of Lévi-Strauss, Foucault and Lacan, an ambition to elevate itself to the status of philosophy, of a 'science of man in general'. It is a well-known fact that this orientation has had a strong influence also on contemporary Marxism, through Althusser & Co. and Godelier. And it is from this sector of French culture that the structuralist craze has spread throughout Europe. The enormous success of structural linguistics itself has been a kind of 'boomerang' success which has repercussed back onto linguistics by way of anthropological (and literary-critical) structuralism.[89]

One need only shift from the writings of a Saussure or a Trubetzkoy or a Hjelmslev or a Bloomfield or a Martinet (I purposely cite structuralist linguists of the most different tendencies) to those of the great French intellectuals cited above and their followers all over Europe, in order at once to feel immersed in an atmosphere of sophisticated charlatanry – only a slight anticipation of which could be found in the linguistic field in Jakobson. This impression is a product of the contrast between the flaunting of an anti-empirical, ultra-theoretical and rigorously mathematizing epistemology, on the one hand, and decadentist and existentialistic poses – 'literary' (in the worst sense of the word) flirtations – on the other. We are not dealing, as in the case of linguistic structuralism, with scientists who, however controversial or reactionary, still possess an indis-

---

[89] Although I refer in the following pages almost exclusively to structural anthropology and structuralistic Marxism and almost entirely ignore the questions raised by literary-critical structuralism, this is not because I fail to recognize its importance, but because a satisfactory treatment of these questions would require me to take a stand on matters of aesthetics in which I do not feel adequately prepared. Furthermore, with regard to the ideological limitations and the limited fruitfulness of the results obtained by literary-critical structuralism there already exist in Italian some outstanding achievements. They range from the more overtly polemical ones of Romano Luperini, in *Nuovo Impegno*, VI–VII (1966–7), pp. 41ff. and *passim*, and of Arcangelo Leone de Castris, in *Problemi*, XV–XVI (May–August 1969), pp. 654ff., which is important also for its remarks on structuralism in general, to those carried out 'from within' by Cesare Segre, *I segni e la critica*, Turin 1969, and by Paolo Ramat, in *Il Protagora*, LIV (December 1967), pp. 68ff. I have the impression, however, that even as regards the study of the formal values (stylistic, metric, etc.) of literary production, structuralism has not advanced beyond other scholars (including Italian ones) who have handled these questions with a much greater respect for the concrete particular and, therefore, in a much more genuinely scientific fashion, which is something quite different from scientistic ostentation.

putable intellectual integrity within their scientific field. Rather, we are dealing with old literary foxes who, as their final and most sophisticated trick, have taken to 'playing at science'.

We see, for example, a Lévi-Strauss indict all previous anthropologists (although not without a good deal of diplomatic bowing and scraping and many partial affirmations of work well done) for having failed to maintain the necessary distance from the object of their research, for having stopped at the empirical given, the level of 'lived experience', and for having thought that abstraction was precisely 'abstraction' from the data of experience and not the construction of *a priori* theoretical models. These are very debatable ideas, as we shall see. But if only they were at least articulated in a coherent fashion, and the style of their presentation was commensurate with the ideas themselves! Nothing of the kind. The austere theoretician, the mathematizer of anthropology, entitles the parts and chapters of the first of his books dedicated to the study of myths (*The Raw and the Cooked*) with musical terms: 'Theme and Variations', 'Recitative', 'Toccata and Fugue', 'Rustic Symphony in Three Movements', and so on and so forth. The book is dedicated *to Music*, and in the *Overture* Lévi-Strauss assures us that all this musicality is not the product of mere fancy, but rather responds to an absolute necessity. If he had divided the book into chapters in a banal fashion, he would have 'weakened and mutilated' the movement of his thought, which needs variations of tempo, counterpoints and harmonies. In short, he would have 'blunted the force of the demonstration'.

He speaks to us in enraptured terms of his 'reverence from childhood on' for Richard Wagner – a reverence not only artistic but also ideological. He informs us that Wagner is the true 'originator of the structural analysis of myths', and that it is not a matter of chance that 'the analysis was made, in the first instance, *in music*'.[90]

90 Claude Lévi-Strauss, *The Raw and the Cooked*, New York 1969, pp. 14–15. Needless to say, Wagner's musical greatness is not at issue, but only that typical Wagnerian idolatry which attained paroxysmal heights in late eighteenth-century bourgeois culture, and which led to a view of Wagner as the representative of Music *par excellence* and to a view of Music as a spiritual manifestation with a privileged position above all others. Wagnerian themes continue, moreover, to re-echo even in the fourth and final volume of mythological studies, *L'homme nu*, Paris 1971. Here, in the highly pretentious and boring *Finale* (pp. 559–621), we find once again, on the one hand, the usual scientistic fanfare, and, on the other hand, the tendency to confuse the study of myths with a kind of religious and aesthetic self-recognition in the myths themselves. Lévi-Strauss

Previously it had been thought that Wagner's way of reviving myths was the product, for better or worse, of irrationalist currents in nineteenth-century European culture, which had won out over an initial confusedly anarcho-communist inspiration. Now, however, we come to understand that it is the precursor and model for a scientific analysis. Furthermore, Lévi-Strauss himself points out just before the above passage that 'it would not be wrong to consider this book itself as a myth' (in the unlikely event we had not already surmised as much). For a scholar who wanted to maintain his distance from 'lived experience' and to reduce the human sciences to exact sciences, all of this does not appear very encouraging.

Foreseeing, however, the charge of arbitrary schematizations and distortions in his interpretations of myths, Lévi-Strauss thinks it a good idea to explain his position even more clearly, putting aside, as he says, all hypocrisy. 'I therefore say in advance to possible critics: what does this matter? For if the final aim of anthropology is to contribute to a better knowledge of objectified thought and its mechanisms, it is in the last resort immaterial whether in this book the thought processes of the South American Indians take shape through the medium of my thought, or whether mine take place through the medium of theirs. What matters is that the human mind, regardless of the identity of those who happen to be giving it expression, should display an increasingly intelligible structure as a result of the doubly reflexive forward movement of two thought processes acting one upon the other, either of which can in turn provide the spark or tinder whose conjunction will shed light on both.'[91] A startling and indeed 'non-hypocritical' conception of 'knowledge of objectified thought', according to which the important thing is to arrive *in whatever way* at an identity of interpreter and interpreted – an identity which, as demonstrated by the expressions themselves ('spark', 'tinder', 'light') is the identity of

states that he has attempted with these books to 'compenser . . . *son* impuissance congénitale à composer une oeuvre musicale' (p. 580). And he concludes thus: 'Je comprends . . . qu'ayant moi aussi composé ma tétralogie, elle doive s'achever sur un crépuscule des dieux comme l'autre', or more precisely on 'un crépuscule des hommes' (p. 620). The question of a possible end of humanity is a serious one, but not when it is handled with such theatrical exhibitionism. Here again one can see the great distance which separates the materialistic pessimism of Giacomo Leopardi from parlour existentialistic pessimisms of this kind.

91 *The Raw and the Cooked*, p. 13.

mysticism. Thus, for example, if I should undertake to make a scientific study of belief in the miracle of San Gennaro, I am at liberty to force my interpretation at will (so that it is more readily consistent with a 'general model of miracles' which I have already constructed *a priori*); or else it may happen, and just as legitimately, that 'the thought' of the believers 'acts upon' me to the point that I become a devotee of San Gennaro myself and share in a 'mutual illumination'. A two-way itinerary, *a parte subiecti* and *a parte obiecti,* in which what is absent at all events is any 'objective' knowledge of the object.

Is Saussure's principle of the arbitrariness of the linguistic sign called into question? As we mentioned above, many objections have been raised against this principle, beginning with Benveniste. The result has been to give it greater specificity and to indicate its limits, without really invalidating it. While Lévi-Strauss does not hesitate to echo these objections in a somewhat approximate form, he adds a more profound and rigorously scientific one of his own. He informs us that for those like him, who are endowed with the ability to say everything in French and English with equal ease, *fromage* and *cheese* possess two strikingly different nuances of meaning. '*Fromage* evokes a certain heaviness, an oily substance not prone to crumble, and a thick flavour'; *cheese,* 'which is lighter, fresher, a little sour, and which crumbles in the mouth (compare the shape of the mouth) reminds me immediately of the French *fromage blanc*', a variety of cottage cheese. Here we can clearly see the advantages of bilingualism combined with a refined palate: depending on whether it is savoured by Lévi-Strauss *à la française* or 'in the English manner', the same piece of cheese is capable of conveying on one occasion the strong and slightly heavy pleasures of the flesh and on another the subtle delights of the spirit (the latter enhanced by a touch of psychoanalytic refinement: the eroticism of 'the shape of the mouth'). And as a result of Lévi-Strauss's habitual tendency to deny in radical terms all subjectivity and at the same time to identify the objective Spirit with his private Ego, it is simply taken for granted that those connotations of *fromage* and *cheese* do not belong to the individual psychology of Lévi-Strauss, but rather to a collective linguistic feeling.[92]

Naturally, this too facile sarcasm (justified, however, by a too

[92] C. Lévi-Strauss, *Structural Anthropology,* New York 1963, p. 93. One must, however, admit that certain far-flung phonetic-symbolist remarks by Jakobson

flagrantly exhibitionistic stance) does not apply to all of Lévi-Strauss. I know very well that before he became absorbed in the unequal struggle to become the Anti-Sartre, Lévi-Strauss made some truly important and scientific contributions to the study of kinship systems among primitive peoples (however intermingled these may have been with bad ideology). I know also that the early Lévi-Strauss was led to anthropology not just by serious scientific impulses but also by a genuine love for primitive people. Although this love was coloured even then by reactionary reveries à la Chateaubriand and by decadentist gratifications, it represented a far from meaningless protest against Eurocentrism and colonialism and against an altogether too linear conception of progress, still persistent among many Marxists.[93] I know that, even from a literary point of view, certain pages of *Tristes Tropiques* bear a mark of genius, not present in later books. I know that, though Foucault's *Les mots et les choses (The Order of Things)* and *L'archéologie du savoir (The Archaeology of Knowledge)* merely represent an (entirely successful) attempt to outstrip Lévi-Strauss in snobism and pretension,[94] the same Foucault has written things about the history of

---

(which Lévi-Strauss himself cites on pp. 91–2) have cleared the way for Lévi-Strauss' reflections on dairy products.

[93] Cf. Sergio Moravia, *La ragione nascosta: scienza e filosofia nel pensiero di C. Lévi-Strauss*, Florence 1969, pp. 88–95. From what follows one can clearly see my debt to this book, which is the best overall work on Lévi-Strauss. With regard to the reactionary side to Lévi-Strauss's 'philo-primitivism', still worth reading are the two articles by Maxime Rodinson, 'Racisme et civilisation' and 'Ethnographie et relativisme', *La Nouvelle Critique* (June and November 1955). Lévi-Strauss's reply in *Structural Anthropology*, pp. 333ff. and 343ff. glosses over the essential points, even if *La Nouvelle Critique* was certainly wrong to refuse to print it. Now see also P. G. Solinas, 'Le strutture elementari della parentela fra natura e cultura', *Problemi*, xix–xx (January–April 1970), pp. 845ff., which is filled with perceptive observations, even if it is too influenced by an anti-materialist and Althusserian interpretation of Marxism.

[94] An excellent analysis of Foucault is to be found in Jean Piaget, *Structuralism*, New York 1970, pp. 128–35. With regard to his less than precise knowledge of structural linguistics, cf. Georges Mounin, *Clefs pour la linguistique*, Paris 1968, p. 13. But no better is his factual background as regards nineteenth-century linguistics; one need only read the section on Franz Bopp in *The Order of Things*, New York 1970, pp. 280–94, in order to see how Foucault's attempt to reduce the opposing ideas of Friedrich Schlegel and Bopp on the origin of the Indo-European inflection to a single formula completely distorts both positions. Cf. also the objections raised by Luigi Rosiello, *Linguistica illuminista*, Bologna 1967, pp. 168ff. It is interesting to see how Lévi-Strauss, when confronted with a 'rival' like Foucault, calls for caution against 'grandiose general interpretations' and against 'a certain philosophy which claims to provide global and definitive interpretations': see *Conversazioni con Lévi-Strauss, Foucault, Lacan*, ed. P. Caruso,

madness and the origins of modern medicine which, even if open to debate, are certainly worthy of attention. Similarly, Roland Barthes can readily be forgiven his *Eléments de sémiologie (Elements of Semiology)* and *Système de la mode* for the sake of some perceptive essays in literary criticism.[95] But the altogether disproportionate fame enjoyed by these authors during the last fifteen years is not a consequence of the scientific side of their work, but rather, for the most part, a consequence of its charlantanesque features: that admixture of abstract scientism and aestheticist spiritualism which, however patently contradictory it may be, nonetheless represents a perfect solution for the needs of a bourgeoisie which at one and the same time worships science and attempts to strip it of its demystificatory and liberating force.

In all his writings, Lévi-Strauss lays great stress on the function of avant-garde science which structural linguistics (the first science of man which, in his opinion, has attained true scientificity) must play in relation to the other sciences of man, which are still immersed in vulgar empiricism and 'atomism'. Even structuralist literary critics look to linguistics as a model. But to *which* structural linguistics? This is the point which has not been emphasized enough. All those currents within linguistic structuralism which kept alive, in differing degree and from differing points of view, certain anti-formalistic requirements are almost totally ignored by non-linguistic structuralists. For them, obviously, Bloomfield does not exist; but even Sapir or Martinet barely exist if at all.[96] Saussure

Milan 1969, pp. 87ff. But was the bad example not already set, to a large degree, by Lévi-Strauss himself, even if one has to admit that Foucault has gone quite a bit further in that direction?

[95] With regard to Barthes, see the excellent analysis by Cesare Segre, op. cit. pp. 37–44. Furthermore, even Barthes the literary critic (certainly much superior to Barthes the theoretician of semiology) leaves one at times with an impression more of flashy paradox than of genuine intellectual perspicacity. What is one to make of his excoriation of Maupassant and of his summary liquidation of all French realism? (cf. *Writing Degree Zero*, London 1967, pp. 73ff.). Here too we are dealing with an ideological aversion: the enemy is 'naturalism'! Someone like Erich Auerbach has shown, however, a great deal more emancipation from preconceptions and a good deal more critical intelligence in relation to this period of French literature.

[96] This does not mean, obviously, that on occasion some of these scholars are not mentioned *en passant* in the writings of non-linguistic structuralists (e.g. Martinet by Barthes, *Elements of Semiology*, London 1967, pp. 39, 52). What one does not find is that anti-formalist, empirical, and – with regard to Bloomfield – materialist influence which these authors could have had on extra-linguistic structuralism.

exists, but it is a Saussure who has been meticulously purged of all those characteristics of realism and socio-cultural concreteness which de Mauro claims for him, and who has been resuscitated through the interpretation of the Danish school. Thus, while linguistic structuralism does not exist as a relatively unitary move- ment, as Lepschy has rightly pointed out, there is nevertheless a retrograde ideological unity present in extra-linguistic struc- turalism, above and beyond unquestionable differences on parti- cular points. I do not think that one can say, as Paolo Caruso does, that 'the unity of structuralism (extra-linguistic, of course) is created from the outside, by opponents, by the uninitiated, by eavesdroppers, by journalists, in short, by those who for one reason or another do not practise it'.[97] The first 'journalists' in this pejorative sense go by the names of Lévi-Strauss and, even worse, Foucault and, worse still, Lacan.[98]

When the non-linguistic structuralists talk about structural linguistics as an avant-garde science, they are referring in reality to a Saussure interpreted only in the sense we have just mentioned and, even more, to the Prague school. The connection with the Prague school is not a matter of chance. There was a genuine collaboration between Jakobson and Lévi-Strauss, and many of Trubetzkoy's and Jakobson's ideas passed into structural anthropology and into the structuralism which was raised to the level of 'general philosophy': among others, the anti-evolutionist and 'anti-atomistic' orientation (also shared by the Danish school) and the tendency to account for the affinities between human institutions not just on the basis of hypotheses bearing on their historical genesis (a common origin or subsequent contact), but also through recourse to universal and atemporal characteristics of the human spirit. Nevertheless, even in Lévi-Strauss's interpretation of Trubetzkoy and Jakobson there are distortions to be found. Sergio Moravia has shown clearly that a cautious reference by Trubetzkoy to the possibility of 'logically deducing' general laws of language (as opposed to deriving them by induction from experience) is distorted by Lévi-Strauss to the point of tendentious use of partial quotations, and that Lévi-Strauss ascribed to the linguists of the Prague school a concept of the 'unconscious' (between the psychoanalytic and

[97] *Conversazioni con Lévi-Strauss, Foucault, Lacan,* Introduction, p. 9.
[98] Among the three, Lacan is the one whose knowledge of linguistics is most imprecise – indeed, at times, utterly erroneous; cf. Mounin, op. cit., p. 13.

the Platonic) which is not to be found in them at all.[99] In Jakobson himself, the declaration of actual or presumed 'universal' laws of language (apart from the objections raised against them by Martinet and others, apparently overlooked by the structural anthropologists) never culminates in an out-and-out metaphysics of the objective Spirit, as it does in Lévi-Strauss. Like Trubetzkoy, Jakobson's historical interests are too great for him to reduce linguistics to a search for a few 'invariant' elements. The Prague school, as we have seen, had as one of its foremost leitmotifs an upgrading of diachrony (if only in an ambiguously teleological and spiritualist sense), not its negation. It was not a matter of chance that Martinet's diachronic-functional linguistics, although in disagreement with the Prague school on many points, was able to develop out of the latter.

It is interesting to see how, precisely with regard to the question of diachrony, Lévi-Strauss has recourse at times to the Prague school and at times to Saussure, without giving any indication that he realizes the difference between the two positions. When Haudricourt and Granai accuse him of having underestimated the diachronic dimension, we find that he is quick to unveil the Prague theses and the subsequent developments made by Jakobson: 'the opposition between synchronic and diachronic is to a large extent illusory'; Haudricourt and Granai, not having moved beyond Saussurianism, 'overemphasize the contrast between the diachronic and synchronic viewpoints'.[100] According to Lévi-Strauss, therefore, it is not a question of denying diachrony, but merely of replacing the 'chaos of discontinuity' characteristic of nineteenth-century linguistics and ethnology with the new concept of 'evolution . . . directed by the *tendency toward a goal*' and endowed with an 'internal logic'.[101] But a few years later, when the debate over 'historicism' had heated up, we see Lévi-Strauss adhering (as against Sartre) to precisely that conception of history as the realm of the discontinuous and the disconnected which he had rejected as an old positivist misconception. In this instance, from the misconceived estimation that *tout se tient* on the synchronic level, he moves to the equally misconceived notion that *rien ne se tient* on the diachronic level. Chapter IX of *The Savage Mind* ('History and

[99] Moravia, op. cit., pp. 287–9.
[100] *Structural Anthropology*, pp. 88–9.
[101] Ibid., pp. 34–5.

Dialectic') is entirely devoted to illustrating this proposition, and it culminates in the *boutade*: 'As we say of certain careers, history may lead to anything, provided you get out of it' ('l'histoire mène à tout, mais à condition d'en sortir').[102]

Although Lévi-Strauss uses this phrase as if it were his own, it is in fact an obvious echo of the phrase of Saussure which we have already cited: 'What is said of journalism applies to diachrony; it may lead to anything, provided you get out of it' ('elle mène à tout à condition qu'on en sorte'). One could say something about the changes Lévi-Strauss introduces – somewhat clumsy and one of them 'history' in place of 'diachrony', conceptually dubious from the Saussinian standpoint – which hardly make him a master of 'allusive art'. But what is certain is that here Lévi-Strauss has given up the Prague conception of diachrony as teleological evolution.

Is this evidence of a development in Lévi-Strauss's thought? I think not. I should say that both the Prague conception and the Saussurian conception are used by Lévi-Strauss for instrumental purposes.[103] What really concerns him is to clear the field *in whatever way possible* of all these hypotheses (whether evolutionist or diffusionist) which attempt to explain similarities and differences between the various human cultures on a historical basis. This is also the explanation for the extremely sophistical nature of his argument against evolutionism (once again in contradiction with the Prague conception). We have seen that the Prague thinkers were convinced that even in biology Darwinism had already been superseded by finalistic evolution, and that the concept of

[102] C. Lévi-Strauss, *The Savage Mind*, London 1966, p. 262.

[103] In fact, in the first conversation with Caruso (op. cit. pp. 41 ff.) held one year after *The Savage Mind,* Lévi-Strauss gives yet another justification for his rejection of diachrony. To start with, he remarks that the distinction between synchrony and diachrony is 'to a large degree arbitrary' and that 'pure synchrony does not exist' (and this is supposed to represent a return to the Prague theses, which are used, however, not in order to open the field to diachronic studies, but to justify the exclusive attention given to synchrony with the pretext that *diachrony is already contained in synchrony*). Then he adds that diachronic research should be put off till a later phase ('for the moment I am entirely a "comparative anatomist". After all, Darwin would not have been possible without Cuvier....'). Thus, it is no longer a question, as in *The Savage Mind,* of 'moving on from history' as soon as possible, but rather of seeing that the moment has not yet arrived for getting into it! The formulation of the relationship diachrony-synchrony is again different on p. 79 of the same *Conversazioni.* The hostility towards history remains the same; only the motives change continuously.

evolution in the human sciences could be modelled on these new biological theories. Although Lévi-Strauss on one occasion follows Trubetzkoy in referring favourably to finalistic evolution,[104] elsewhere he prefers to concede the validity of Darwinism and to contrast it with the 'false evolutionism' of the human sciences. 'When we turn from biology to culture, things become far more complicated. . . . An axe does not give birth to an axe in the physical sense that an animal gives birth to an animal. Therefore, to say that an axe has developed out of another axe is to speak meta-phorically and with a rough approximation to truth, but without the scientific exactitude which a similar expression has in biological parlance. What is true of material objects whose physical presence in the earth can be related to determinable periods, is even more true of institutions, beliefs and customs, whose past history is generally a closed book to us. . . . The concept of social or cultural evolution offers at best a tempting, but suspiciously convenient method of presenting facts.'[105]

This line of argument is designed to oppose not just social Darwinism and the erroneous view which sees all cultures as stages of a *single* line of development. Rather, in a grotesque fashion it is designed to oppose all historical development which is not reduc-ible to 'physical procreation'. Since the *Signorie* were not sexually engendered by the *Comuni*, nor bourgeois society by feudal society, nor was Lenin the son of Marx or Engels in a material sense, one would have to conclude that there is no derivational relationship between the one and the other of these socio-economic institutions or formations or cultural figures. Even to raise the question would amount to a relapse into false evolutionism! Lévi-Strauss adds another incredible argument: the difference between true and false evolutionism 'can be explained on the basis of their respective dates of appearance'. Sociological evolutionism precedes biological evolutionism; it goes back to Vico and develops through Con-dorcet and Comte; it is pre-Darwinian and therefore pre-scientific.[106] As we all know, the notion of historicity developed in the human sciences before it developed in the natural sciences, in which it was less readily discernible. And as we all know, the

---

[104] *Structural Anthropology*, pp. 34–5.
[105] C. Lévi-Strauss, 'Race and History', in *Race and Science*, New York 1969, p. 227. See also note 107.
[106] Ibid., pp. 227–8.

philosophies of history of the eighteenth and early nineteenth centuries – and even many of more recent date – are heavily weighed down with schematism and a metaphysical spirit. But that does not justify placing biological evolutionism on one side, as the only kind endowed with 'scientificity', and on the other side, all together, the 'non-scientific' historical explanations of human history and culture – including, presumably, Marxism (although Lévi-Strauss is prudently silent on this point). For a long time, before Lyell and Darwin, there prevailed an antithesis between nature, which was presumed to repeat itself in an eternal cycle, and human history, in which there was presumed to be evolution and progress. The innovation brought about by geological and biological evolutionism consisted precisely in its historicization of nature. Now Lévi-Strauss proposes to turn that old position upside-down: the historicity of nature is 'a hypothesis characterized by one of the highest coefficients of probability which can be found in the field of the natural sciences', whereas the historicity of human institutions is non-existent or unprovable. And all this does not strike Lévi-Strauss as being in contradiction with his intention of overcoming the antithesis between nature and culture![107]

On the other hand, the argument against unilinearism does not at all entail a general disesteem for historical knowledge (assuming that the argument is not used simply as a pretext). To begin with, Darwinism itself is not at all 'unilinearist'. Neither Darwin nor any serious Darwinist has ever thought of placing all species, extant and extinct, on a single line of evolution. Furthermore, there exists another conception of human history, apart from anti-materialist historicism, that salvages the connection with natural history and also brings out the fundamental differentiating element. This conception is Marxism – not given as an already perfected system, but rather as open to further developments and susceptible even to relapses into erroneous conceptions. The homage paid by Lévi-Strauss to Marx as a theoretician of socio-economic

[107] This intention is expressed, among other places, in *Conversazioni,* p. 90. One should note how Lévi-Strauss, in order to discredit what he calls false evolutionism, goes so far as to exaggerate the degree of relative certainty of biological evolutionism. To take up the example that he uses, the fact that the presumed descent of *Equus caballus* from *Hipparion* is a 'physical descent' does not increase, in and of itself, the degree of probability, since no one possesses any direct evidence of this derivation. Many relationships of 'non-physical descent', i.e. of cultural-historical derivation, are certainly much better established!

structures (while he, Lévi-Strauss, claims to bring about an integration of Marxism with the study of superstructures)[108] disguises, beneath its diplomatic form, an essential anti-Marxism. This is the case both because Lévi-Strauss lacks all interest in the superstructures *qua superstructures of socio-economic structures*,[109] and because Lévi-Strauss's spiritualistic metaphysics and anti-historicity are irreconcilable with an historical-materialist position.

Obviously, this is not at all meant to deny the importance which kinship relationships have in primitive societies and the difficulty, already noted by Engels, of establishing an exact correspondence between kinship relationships and the economic structure in these societies. This is a question which has been taken up again recently, and which promises to lead to interesting developments. We only hope that theoretical-terminological concerns do not, in Althusserian fashion, end by stifling interest in the empirical data.[110] But it is precisely the need for further study of this kind which Lévi-Strauss does not sense. For him, the study of kinship relationships is blissfully self-sufficient. Marx and Engels's recognition of the *relative* autonomy of kinship relationships vis-à-vis relations of production in primitive societies serves Lévi-Strauss simply as a 'licence' for dealing exclusively with the former and for turning them into the essential distinguishing feature of human culture.[111] This accounts also for the somewhat ridiculous emphatic manner in which Lévi-Strauss constantly returns to his favourite theme of the incest prohibition. The latter, it appears, represents the feature which actually distinguishes nature from culture – i.e. serves as a substitute for what labour is for Marx and Engels and language for other thinkers – and at the same time apparently derives a great deal of its fascination from the inexplicability of its origins. It is a kind of mysterious creation of the unconscious wisdom of the objective Spirit.

We have already seen how cautious Saussure was in drawing up his plan for the future science of semiology, and how this caution

[108] Cf. *The Savage Mind*, p. 130; *Structural Anthropology*, pp. 333ff., 377 and *passim*.

[109] In this regard, see Lucien Sève, *Marxisme et théorie de la personnalité*, Paris 1968, pp. 484ff.

[110] I am referring in particular to E. Terray, *Marxism and 'Primitive' Societies*, pp. 143–56; cf. also Raoul Makarius, 'Parenté et infrastructure', *La Pensée* CXLIX (February 1970), pp. 51ff.

[111] This is particularly evident in *Structural Anthropology*, pp. 334–7.

had already been disregarded by the Copenhagen school. But although Hjelmslev tended towards a reduction of all science to semiology, basically he remained a linguist interested in the relationships between linguistics and logic. If, however, one attempts to reduce to semiology human sciences with much more 'content' to them, much richer in socio-historical implications, such as ethnology or literary history or political economy, then one finds oneself faced with a dilemma. Either one maintains a certain awareness of the specificity of semiology – an awareness of what distinguishes the 'sign' from the 'symbol' and from the 'token' and from all other elements of a system – in which case one ends ends up with the altogether disappointing result represented by Roland Barthes's little book *Elements of Semiology*. Such a book does nothing more in substance than summarize Saussure and some more recent linguists; remaining within the sphere of linguistics, it merely adds here and there a few fleeting hints on possible extensions of semiology to the fields of fashion and cuisine. This is the objection, in my opinion decisive, raised by Cesare Segre to Barthes's little volume.[112] And although Barthes has attempted to develop a structuralist theory of fashion in another book, and although 'culinary structuralism' has been amply developed in the latest books of Lévi-Strauss, it seems to me that the future of semiology would be somewhat cloudy should it continue to cavort about with contrasts between skirts and blouses, blouses and pullovers, soups and entrees, etc., learnedly distinguishing 'paradigmatic' relationships from 'syntagmatic' ones.

Or else, on the other hand, one attempts to move bravely in the direction of the semiologization of those things which are least readily semiologizable. In this case, it becomes necessary to distort Saussure's concept of the 'sign' and turn it simply into a term indicating a relationship between *similar* things, overlooking the fact that for Saussure it is also a relationship between a *similar* and a *dissimilar* thing. It becomes necessary to give a completely one-sided reading to the chapter of the *Cours* dealing with 'Linguistic Value' and to sacrifice the relationship signifier-signified to the exclusive advantage of the relationship between each sign and the

---

[112] On the distinction between 'signs' in the strict sense and 'tokens' or 'indicators', see Segre, op. cit., pp. 45, 68–70, where he develops certain remarks made by Éric Buyssens in *La communication et l'articulation linguistique,* Paris 1967; cf. also Mounin, *Clefs pour la linguistique,* p. 37 and his *Saussure,* Paris 1968, p. 81.

others with which it forms a system. That there is a danger of sliding down this slope already in Saussure has been pointed out above. But in extra-linguistic structuralism it is no longer merely a danger.

Here we find language and kinship systems identified with one another, in that both of them represent 'a set of processes permitting the establishment, between individuals and groups, of a certain type of communication'.[113] Here we find, lumped all together under the general category of 'exchange', linguistic rules, marriage rules and economic rules (with an obfuscation of the much more crucial links which connect the exchange of goods with the *production* of goods and with social relations among men).[114] Here we find women identified with 'signs', in that they are objects of exchange.[115] And if objections are made to the 'anti-feminist' character of this conception, Lévi-Strauss will be quick to reply that words, while reduced through usage to signs, were also once 'values' (and continue to be so for poets). Thus, women too are values as well as signs. This 'ambiguity' allows us to 'achieve insight into a problem that is still very obscure, that of the origin of language'. For men living in Vico's feral age words had the same corporeality and the same 'immediate' evocative power as women (we do not know if they had the same power of sexual attraction).[116] Thus, having first taken away all specificity from the concept of a sign, we have now achieved the same spectacular result with the concept of value; and, in this utter confusion, there is no longer any obstacle to the assimilation of everything humanly knowable to the realm of semiology.

Obviously, the concept of sign which lends itself most readily to this semiology is that of the sign which has no meaning. Foucault, who has made it his mission to represent an unwitting caricature of Lévi-Strauss while deceiving himself into thinking he has gone beyond the latter, ends by declaring that he is a non-structuralist precisely with regard to that (none too great) measure of interest which linguistic structuralism maintains for the question of the signified. 'What there is in me of a non-structuralist, of a non-

---

[113] *Structural Anthropology*, p. 61.

[114] Ibid. p. 83.

[115] On the distortion involved in this identification (already present in his book *Elementary Structures of Kinship*, which is nonetheless one of Lévi-Strauss's earlier and better works), cf. Moravia, op. cit. p. 200.

[116] *Structural Anthropology*, pp. 61–2.

linguist, becomes ecstatic [*sic*] over such a use of signs: i.e. signs in their modality as signs, and not in their capacity to transmit meaning.'[117]

The split between linguistic structuralism and non-linguistic structuralism which has developed despite their common starting points is brought out very clearly by Lévi-Strauss in a paper given at a conference of linguistics and anthropologists. 'So you may see that the motivations of the anthropologists, insofar as I am able to interpret them correctly, are rather contradictory to the motivations of the linguists. The linguists try to join the anthropologists in order to make their study more concrete, while the anthropologists are trying to rejoin the linguists precisely because the linguists appear to show them a way to get out of the confusion resulting from too much acquaintance and familiarity with concrete and empirical data. Sometimes it seems to me this has resulted, during this Conference, in a somewhat – shall I call it – unhappy merry-go-round, where the anthropolgists were running after the linguists while the linguists were running after the anthropologists, each group trying to get from the other precisely what it was trying itself to get rid of.'[118]

In point of fact, there have often been close links between linguistics and anthropology, even long before the rise of structuralism. For example, such men as Cattaneo, Pictet[119] and Ascoli were both linguists and anthropologists. But the concept of science which supplied the foundation for collaboration between the two disciplines has been progressively changing. Here we have, on the one hand, contemporary linguists who bridle at the excessive formalism which threatens to swallow up their discipline; on the other hand, the anthropologist (whose science should be less vulnerable in and of itself to the risks of formalism and much more closely linked to socio-economic and socio-cultural questions than linguistics could ever be) who calls the linguists to order and invites them not to furnish historical or empirical merchandise but rather *a priori* models, inventories by means of which all cultures can appear as the result of various random combinations of a few

---

[117] *Conversazioni*, p. 119. The remark was made with particular regard to the extension of the concept of 'sign' to Paul Klee's painting.

[118] *Structural Anthropology*, p. 70.

[119] Adolphe Pictet (1799–1875): Swiss philologist who inaugurated what is known as linguistic paleontology in his attempts to reconstruct ancient Aryan civilization on the basis of a study of ancient Indo-European languages. (NLB).

invariant elements.

What is actually at issue here is the very concept of science which has characterized European linguistic structuralism and much of twentieth-century epistemology and which has been strained to the limits by non-linguistic structuralists. A debate of such dimensions goes beyond the confines of the present essay and requires a depth of knowledge which I am far from possessing.[120] One must, however, at least point out the sophistry with which structuralists like Lévi-Strauss and structuralistic Marxists have attempted to legitimize their concept of science. They have sought to blur together under the pejorative label of 'empirical' both 'lived experience' in the irrationalist sense and the 'experimental'. They have defined science only as anti-empiricism, as pure theory, as the search for *another reality* truer than phenomenological appearances – dismissing its function as anti-myth, anti-magic, knowledge related to action through a process of reciprocal verification. Search for the reality behind appearances – formulated in such general terms, this could be the programme of the scientist who distinguishes phenomena from one another, who through a process involving induction and deduction, experience and mathematics, eliminates the subjective and illusory side to our sensations and finds laws hidden from our immediate experience (although still subject to experimental verification), and who makes abstractions in order to return to the concrete (a fact which does not preclude the *relative* autonomy of abstractions). But it could also be the programme of the metaphysician who, as a result of an alliance between mathematics and mysticism which has taken shape numerous times in the history of thought ever since the ancient Greeks, denies empirical reality in the name of a higher, trans-cendental Reality. Unless the two programmes and the two attitudes of mind are distinguished, one arrives at an identification of science with religion through a process of countless polemics against the irrationalism of 'lived experience'. It is not a matter of chance that on a number of occasions Lévi-Strauss refers with a touch of the mystical to that 'uninvited guest which has been seated during this Conference beside us and which is the *human*

---

[120] For a revival of this question, I should like to call attention to the importance of the book by Ludovico Geymonat, *Filosofia e filosofia della scienza*; see, in particular, pp. 89ff. and appendices II and III. Cf. also Geymonat's *Storia del pensiero filosofico e scientifico*, Milan 1972, VI, pp. 145–51 and *passim*.

*mind (esprit)'*. In reality, this guest or, as Lévi-Strauss terms it immediately thereafter, this 'unexpected phantom' has always kept its distance from serious scientific exchanges.[121] If it makes an appearance at the spiritualist sessions of structural anthropology, it does not take much to figure out who has called it forth. What is the point, therefore, of exalting structuralism as a reaction against Bergsonism and subjective idealism,[122] if this reaction only leads to an objective idealism which is laden with romantic-existentialist overtones? It is particularly important to bear this in mind when comparing linguistic structuralism with extra-linguistic structuralism. As we have seen, in both instances the term 'Platonism' can properly be applied. But this term remains too vague. There is a Platonism – that of a Leibnitz or a Bertrand Russell, shall we say – which maintains a mathematical-rationalist lucidity, despite its metaphysical implications. In certain regards, Saussure and, to an even greater extent, Hjelmslev and Halliday[123] belong to this variant. And there is a mystifying Platonism, which makes use of mathematics as an exercise in 'maintaining its distance from the sensate', ultimately arriving at an adoration of the divinity – this is Lévi-Strauss's kind of Platonism. The ultimate implications of his concept of science can best be seen in his first conversation with Paolo Caruso, in which he acknowledges that he could be called 'a scientist *or* a theologian', and he goes on to state: 'I am a theologian insofar as I maintain that the important thing is not man's point of view but that of God.'[124] Similarly, that neo-positivist inspiration, which Lepschy rightly perceives in much of linguistic structuralism,[125] is strangely redirected in non-linguistic struc-

[121] *Structural Anthropology*, p. 71. [The term 'unexpected phantom' does not appear in the English text, but 'fantôme imprévu' does appear in the revised French edition, Paris 1958, of this lecture originally given in English – NLB]

[122] This is the case, for example, in Caruso's introduction to the *Conversazioni*, pp. 19–21. But see Henri Lefebvre, 'Claude Lévi-Strauss et le nouvel éléatisme', in his book *Au-delà du structuralisme*, Paris 1971, pp. 261–331.

[123] The reference is to M. A. K. Halliday, a contemporary British linguist. (NLB).

[124] *Conversazioni*, pp. 36ff. Leone de Castris (cited in note 89) is right when he says Lévi-Strauss represents 'a very dangerous theology, which is all the more anachronistic and menacing in that it is disguised by the modern, technocratic attire of the white-collar worker and by the neutral austerity of *objective* research laboratories'. Other deft flirtations with religion can be found in *L'homme nu*, e.g. p. 615.

[125] *La linguistica strutturale*, p. 41, note 7. Certain reservations (particularly with regard to the influence of W. von Humboldt) have been expressed by de Mauro, *La cultura*, v (1967), pp. 114ff.

turalism towards existentialistic channels. The very style of Lévi-Strauss, Foucault, Lacan, etc. lacks altogether that 'English' irony characteristic of the neo-positivists (which also, needless to say, can often be quite annoying), and instead inherits the feeble rhetoric and false pathos characteristic of a particular French existentialist tradition. The great French Enlightenment could have provided very different models!

Closely connected with the rejection of the empirical (in the ambiguous sense we have indicated above) is the rejection, in the structuralist conception of science, of the individual. A struggle had to be waged, of course, against 'historicist' philosophies which saw the triumph of the particular in history in an irrationalist sense (as the absolutely new, the unrepeatable). It was necessary to emphasize that no science is possible without abstraction and generalization, and that such was the case also for the human sciences. But it is one thing to deny the miraculist conception of the particular, another to deny the legitimacy of a *scientific* interest in the particular as an often extremely complex product of a great number of causal links. While all sciences, both the human and the natural, require that scientific explanation go beyond mere recognition of the singularity of an object or an event, not all sciences demand the same degree of particularization. This diversity does not derive from a 'philosophic' decision in favour of either particularizing or generalizing knowledge, but rather from the very nature of the objects under examination and from the aims of the research. For a physicist studying the laws of falling objects, the individual objects are of interest only insofar as they help to establish general laws. But the physician attending an individual patient cannot help but have a much more 'particularizing' interest, not as a result of vestiges of humanism or spiritualism (which he may very well have), but for the purpose of an exact knowledge of *that* clinical case and its cure. Similarly, whereas a folksong without distinct individuality may be of interest only as an example of a 'genre', the *Iliad* is of interest not only as an example of an epic poem but also simply as the *Iliad*. From a biological standpoint (and from the standpoint of certain psychological, hedonistic, etc. consequences stemming from man's biological constitution), it is legitimate to talk about 'man in general'. From a socio-economic standpoint (and with the corresponding 'superstructural' consequences), fewer generalizations can be made, and it becomes necessary to examine the feudal or the capitalist mode of production, the bourgeoisie and the proletariat and their various strata. But even the Marxist can have an interest in a single individual or a single work, and this too represents a scientific interest as long as it relates the individual person or work to all the influences which have converged to shape him or her or it.[126] Thus, the uncritical adoption of linguistics as the model for other human sciences which *must* objectively be more concerned with the particular (because they deal with more complex facts over a shorter span of time – facts in which man's conscious activity has a greater role) can lead to mistaken or deceptive results.

Nor should one forget that in the past many human sciences (for example, philology, the one of which I have the greatest knowledge) have suffered not only from an aestheticist and anti-scientific historicism, but also from a claim to see 'laws' where there are none (and there are none not because the 'freedom of the Spirit' reigns, but because the causal links are too entangled and contradictory and mutually cancelling to allow easy simplifications). In studies of syntax, metre, textual criticism, etc., it has often been necessary to recognize that 'anomaly' prevails over 'analogy', and that it is possible only to arrive at the formulation of 'tendencies' and not laws (a conclusion based not on idealist preconceptions but on that necessary respect for empirical data which is such a source of irritation to many extra-linguistic structuralists). This recognition has represented a *higher,* not lower, degree of scientificity. It is also for this reason that I think that the path towards greater scientificity in the human sciences does not always lie in the direction of a premature (and often merely exhibitionist) mathematicization, but rather in the direction of an exchange of findings with other *inexact* sciences, more closely linked to empirical elements and the historical dimension.

Of course, linguistics and anthropology (like political economy, in certain respects) are less particularizing than other human sciences, since they deal with phenomena which are largely collective and unconscious in nature. But in Lévi-Strauss there is a

---

[126] On this point see Sève, op. cit., 362ff. With regard to the question of abstraction and generalization one cannot overlook the contribution of Galvano Della Volpe and his school, which may be debatable in many of its particulars, but is commendable for having rejected the false alternatives of 'Either irrationalist and particularizing historicism, or Platonizing scientism'.

tendency (already noted by a number of critics) towards universalization in a metaphysical sense, which goes beyond the need for generalization in the scientific sense. His objective is not the formulation of laws capable of 'grasping reality', but rather the formulation of eternal Principles very similar to Plotinus' One or Cioberti's Being – a circumstance which is obviously connected with the previously noted religious character of his thought. There is reason to fear that this tendency has had negative repercussions also on his concrete work as an anthropologist. Frequently, the step forward he claims to have made in relation to former scholars amounts to a step in the direction of generalities and explanations *bonnes à tout faire*, which could serve equally well to explain a phenomenon and its opposite. Here, one should probably recognize the influence of the most debateable side to Freud.[127] Note, for example, the connection (of a *lucus a non lucendo* type) which he establishes between the elevated position occupied by women in a particular society and the 'inability to think of women as belonging to only one logical category' allegedly revealed in the language of that tribe, which is supposed to represent a kind of 'price' or unconscious revenge exacted on the linguistic plane in exchange for what men have conceded to women on the social plane.[128] Is this a scientific explanation or simply a paradoxical quip? Is Lévi-Strauss, who suggested it, more of a scientist than his colleague, Lounsbury, who was satisfied with simply calling attention to the facts without being able to explain them? Or again, consider the 'structural sketch' which is drawn for us in 'Four Winnebago Myths'. Paul Radin had traced back three Winnebago myths to a common matrix; a fourth one appeared to him to be different. Lévi-Strauss 'succeeds' in finding a common denominator for the fourth myth as well – but at the price of generalizations and 'transformations' capable of linking up any given myth with any other.[129] Does this represent scientific progress? A reading of

[127] I am thinking in particular of the explanations of slips of the tongue (often altogether far-fetched and unproven) contained in his *Psychopathology of Everyday Life*. See my short work *The Freudian Slip.*, London 1976, which seeks merely to open, and not to conclude, debate on this question.

[128] *Structural Anthropology*, p. 72.

[129] See *Culture and History. Essays in Honour of Paul Radin,* ed. S. Diamond, London 1960, pp. 351ff. The logico-mathematical procedure of 'transformation' becomes, in Lévi-Strauss's hands (especially in *The Raw and the Cooked* and *From Honey to Ashes*), a facile method of connecting and uniting everything with everything.

Domenico Comparetti[130] on *Edipo e la mitologia comparata (Oedipus and Comparative Mythology)*, written in 1867 against opponents quite different in their cultural orientation but akin in their simplistic identifications and permutations, would be very useful to today's mythologists too.[131]

In actual fact, the partially legitimate element in the anti-historicism of the structuralists can be put to use only by bringing it down to a more modest level of empirical observations. At issue is not the question of atemporal Platonic models, but the ability to recognize that proper attention should be given in human history to what Braudel in a famous essay called '*la longue durée*' and '*la très longue durée*': to 'semi-permanent forces', 'long-term movements' and 'natural phenomena', as Arnaldo Momigliano says.[132] At issue here is the question of re-examining, in materialist rather than objective-idealist terms, those more or less 'long-lasting' features of human reality which have been played down by a historicism overly eager to assert with Heraclitus that everything moves. At the same time, we must bear in mind that this *relatively* static state is neither eternal nor extra-historical. A similar argument has to be made with regard to claims that reality must be studied as a systematic and organic whole, that the *tout se tient,* that there exists a 'priority of the whole with respect to the parts'. Here too a generic statement about the unity of reality is of little help, even

---

[130] Domenico Comparetti (1835–1929): Italian classical scholar and autodidact. (NLB).

[131] Domenico Comparetti, *Poesia e pensiero del mondo antico,* Naples 1944, pp. 234ff. Comparetti's polemic was directed against a great linguist, Michel Bréal, whose interpretation of the Oedipus myth did not, however, advance far beyond the simplistic comparativism of his day. As against Lévi-Strauss's interpretations of myths, see G. S. Kirk, *Myth: Its Meaning and Function in Ancient and Other Cultures,* Berkeley 1970; with regard to Lévi-Strauss, see especially Ch. II; and with regard to the impossibility of establishing a strict analogy between myth and language, see his perceptive remarks on p. 70. A lively and incisive argument against the mythological structuralism of J.-P. Vernant and M. Detienne has been written by Giulia Piccaluga, 'Adonis e i profumi di un certo strutturalismo', *Maia,* XXVI (1974), pp. 33ff.

[132] Cf. Fernand Braudel, 'La longue durée', *Annales,* XIII (1958), pp. 725ff.; Arnaldo Momigliano, *Terzo contributo alla storia degli studi classici,* Rome 1966, I, pp. 295 and 301. For some time now in his studies of the history of historiography, Momigliano has emphasized the difference, which has existed since ancient times, between 'history' (as the narration of a succession of events) and 'antiquaria' (as the description of a system of institutions). The structuralists have been wrong not to have taken into account this very interesting body of research.

if it is accompanied by the qualification that this is an articulated and structured unity, which sets it off from the elements of mysticism which are apparently present in the Hegelian concept of unity (a qualification to which the Hegelians can make their own polemical responses). What is important is to recognize that, in nature as well as in human institutions, there exist quite different degrees of cohesion and interdependence of the individual elements. There are aggregates and systems, mixtures and compounds, very tight inter-connections and slack or practically non-existent inter-connections. To opt on an *a priori* basis in every case in favour of a maximum of organicity and systematicity, and to dismiss on an *a priori* basis every so-called 'atomistic' interpretation, leads inevitably to strained and arbitrary arguments.

\*        \*        \*

This cultural orientation (particularly French extra-linguistic structuralism), which is so different from Marxism, has had an extraordinary influence on certain French Marxists, during a period in which Marxism was in crisis much more for political than for cultural reasons. The influence can already be detected in certain outward features of their writings. Of course, Althusser and his collaborators have an altogether different seriousness and sobriety about them from what can be found in Lévi-Strauss, Foucault and Lacan. We will not find them becoming 'ecstatic' over signs which mean nothing, or be informed that they have found in Richard Wagner a master of 'scientific analysis carried out in music'. Nevertheless, something of Lévi-Strauss's existentialistic false pathos has undoubtedly passed over into Althusser, *even in his style*. Indeed, certain of Althusser's recent writings (for example *Lenin and Philosophy* and the paper on 'Marx's Relation to Hegel') actually represent an exacerbation of this tendency. The stylistic pomposity and the theoretical pretensions develop *pari passu*. 'I shall renounce rhetoric', Althusser proclaims in the second of these two writings. But what does this mean when the author, immediately after delivering this forthright pronouncement, makes it clear that he gives a great deal of importance to the metaphor of 'great scientific continents', and dwells on it as if it represented not just a simple metaphor but an advance in knowledge? What does it mean when he explains to us with diagrams and formulae that '*Capital* is the product of the work of Hegel (German

Philosophy) on English Political Economy + French Socialism', i.e. the product of the work of 'instruments of theoretical production H' on the 'raw material R + FS', whereas *Reading Capital* was the result of 'setting to "work" on our raw material G'1 (i.e. the *Marx-Hegel* relationship) means of theoretical production G'2 (Marx himself + certain other categories) to produce a result G'3'' (i.e. as Althusser modestly states, 'whatever *Reading Capital* contains that is not aberrant')?[133] Futhermore, the productive processes is not finished; now, Althusser says, one has to take G'2 as the raw material and put it through the machinery G'3. . . .

Althusser's use of terms like 'epistemological break', borrowed from Bachelard, 'overdetermination', borrowed from psychoanalysis, and many others of this kind, already justified the suspicion that his terminological acquisitions were far more numerous than his actual conceptual advances. But in this last writing one really has to ask oneself where that sense of the ridiculous has gone with which Marx, Engels, Labriola, Lenin and Gramsci were so amply endowed. Can one serious imagine that all these 'mechanical' metaphors carry forward the question of Marx's sources and cultural and theoretical development even one small step? In reality this last essay, to a much greater degree than the earlier ones, conceals behind the metaphors a disturbing lack of originality. The notion that in Hegel there is the idea of a 'process without a subject' is only an exaggerated and awkward way of repeating something which had already been maintained by all those Hegelian-Marxists from whom Althusser, till recently, was (legitimately) eager to dissociate himself. And the fact that both the limitation and the strength of Feuerbach lay in the simplicity of his anti-Hegelian polemic is something which all of us have known at least since Engels.

But this is not the essential. Althusser's structuralism emerges most prominently in his concept of science (anti-empiricist, in the misguided sense we have already indicated in Lévi-Strauss & Co.), in his low estimation of diachrony, and in his expulsion of man from the human sciences. These are questions to which we have alluded, if only briefly, throughout the preceding essays, and which have been discussed more thoroughly by other scholars, particularly

---

[133] Louis Althusser, 'Marx's Relation to Hegel', in *Politics and History*, NLB 1972, pp. 166, 170. With regard to Althusser's reply to John Lewis, see below, note 40 to the essay on Korsch and Lenin.

Lucien Sève and (on a less specifically philosophic plane but no less effectively) Ernest Mandel and Eric Hobsbawm.[134] Unquestionably, structuralistic Marxism has served a useful critical function in relation to other twentieth-century pseudo-Marxisms. It has raised the question of the distinction between science and ideology (although resolving it poorly), it has brought to light the ambiguities of 'humanist' and 'historicist' Marxism, and it has emphasized the distance separating Marx from Hegel (a point, however, which had previously been made by the school of Della Volpe) and the various phases of Marx's thought from one another. But each of these advances has been accompanied by a regression, as a consequence of the fact (discussed above) that one idealist interpretation of Marx has been contested in the name of another one. Worse still from a methodological standpoint, structuralist Marxism has exasperated the tendency (already present in a good deal of twentieth-century Marxism) to represent modifications and additions to Marx's thought as 'interpretations' or 'readings' of Marx's texts. *Reading Capital*: there is already a gross misrepresentation in the title. A *reading,* which once indicated the most respectful and discerning treatment of a text, has become a highly suspect term since Althusser conjured up his 'symptomatic reading' or theoreticist forcing of texts. This is an operation which (however changed the setting) takes us back to the worst Italian neo-idealism of the early twentieth century. Then every reading represented a re-creation of the text; in other words, those neo-idealists distorted in a subjectivist direction a serious question, the 'contemporaneity' of the past, which requires a preliminary *objective*, historico-philological interpretation, if it is to be dealt with in a responsible fashion.

One can very easily put together a compendium of statements by Marx and Engels against the empiricism of vulgar economics, which 'stops at appearances'; one can call to mind that for Marx no

---

[134] Sève, *Marxisme et théorie de la personnalité*, pp. 482ff., 376ff.; cf. also the debate with Godelier in *Marxismo e strutturalismo*. Eric Hobsbawm, 'Karl Marx's Contribution to Historiography', in R. Blackburn (ed.), *Ideology in Social Science*, London 1972. Not everything in the Hobsbawm essay seems to me to be equally acceptable, but his argument against structuralism and structuralistic Marxism (pp. 275–80) is particularly incisive. With regard to Mandel, see *The Formation of the Economic Thought of Karl Marx*, NLB 1971, pp. 158–9, note 15. See also H. Lefebvre, 'Les paradoxes d'Althusser' in *Au-delà du structuralisme*, pp. 371–417, and particularly his incisive remarks on 'symptomatic reading', pp. 398ff.

individual and no society divided into classes is what it thinks it is. But when these statements are used to draw the conclusion that Marxism is an 'anti-empiricist' theory in the broad sense of contemporary structuralism (i.e. a search for the Other Reality which lies behind phenomena), then the distortion that results is similar to (although much more serious than) the one produced by those who claim Galileo as a 'Platonist'. It is overlooked that Marx was not searching for abstract models independent of experience and applicable to the 'human Spirit' in general. Rather, he was looking for an abstract model which would help him to understand that *transient* socio-historical formation which is capitalism. Transient, meaning that it does not reproduce itself in a perfect cyclical process, but tends towards increasing disequilibrium. The mechanism of this increasing disequilibrium (the part played respectively by objective economic processes such as the falling rate of profit and by the formation of the oppressed class's revolutionary consciousness) has been an open question since the end of the nineteenth century and still is today, both because Marx himself did not sufficiently develop this part of his theory, and because since his time capitalism has developed various ways of partially immunizing itself and putting off its demise. However, even the moulding of the proletariat into a political party was always seen by Marx, Engels and Lenin (as it still is today by Mao, although not always by western Maoists) as an objective, 'caused' process, and not as a mere act of will which attempts to destroy an economic system capable of functioning *ad infinitum* with perfect rationality.

Furthermore, it is hardly necessary to call to mind that Marx regarded precisely his demonstration of the 'non-naturalness' of the bourgeois economy (in the sense of its non-eternal and historical character) as the essential point separating his theory from classical economics. The enthusiasm of Marx and Engels for Darwin indicate that they recognized a feature shared by historical materialism and Darwinism which went beyond all the differences in subject matter and mentality clearly perceived by them: the extension of the notion of historicity to sciences (political economy on the one hand, biology on the other) which traditionally had excluded it.[135] To disregard all that and turn Marxism into a purely

[135] The 'anti-naturalism' (not in a spiritualistic sense, but in an anti-static sense) of the Marxist critique of political economy has been brought out effectively by Nicola Badaloni, *Marxismo come storicismo*, Milan 1962 – a book which should

'synchronic' science represents a complete distortion. The distortion is even more absurd on historiographic grounds. Marx, undoubtedly, superseded the science of his time in a decisive fashion, and *Capital* represents also a great lesson in epistemology. But can one possibly see him as the precursor of a theory like structuralism, which emerged from the anti-materialist (and, more of less indirectly, anti-Marxist) reaction of the late nineteenth century and represents a renewal of the schism between history and science?

Behind this denial or underestimation of historicity – which paradoxically brings together bourgeois and revolutionaries in the West – lie motives which are not merely cultural but political. Present-day capitalism no longer needs nor desires to justify itself in 'historicist' terms. The technocracy has its own pseudo-Enlightenment ideology, which identifies the system's needs for rationalization with Reason and Science *tout court*. On the other hand, the extreme revolutionary left is led, by virtue of its weakness and the difficulties it has in penetrating the working class and combating reformism, to a belief in the myth that the capitalist system works perfectly and that it can be destroyed only through an act of pure voluntarism. Although Marcuse and Althusser may differ sharply in their cultural-political background and in their posture towards science, they both start off from a substantially shared vision of present-day capitalism and its absence of 'objective' crises.

*   *   *

However, ideological fashions succeed one another more quickly in the present-day neo-capitalist West than in the old brand of bourgeois culture, even though certain basic tendencies remain. Thus, although structuralism appears still to be in good health in Italy, where it arrived late, in the countries where it had an early and vigorous development it is already tending to decline. In the United States, although Chomsky's transformational grammar has certain features of continuity with a strain of American structuralism which dates back to Sapir, it explicitly sets itself in antithesis to structuralism as a whole, accusing it of the same mechanism and vulgar associationism from which the despised

be judged on the basis of its content, and not on the basis of its title and the narrow meaning taken on by the term 'historicism' in the debates of the last few years.

neo-grammarians suffered, and reasserting the creativity of language. In France, it is no longer just Sartre who argues against structuralism. An entire group of scholars who draw on Merleau-Ponty and, even further back, on Husserl, repudiate structuralism as an objectivist philosophy which downgrades human activity and its power to transform reality. As early as 1967, a special issue of *Esprit* dedicated to structuralism was marked on the whole by strong criticisms (first in the introductory article by J.-M. Domenach and then, even more explicitly, in an essay by Paul Ricoeur on 'La structure, le mot, l'événement').[136] Then we find a lecturer from the University of Nanterre, in an effective piece on the French May under the pseudonym of Epistémon, expressing himself in even more extreme terms. The characteristics of 'bureaucracy' (both academic and party) are to be found in the structuralist approach; the French university on the eve of May 'had become something akin to the most radical structuralists' object of study: a language sufficient unto itself, whose function and purpose is not signification . . . May '68 is not only the revolt of the students of Paris and the beginning of a transformation of the French university, but also the swan song of structuralism'. Epistémon also associates himself with Husserl and Merleau-Ponty, stating that 'phenomenological method and structuralist method are poles apart from one another'. And he attributes to a group of Nanterre professors (which includes Ricoeur himself) a role of cultural-political preparation for the May revolt – in which Nanterre played a vanguard function – as a result of the polemic they had waged for some time against 'structuralist terrorism'.[137] On the other

---

[136] *Esprit*, May 1967: 'Structuralisme: idéologie et méthode'. See also, for example, Jean Dubois, 'Structuralisme et linguistique', *La Pensée*, CXXXV (October 1967), p. 20: 'La grammaire générale et le transformationnalisme marquent les années 60 comme le structuralisme a marqué les années 50.' The dates have, perhaps, been pushed forward somewhat (even for France, but obviously also for Italy, where these cultural movements arrived late), but on the whole the statement is accurate. A book which in certain respects stands apart, even though it too talks of a crisis within structuralism, is Raymond Boudon's *The Uses of Structuralism*, London 1971 – originally written in 1968. The author is well versed in epistemology and sociology, and points out very effectively the illusions and (unintended) fakery of those whom he calls 'magical structuralists'. In my opinion, however, he is wrong to regard as typical exponents of the best in structuralism Lévi-Strauss (who in many respects fits into the category of 'magical structuralism') and Chomsky (who already represents the beginning of a polemical reaction against structuralism).

[137] Epistémon, *Ces idées qui ont ébranlé la France*, Paris 1968, pp. 27–32.

hand, even in the camp of theoretical Marxism it is easy to perceive in the Godelier-Sève debate and other similar events, a decline in the fortunes of Althusserian positions.

Even from this cursory and incomplete survey of the new opponents of structuralism it becomes clear that, although many of the particular objections they raise against structuralism are quite correct, the general theoretical orientation underlying their criticisms cannot be shared by a materialist-Marxist. In point of fact, we are witnessing once again the occurrence of a phenomenon which has reappeared cyclically in bourgeois culture and in a great deal of western Marxist culture since the beginning of our century: one idealism is 'unmasked' and opposed in the name of another idealism. And since the fundamental types of idealist conceptions are not limitless in number, the primary result is the monotonous spectacle of a culture which, although it moves forward on a purely technical plane, turns in a void on the ideological-political plane.

Structuralism, in the form given it by Lévi-Strauss in particular, represented a kind of objective idealism. Now, however, the predominant tendency is to oppose it not insofar as it is idealism but insofar as it is objective. A polemic is waged not against the conception of True Reality as a metaphysical essence, as a 'hidden Reason', but against the 'illusion' that there is a reality which pre-exists us, is independent of us and conditions us. No attempt is made to distinguish language from other human institutions and activities, and to point out, therefore, what makes linguistics inappropriate as a model for the other sciences of man. On the contrary, the equation of language with institutions is implicitly accepted, and the 'creativity' in language (*energeia* as against *ergon,* to repeat the too often repeated distinction of Wilhelm von Humboldt) is exalted in a one-sided fashion, although obviously in a form much less simplistic than was the case with Croce. The old cries of mechanism, which the structuralists (with the exception of Bloomfield and only a few others) had turned against materialism and nineteenth-century positivism, are now turned against linguistics and structural anthropology. And thus, after his hosannas to the human Spirit always present amongst us, after his self-definition as a theologian, and after his numerous expressions of disdain for empirical reality, it becomes Lévi-Strauss's sad fate to be lynched for 'naturalism'!

Of course, not all the new anti-structuralists fall within this summary characterization. In particular, Chomsky's case is quite complex; moreover, the positions of the various Chomskians do not coincide in every respect with those of Chomsky. Unfortunately, I lack a background in mathematical logic, which would be indispensable for understanding and evaluating the most technical (and probably the most valid) side to Chomsky's linguistics. I cannot, therefore, make judgements, but only express impressions and doubts – which, moreover, are not just my own, but have already been expressed in part by scholars far more qualified than I.[138] There is a Chomsky who is on the front lines of the anti-imperialist struggle within the United States, and who associates himself with a 'Marxist-anarchist' perspective informed by the thought of Rosa Luxemburg and Lenin's *State and Revolution* (even though he is not and does not declare himself to be a Marxist in the strict sense);[139] a Chomsky who with great courage and extraordinary lucidity lays bare the responsibilities of intellectuals in capitalist society. There is also a Chomsky who, in order to explain what he calls 'linguistic competence', i.e. the capacity to produce sentences which are not simply the repetition of sentences already heard, has resort to the most metaphysical and retrograde side of Cartesianism: the doctrine of innate ideas and the *absolute* distinction between spirit and 'mechanism', between man and animal. In other words, he resorts to a spiritualistic metaphysics which has been abandoned for some time now by the more discerning elements of spiritualist culture itself, which, under the pressure of objections raised by empiricism and materialism, have created those much more polished forms of spiritualism represented by the Kantian critique, post-Kantian idealism and the various tendencies customarily referred to as neo-positivism.

When interviewed on the relationship between his linguistic theory and his political convictions, Chomsky replies that, although

[138] See, for example, Piaget, *Structuralism,* pp. 87ff.; Mounin, *Clefs pour la linguistique*, p. 140; Paolo Ramat, in *Problemi*, XIV (March–April 1969), pp. 621–3 and note 20, with which I strongly agree on this point; J. Peter Maher, 'The Paradox of Creation and Tradition: Sound Pattern of a Palimpsest', *Language Sciences,* October 1969, pp. 15ff. I shall attempt to develop some of the points raised by the authors I have cited.

[139] See the interview published in *New Left Review* No. 57 (September–October 1969), pp. 21–34; the reference to Luxemburg and Lenin is on pp. 28–9, and to a 'Marxist-anarchist perspective', on p. 31.

they have developed independently of one another, they have a common point of departure: the idea that 'the fundamental human capacity is the capacity and the need for creative self-expression, for free control of all aspects of one's life and thought'. Corresponding to the creativity of language, which, however, unfolds within the limits of a system of universal rules valid for all languages, there must also exist a social system which guarantees the free development of all men within the limits of a moral-intellectual structure common to all. 'I would like to assume on the basis of fact and hope on the basis of confidence in the human species that there are innate structures of mind. If there are not, if humans are just plastic and random organisms, then they are fit subjects for the shaping of behaviour. If humans only become as they are by random changes, then why not control that randomness by the state authority or the behaviourist technologist or anything else?'[140] This is a reply which is not only profoundly sincere but also quite understandable within a technocratic society which aims at reducing man increasingly to a machine, and which evokes, therefore, a polemical reaction in a humanistic sense amongst those who struggle against it (given their present inability to bring about a union of vanguard intellectuals and the working class). Only if there exists in man a spiritual structure which is absolutely irreducible to an animal and automatistic nature can one hope that the manipulators of men's consciousness will not win out! And to the extent that this conviction sustains Chomsky in his struggle, it is certainly more revolutionary than the professorial Marxism of those who do not take part in the struggle itself or who take part in it behind the front lines. The same thing should be said for those who are revolutionary communists while still professing belief in Christianity or other religions.

But if Marxism is to be something more than the many utopian socialisms (some of which, moreover, were already oriented in a materialist direction), if it is to be a theory of scientific socialism, then the connection made by Chomsky between his metaphysics and his political position does not appear acceptable. From the 'negation of man' which was the product of structuralist Marxism we now lapse back into one of the oldest and most anti-scientific forms of humanism.

[140] Ibid., pp. 31–2.

Chomsky likes to associate himself with Rousseau and Wilhelm von Humboldt as precursors of his libertarian spiritualism.[141] Apart from the question of the enormous distance separating the revolutionary potential of Rousseau's thought from the tempered liberalism of von Humboldt, it is only too easy to point out that practically no one amongst the worst theoreticians of inequality and oppression ever stated that man is a 'plastic and random organism' – a statement which, moreover, represents merely a caricature of the materialist definition of man. From the reverend Jesuit fathers to the priests of the ungodly modern religion that is nationalism, almost all have asserted the spirituality of man, the freedom of his will, and many other fine things of the kind; it is in the name of these sacred principles that they have manipulated and oppressed him. In an exaltation of activism, idealism and a disdain for any naturalistic conception, the intelligentsia of all Europe slaughtered itself and caused the slaughter of millions of proletarians during World War I. Present-day experience indicates that the old spiritualistic techniques used to 'manipulate behaviour' are perfectly reconcilable with more up-to-date techniques.

As far as the philosophy of language in particular is concerned, one can admit that Chomsky was initially correct in reacting against the overly simplified behaviourism of Bloomfield and, even more, that of his followers. But it is disappointing to see how his polemic against attempts at scientific explanation (summary though these may be) led him immediately to embrace the illusion that everything could be resolved by taking refuge in old dogmas. With an obsessive persistence he repeats that 'it means absolutely nothing' to talk about a gradual evolution from elementary forms of communication to human language, about linguistic habits learned through repetition, about associations and extensions by analogy.[142] He assumes that there exists an absolute hiatus separating animality from humanity, which no kind of mediation can bridge. Of course, we still do not possess an exhaustive description of the brain's activity; furthermore, we are still quite distant from this goal. But can one regard as an explanation Chomsky's assumption

---

[141] Cf. Noam Chomsky, *Cartesian Linguistics,* New York 1966, pp. 26–30, 91–3 (note 51), where, in addition to Rousseau, he invokes the Marx of the *Economic and Philosophic Manuscripts;* cf. also the interview cited above, p. 31.

[142] See, for example, *Cartesian Linguistics,* pp. 13, 55, 73, 109 (note 114), and *Language and Mind,* New York 1972, pp. 4 and 36.

of 'innate linguistic competence' as an unconditioned *primum*? When the pre-Socratics endeavoured to give naturalistic explanations of meteorological phenomena or of the origin of living beings, a Chomsky of that age would have amused himself by scoffing at such attempts and concluding that, given their inadequacy, it must be assumed that lightning is launched by Zeus and that plants, animals and men are divine creations. The history of science, however, has shown the fruitfulness of that imperfect materialism and, vice versa, the halting and sidetracking function of religious or metaphysical explanations.

Chomsky does not share this view. Towards the conclusion of his study on *Language and Mind* he declares with extraordinary self-assurance the failure of evolutionism. 'The process by which the human mind achieved its present stage of complexity and its particular form of innate organization are a total mystery, as much so as the analogous questions about the physical or mental organization of any other complex organism. It is perfectly safe to attribute this development to "natural selection", so long as we realize that there is no substance in this assertion.'[143] And to those who raise the question of a possible 'physical' explanation of innatism, he replies ironically. 'We can, however, be fairly sure that there will be a physical explanation for the phenomena in question, if they can be explained at all, for an uninteresting terminological reason, namely that the concept of "physical explanation" will no doubt be extended to incorporate whatever is discovered in this domain, exactly as it was extended to accommodate gravitational and electromagnetic force, massless particles, and numerous other entities and processes that would have offended the common sense of earlier generations.'[144]

Thus according to this view science has not, over the course of its history, made real advances to the detriment of myth and religious faith. Rather, it has only pulled off a series of verbal tricks; since it could not deny the reality of certain 'spiritual' phenomena and would not admit its own defeat, it has had recourse to such shrewd manoeuvres as incorporating these phenomena by expanding its own boundaries.[145] It is, of course, beyond question that no

[143] *Language and Mind,* p. 97.
[144] Ibid., p. 98.
[145] I am still unable to give any other interpretation to the highly sarcastic words used by Chomsky, despite the different opinion expressed by Lepschy in *Comunità*, CLXV (November 1971), p. 301, note 34.

great scientific advance can be reduced to a mere addition to the previous scientific heritage, since it brings about an entire methodological revision of the principles of science itself. But such revisions have never erased the distinction between science and non-science, and they have never signalled the triumph of spiritualism – unless one confuses, for example, Heisenberg's principle with the amateurish extrapolations which have been made from it with regard to 'free will'. This has been the case least of all in biology, in which vitalism has suffered the heaviest blows precisely in these last few decades. To speak today with such disdain for Darwinism, and to deny with such self-assurance that cybernetics can make a contribution to a materialist explanation of mental processes,[146] means that one has adopted an obscurantist position which makes the struggle for communism all the more difficult.

Chomsky himself presents the essay on *Cartesian Linguistics* not as an actual historiographic study, but as a rediscovery of ideas unjustly overlooked by the nineteenth and early twentieth centuries which find their confirmation and full development in present-day transformational grammar. But if this character of the essay legitimately removes it from all pedantic objections as to matters of detail, it does not justify the crudest forms of misinterpretation, such as the unbroken link which is made between the Jansenists of Port-Royal, the German Romantics and von Humboldt, or the failure to take into account all the contributions to seventeenth- and eighteenth-century general linguistics made by empiricist thought, etc.[147] Furthermore, although Chomsky does

---

[146] Ibid., p. 4 and *passim*.

[147] See the objections raised by Luigi Rosiello, *Linguistica illuminista*, Bologna 1967, especially pp. 8, 14, 114, 119, 187 (Rosiello is right to criticize Chomsky for confusing Cartesian innatism with von Humboldt's concept of 'inner form', and he points out that between the two of them lies 'Kant's critique'); Paolo Rossi, 'Linguisti d'oggi e filosofi del Seicento', *Lingua e stile*, III (1968), pp. 1ff. (a debate with Rosiello and de Mauro, but also with Chomsky on a number of points); Lia Formigari, *Linguistica ed empirismo nel Seicento inglese*, Bari 1970 – while not arguing directly against the ideas of Chomsky, she clearly brings out the merits of empiricism and of its anti-innatist polemic. Obviously, no one today conceives of the human mind as a *tabula rasa* in the literal and banal meaning of the term. Neither language nor knowledge is possible without that extremely complex nervous structure which is the human brain, and which has taken shape through a process of biological evolution. But it is clear that 'innatism' (assuming one wishes to use this term) in this biological sense has nothing to do with the innatism of the philosophical tradition and with its spiritualist pre-

not fail to make a few references (negative, of course) to La Mettrie, he does not appear to take seriously enough that process of thought whereby, under the stimulus of the difficulties created by Cartesian dualism and the theory of the 'animal-machine', La Mettrie's 'man-the-machine' and Diderot's far from crude materialist biology were arrived at. In this process of thought, as Aram Vartanian has pointed out,[148] the empiricism of Locke played a less decisive role than has been generally believed. Those same difficulties must be confronted by whoever, like Chomsky, attempts to resuscitate Cartesianism. Once one has admitted a rigorously mechanistic explanation for all the vital processes and modes of behaviour of an animal, how is one to prevent the 'materialist infection' from spreading to man? If, on the other hand, one becomes converted to a vitalist biology, how is one to prevent the fundamental distinction from becoming one between life and non-life, so that within the framework of a spiritualist conception of life a continuity (however spurious the scientific and philosophic grounds may be) is established between man and animal? And if we begin to distinguish in the human psyche what is still explicable in automatist terms from what is not, then how are we to avoid declaring that some men (individuals or nations or races) are 'more equal than others', i.e. the bearers to a greater degree than others of mankind's 'divine' as opposed to merely 'feral' characteristics? This latter and worst form of spiritualism also existed in Romantic linguistics even before it made its appearance in racism pure and simple. Its founder, Friedrich Schlegel, in his work *Uber die Sprache und Weisheit der Indier* characterized as purely 'mechanistic' the

---

suppositions. In any case, recent studies in bio-linguistics have tended to play down the conventional or 'arbitrary' (in Saussure's sense) elements in the various spoken languages of the world; and, thus, they have lapsed into a retrograde biologism. With regard to certain forced interpretations of the *Grammaire de Port-Royal* made by Chomsky, see Raffaele Simone's introduction to *Grammatica e Logica di Port-Royal*, Rome 1969. See also P. Ramat, 'Del problema della tipologia linguistica in Wilhelm von Humboldt e d'altro ancora', *Lingua e stile*, VIII (1973), pp. 37ff.

[148] Aram Vartanian, *Diderot and Descartes*, Princeton 1953. This excellent essay has generally been overlooked both by Chomsky and his critics. In the debate provoked by *Cartesian Linguistics*, emphasis has been given to the anti-Cartesian empiricists, rather than to the materialist developments which, paradoxically but understandably, emerged from one of the currents in Cartesianism itself. One need only think of how lively the debate was in the eighteenth century over the question of the 'soul of animals', and how strong an influence it had on the thought of Giacomo Leopardi.

languages which were later termed isolating or agglutinative. He ascribed genuinely creative qualities only to Sanskrit (and, to a lesser extent, to the other Indo-European languages, which he believed to be the children and not the siblings of Sanskrit). This distinction continued, in various forms, to hold sway over a good deal of nineteenth-century linguistics. If one wants to pose correctly the problem of man's animality and a non-metaphysical distinction between man and animal, one has to be Darwinian and Marxist. But this is impossible as long as one continues to talk about innate ideas and the present-day validity of Cartesian dualism, however fine one's ethico-political intentions may be.

It would certainly be an error to place Chomsky's 'linguistic creativity', which is anchored to a logico-linguistic 'deep structure' and a body of transformational rules which allows one to shift to the 'surface structures' of different languages, on the same plane with Crocean aestheticist and pre-logical creativity. Yet it is striking to see how Chomsky adheres to the Romantic identification of language with poetic creation – tracing, moreover, this typically Romantic (or, at the most, sensist-Viconian) concept back to the Cartesians. And it is just as striking to see how he regards as one of the virtues of that body of theories which he refers to as 'Cartesian linguistics', its insistence on the fact that language 'is not restricted to any practical communicative function, in contrast, for example, to the pseudo language of animals'.[149] Nor is this just a fortuitous consequence. Every one-sided assertion on behalf of the creativity and spirituality of language always ends by regarding the 'highest' and most 'disinterested' forms of human language as typical and by abandoning to the sphere of animality all those 'practical communicative' forms which must serve as the starting point for a *linguistic* study of language. Schuchardt said that language, 'born from necessity, culminates in art'; when all's said and done he was being less idealist not only than Croce and Vossler, but also than Chomsky.

We have seen in the first part of this essay how Saussure's theory, and later structuralism, arose in reaction to the preceding nineteenth-century linguistics with its 'atomism' and mechanicism. But to an 'unbridled spiritualist' like Chomsky, Bopp and Schleicher, the neo-grammarians, Whitney and Saussure all appear as a single bloc

[149] *Cartesian Linguistics,* pp. 17 and 29.

of vulgar empiricists and materialists. 'The death-knell of philosophical grammar was sounded with the remarkable successes of comparative Indo-European studies, which surely rank among the outstanding achievements of nineteenth-century science. The impoverished and thoroughly inadequate conception of language expressed by Whitney and Saussure and numerous others proved to be entirely appropriate to the current stage of linguistic research.'[150] It was to no purpose that Saussure had been one of the earliest champions of the *Grammaire de Port-Royal*[151] after it had fallen into disrepute during the nineteenth century – even though he was not so acritical a champion as Chomsky.[152] That fact does not at all prevent Chomsky from drawing up a periodization of the history of linguistics which places on one side 'philosophical grammar' from the seventeenth century down to Romanticism and von Humboldt, and on the other side everything that has occurred since von Humboldt, right down to 1950.[153] This second period, which supposedly represents a period of total decline, is referred to by Chomsky with the all-encompassing term of 'structuralist' – a term which he himself says is used 'rather misleadingly', but not in an altogether absurd fashion. This is a typical manifestation of the phenomenon alluded to above: although structuralism is strongly antagonistic (with only a few exceptions) towards any naturalistic conception of language, it has been 'overtaken on the right' by those who still find it too positivist. One element which may have contributed to this mistaken outlook is the fact that in America Bloomfield adopted uncritically a great deal of the teachings of the neo-grammarians. But it is equally paradoxical that Chomsky does not see the differences in ideological formulation which exist between Bloomfield and European structuralism, between Whitney and Schleicher or Ascoli. Or rather, this levelling of all distinctions is to be explained on the basis of Chomsky's metaphysical extremism.

In its original form, Chomsky's 'philosophical grammar' has limited prospects for success. It is not conceivable that innatism

[150] *Language and Mind*, p. 20; but see also pp. 19ff.
[151] The intellectual religious community of Port-Royal was founded in 1637. Among the works produced there was a philosophic, logical grammar (1660), which attempted to establish the general grammatical forms common to all languages. (NLB).
[152] *Course in General Linguistics*, p. 82.
[153] *Language and Mind*, p. 22.

and Cartesian dualism, which are too antiquated by now for bourgeois thought itself, could become philosophically fashionable. This accounts for the various attempts at a 'modernized Chomskyism' which we have witnessed over the last few years.

First of all, there is the attempt, now viewed favourably by Chomsky himself, to translate innatism into biological terms. Lepschy, who is aware, however, of the difficulties posed by this task, remarks: 'Chomsky prefers to talk about *innate ideas* or, as one might say in naturalistic terms, about a hereditary predisposition – which emphasizes the existence at least of an open question. . . .' Elsewhere he states: 'This characteristic [i.e. 'linguistic competence'] cannot be *learned*, just as one does not *learn* to walk, and just as a cat tossed into the air *knows how* to land on his paws without ever having *learned* to do so.'[154] But in what type of biology would one locate this biological translation of Chomskyism? In a creationist biology, according to which the species *homo sapiens* had linguistic ability from the beginning? One hopes not. In an evolutionist biology? In that case, linguistic ability would have evolved (albeit by the most complex and least unilinear paths) from those rudimentary forms of animal language which Chomsky regards as totally different from human language; one could no longer talk with such utter disdain about mechanisms of stimulus and response, about practical needs, etc., since one would have to have recourse (at least at the phylogenetic, if not at the ontogenetic, level) to precisely these 'crude' mechanisms in order to explain the origin of linguistic ability. But would such a Darwinian revision of innatism really be sufficient in and of itself? No,' because it would reduce language to an instinctual activity, dismissing everything we have known for some time now about its conventional, social and non-biological nature. The comparison with the cat which, once it is

---

[154] *La linguistica strutturale*, p. 176 (see pp. 135–6 of the English edition); Lepschy's preface to the Italian edition of Chomsky, in *Saggi linguistici*, Turin 1969, I, p. 14. 'Biological Chomskyism' has been developed particularly by E. H. Lenneberg, *Biological Foundations of Language*, New York 1967; but this book too fails to overcome the fundamental difficulties and it leaves the reader with the impression of an attempt at the '*a posteriori* scientifization' of a theory which developed out of a marked hostility towards the biological sciences and cannot readily be detached from its origins – or, if it is detached without a thorough reconsideration of the relationship between nature and society, it runs the risk of falling into a no less serious but opposite error: i.e. biologism. For a more favourable judgement on Lenneberg, see Ramat, 'Del problema della tipologia linguistica', p. 51, note 53.

thrown into the air, 'knows how' to land on its four paws is quite appropriate for showing how no baby 'knows how' to speak in this sense, but rather has to learn to do so (even though this statement obviously does not resolve, but simply opens up a whole series of neuro-physiological problems, on the one hand, and psycho-social ones, on the other). The difficulty is a serious one for another reason too: because Chomsky's humanism, although it rests on the nature of language, inevitably tends towards an innatism to moral and political principles, in which it sees, with much naïveté, the sole guarantee of man's 'non-manipulability'.

The interview which we have cited speaks clearly on this point: 'A serious study of morals or of social systems would attempt the same thing. . . . I think that among the biological characteristics that determine the nature of the human organism there are some that relate to intellectual development, some that relate to moral development, some that relate to development as a member of human society, some that relate to aesthetic development. I suspect that they are restrictive and that we shall find that all of these constraints can be said to constitute human nature. To a large extent, they are immutable. That is to say, they are just part of being human the same way that having legs and arms is part of being human.'[155] Lacking any clear idea about what Engels called 'the part played by labour in the transition from ape to man' (and therefore about the link between relations of production and moral, juridical and political concepts), Chomsky wavers between an antediluvian spiritualism and a genuinely 'vulgar' materialism – not in the polemical sense in which we have espoused it in this book, but in the literal sense of an *immediate* biologizing of mankind's social and cultural characteristics.

Of course, like all cognitive and communicative processes, language too must be the object of neuro-physiological study. It is, however, quite likely that, as it develops, such study will not confer biological legitimacy on Chomsky's innatism. Rather, it will increasingly call into question that kind of 'elementary logical analysis' (an unfortunate heritage from Port-Royal) which charac-terizes the so-called deep structures in Chomsky's theory.[156] And

---

[155] 'Linguistics and Politics – Interview with Noam Chomsky', pp. 32, 33–4.
[156] With regard to Chomsky's distinction between deep and surface structures, reservations have been expressed even by the Chomskyan M. Wandruszka, 'Der Ertrag des Strukturalismus', cit., p. 107, who prefers to talk about *Erlebnis-*

it will restore to sense data, to the individual's reactions to pleasure and pain, and to stimuli from the natural and social environment that primacy which Chomsky would deny them in favour of a logical and linguistic *a priori*.

The kind of modernizing of Chomsky's theory which will have most success, however, will not entail the biologizing of innatism. Rather, it will be the tendency to set aside innatism as well as the more strictly technical side to transformational grammar, and to confine Chomsky's value to his espousal of the *creative* side of linguistic activity. In this way, Chomskyism will rid itself both of the metaphysical naïvetés which make it unacceptable to European intellectuals and of the logical and mathematical complexities which make it too difficult for them. Then, without too much effort, one will be able to reincorporate language into the realm of that 'praxis' which encompasses everything.

Naturally, within this general tendency there can be and are many nuances. There is an anti-structuralism which takes to task not just the structuralist conception of science but *all science*, accusing it of being nothing more than false bourgeois objectivity. These are positions which have demonstrated only too often their inability to provide a theory of the proletarian revolution. If anti-structuralism were to mean simply a 'return to Frankfurt' (or even a return to 'revolutionary' developments stemming from the Frankfurt matrix), not very much would be gained. Even Sartre, who cannot be identified in any way with these positions, and who has had the virtue of opposing the structuralist fashion and raising extremely valid objections to Lévi-Strauss, is too anti-materialist, too imbued with existentialist activism to be able to represent a genuine alternative to Lévi-Strauss and Althusser.[157]

In addition, there is a great proliferation of 'de-objectifying' interpretations of structuralism, many of which are easily satisfied indeed. If Lévi-Strauss's theory has been defined as 'Kantianism without a transcendental subject', then the idea can readily take hold that everything can be settled with a return to a Kantianism

---

*und Denkstruktur* (experiential-thought structure) and *Werkzeugstruktur* (instrumental structure).

[157] This has been rightly pointed out by J.-M. Domenach in *Esprit,* May 1967, pp. 771, 774, and by Sève, op. cit., at the beginning of the final chapter. This does not detract from the fact that certain of the objections contained in Sartre's reply to Lévi-Strauss (in *L'Arc*, xxx, pp. 87ff.) are perfectly valid.

with a transcendental subject, more or less imbued with empirio-pragmatism. In point of fact, several scholars ask of Lévi-Strauss only that he deny ontological reality to the structures and make them into structures of *our* thought which we construct – structures which are not objective but inter-subjective, not stationary but dynamic (this latter feature concerns also Chomsky's innate ideas).[158]

This type of reform of structuralism is to be found to some extent also in Jean Piaget. On the one hand, it is undeniable that his expertise in matters of biology and his well-known studies on the sensorial and mental development of the child suggest to him materialist objections against structuralism. He notes, for example, that Lévi-Strauss's atemporal Reason is incompatible with the evolution of animal species.[159] On the other hand, however, these same studies on child psychology lead him to transform the process whereby the child acquires 'consciousness' of reality into a process of the 'construction' of reality itself. The dynamism of structures which he espouses does not have to do with their objective histo-ricity, but rather with our 'making' of them. Of course, the objec-tivity of the external world is never radically denied by Piaget, but tends instead to be reduced to an orderless given, to shapeless matter. For him, the great dilemma is the choice between a predetermina-tion of structures in a Platonist sense (Lévi-Strauss) and a 'construc-tivism', with everything of a semi-idealist nature which this concept implies. Once again, materialism is either absent or too timidly asserted.

The philosophy which has the greatest chance for success in this contest to recoup the legacy of structuralism is phenomenology; Epistémon was right in predicting this in the essay cited above. Furthermore, the likely success of phenomenology has been pre-pared through a debate with structuralism which has been going on for a number of years.[160] In comparison with the forms of

[158] Moving in this direction, with differing emphases, are the critiques of Umberto Eco, *La struttura assente*, Milan 1968, and Paolo Ramat, *Problemi*, xiv (March–April 1969).

[159] *Structuralism*, pp. 118–9, 141.

[160] One need only think of Husserl's concept of 'meaningful intentionality' and the elaborations of it formulated by Maurice Merleau-Ponty, especially in *Signs*, Evanston 1964. See also P. Ricoeur in *Esprit*, May 1967, pp. 801ff. and particularly 809ff.; Epistémon, op. cit., pp. 27ff.; Enzo Paci, 'Nota su de Saussure', in *Catalogo generale 1958–1965* of the publishing house *Il Saggiatore*, Milan 1965, pp. lxixff.; Paci, 'Antropologia strutturale e fenomenologia', *Aut-Aut*, lxxxviii (July 1965), pp. 42ff.

'naïve idealism' which we are familiar with in Italy, phenomenology has the tactical advantage of representing what might be
called a 'cunning idealism' – not in the sense, obviously, of a
commonplace subjective cunning (no one could ever call into
question the tormented sincerity and exasperated self-critical spirit
of thinkers like Husserl or Merleau-Ponty), but in the sense that
the phenomenologists oppose materialism not with an out-and-out
repudiation of it (which is by now untenable) but with an elastic
defence against it. They appear to concede a great deal to it, only
later to backtrack and to remetaphysize everything, making the
materialist vision of the world and of man appear as a dead sediment
which must be 'reactivated' through a magical philosophical
operation. Thus, it is quite likely that the calls for a reassessment of
creativity and subjective praxis which have been provoked by the
structuralists' theological objectivism – both as a natural reaction
and, even more, in response to the new political climate of these past
few years – will at least initially be channelled in the direction of
phenomenology.

From the materialist standpoint which this book seeks to uphold,
the alternative between empirio-pragmatism and Platonism must,
obviously, be rejected *in toto*. The reabsorption of experienced
reality into the experiential activity of man is no more acceptable
than the dichotomy between a 'vulgar' reality, accessible to everyday experience, and an ideal reality, which today is deemed accessible to mathematics, tomorrow will be deemed accessible only to
art, and after that perhaps only to religion. One cannot accept the
antithesis between a synchrony conceived as a closed system (when
not even language corresponds to this model) and a diachrony
conceived as the realm of discontinuity; but neither can one accept
any attempt to overcome this antithesis by conceiving diachrony
in teleological terms. Biological evolutionism offers us a model of
development which is *neither orderless nor teleological,* and which
has no need for any 'hidden Reason' in order to account for things.
The historical materialism of Marx and Engels offers us another
model, capable of explaining what there is that is new in mankind's
development since man began to work and live socially. In this
model finalism is given its part – not in the sense of a mythological
'free will', but in the sense of a capacity to distinguish among means
and ends and to make conscious plans. At the same time, however,
great emphasis is given to the large part played in human history

by unconscious occurrences, constraints, and everything which justifies us in calling 'pre-historical' the epoch of class societies. The evolution of language is at a halfway point between biological evolution and the evolution of human 'institutions', because of the major role played in it by non-finalistic and unconscious changes; therefore, the 'Prague' teleological schema, which once again presupposes a hidden Reason, is not applicable to linguistic evolution. The distinction and at the same time fusion of these two types of development is the task of a historical materialism which also encompasses the study of nature and attempts to overcome the antithesis between history and science. This implies an attack, not on the scientific achievements of this century, but on the ideological use to which they have been put by contemporary philosophies of science, including structuralism; it further implies an attack on the recurrent anti-scientific temptations of voluntarism, whether of a 'Frankfurt' or phenomenological stamp.

\*       \*       \*

In the Marxist camp, however, the reaction against structuralism has not been limited to the revival of Adornian-Marcusian or Husserlian themes. There has also been a different position taken up by Lucien Sève, which is of particular interest precisely because of its two-fold attack on structuralist and on voluntarist Marxism.[161]

The seriousness with which Sève confronts this undertaking should not lead us to overlook certain negative features: an extraordinary prolixity (in *Marxisme et théorie de la personnalité* one finds the same things repeated dozens of times); and a defence of orthodoxy connected with Sève's political alignment within the PCF. Nevertheless, a hasty negative reaction on the part of the extreme left would, in my opinion, be mistaken. The defence of orthodoxy, although clearly incapable of resolving the problems of the communist revolution in advanced capitalist countries or of understanding the new developments introduced by Maoism, has, however, a positive side on the level of *interpretation* of the classics. It represents a necessary insistence on calling a halt to falsificatory 'symptomatic readings'; on reading in Marx, Engels, Lenin and Mao what they have actually written; and on presenting new developments, divergences, and even attempts to found new

---

[161] See Sève's works cited in notes 5 and 109 above.

non-Marxist revolutionary theories, as what they actually are, instead of disguising them as interpretations or 'discoveries of the real Marx'. When Godelier begins his exposition of a Marxism in which there is practically nothing Marxist left with a statement that 'the traditional exegeses of Marx are falling before our eyes, and from their ruins will arise a Marx largely unknown to Marxists and capable of providing unexpected and fruitful elements necessary to the most advanced scientific reflections', Sève is perfectly right to remind him that an objective reading is imperative. The same criticism applies, as we have said, to Althusser and to the Frankfurt and phenomenological Marxists. Sève's polemics against Althusser, against Sartre, against Garaudy and against hasty syntheses of Marxism and psychoanalysis are, therefore, accurate and compelling.[162] He is also quite correct in what he says about the *Economic and Philosophical Manuscripts*: about their unquestionable difference from the mature Marx and the reasons for their persistent vitality even for those who adhere to the point of view of the mature Marx.[163]

But there is not just this interpretative honesty in Sève. His intellectual formation was strongly marked by the influence of Georges Politzer, who, in his tormented path from psychoanalysis to Marxism, laid great emphasis on the need for a 'concrete' psychology. Such an emphasis involved a considerable risk of rejecting every attempt at scientific generalization as abstract and of reducing psychological science to the study of a series of 'individual dramas'; but it also involved a powerful reminder of the need to construct a materialist theory of the person, with a re-emergence of hedonistic motifs (the desire for *happiness*) too long neglected in the Marxist camp. This is the undertaking, barely outlined by Politzer before his death in the struggle against Nazism brought a premature halt to his activity, which has now been resumed by Sève.

In all likelihood, this undertaking has not been brought to a close even with the present book, which Sève himself presents as a phase in a work in progress. But the progress that has been made is unquestionably considerable. Sève is quite right to state forcefully that a Marxist science of man cannot base itself solely on the require-

---

[162] *Marxisme et théorie de la personnalité*, pp. 206, 326ff., 340 (note 3), 376ff., and all of the final chapter; cf. the debate with Godelier, cited above.

[163] *Marxisme et théorie de la personnalité*, pp. 82ff., 190ff.

ment of 'generalization', overlooking the individual (not as a spiritual 'person', but as that particular nexus of social relationships which is different from all the others). This is a requirement to which I have attempted to call attention in an earlier essay in this volume, independently of Sève and starting off from somewhat different premises. But in Sève's book this subject is developed much more fully. Furthermore, even though he regards the sixth thesis on Feuerbach ('the human essence is the aggregate [*Ensemble*] of social relationships') as the basis of a Marxist psychology, Sève does not disregard the fact that a theory of the person cannot overlook the biologically conditioned component in every individual: 'Social individuality itself develops within *biological individuals*, who, as such, are not at all the product of the social base and its contradictions, but rather are an altogether distinct reality.'[164] He is also quite clear in recognizing that between the needs of the individual and those of society there is a discontinuity constituted 'by the very fact of individuality', which implies 'a limitation constituted by the human life span and the eventual death of each individual, a fundamental fact which stands in opposition to the perennity of the social world as a result of the continuous, imperceptible succession of generations. . . . Here is an inexhaustible source of disharmony between individual psychology and social conditions, as well as a source of the unequal importance given to objective data – what counts most from the standpoint of the social formation is at times quite secondary from the standpoint of the person, and vice versa.'[165] As one can see, here we are very close to a recognition of those 'Leopardian' motifs which Marxism, in our opinion, cannot overlook, and which we have attempted to bring out in this book and other, previous works.

On the other hand, however, it is precisely on the question of the relationship between biological man and social man that there is a vacillation in Sève's book; this stems from the fact that in him too, just as in every western Marxist of our period, the anti-biological phobia is excessive and ends by compromising his materialism. Sève takes pains to emphasize that historically man had a biological 'point of departure', but that this original base has since been overcome and reabsorbed by the new social base. 'The natural point

---

[164] Ibid., p. 200.
[165] Ibid., p. 321.

of departure . . . is something altogether different from the real base of the developed totality, since the process of forming the totality consists precisely in a reversal of the relationship between the "natural" and the "social", a gradual transformation of natural data into historical results. In the developed individual even the physical organism has become largely the *product* of the person.'[166] This statement is generally correct, provided one bears in mind that such a generalization does not extend to certain givens of the human condition which are *still* very important and whose disappearance is still not foreseeable (the same ones, for example, which Sève referred to in a passage cited above). The 'reversal' which Sève talks about is only a partial one, therefore, and it has taken place to a quite unequal degree in the various fields of human life and activity, as we attempted to show in the first two essays of this book.

In order to avoid the suspicion that he regards man's biological constitution in any way as a base underlying the socio-economic base, Sève has recourse to a peculiar metaphor. Individuals, he says, 'are in a certain sense fitted in sideways' into the socio-economic base; and he suggests the term *juxtastructure* to designate this relationship. In a relationship of this kind, 'by definition one of the two structures is entirely subordinated to the other, even though its foundation has an independent existence and origin'. The relationship between structure and *juxtastructure* is reciprocal, but 'it follows a guided circular course: one of the two structures is always the determining structure in the final analysis'.[167] Thus, we lose again that awareness which we seemed to have acquired of the conditioning power which nature still exercises over man. The fact that Sève ends by saying about the *juxtastructure* what Engels says, in well-known passages, about the superstructure, indicates that the new term he has introduced does not help to clarify matters.

The extreme defensiveness with respect to biologism can be seen in many other points of the book, for instance in the criticisms directed against psychoanalysis (accused once again *only* of a lack of interest in social reality, and not also of a lack of materialism) and against Lévi-Strauss. Sève is quite correct in his remark that

[166] Ibid., pp. 266ff.
[167] Ibid., p. 200.

Lévi-Strauss's anthropology 'is characterized by a great lacuna: social labour and, therefore, the relations of production – i.e. what is essential to Marxism'. But he is not so correct, for the reasons stated above, when he accuses Lévi-Strauss of biologism, concluding that 'in the human sciences biologism is always the companion of idealism'.[168] In reality, despite an occasional fleeting and inessential allusion to the 'climate' and the 'geographic environment', only one of the two 'companions' is alive and present in Lévi-Strauss – as with all bourgeois thought of the twentieth century. To apply the over-used schema of 'opposing extremisms which merge with one another' to the critique of contemporary bourgeois ideologies leads to a fabrication of non-existent vulgar-materialist positions as a counterweight to an existent and dominant spiritualism, which is the real opponent today.

I do not think it is very useful to make Byzantine distinctions with regard to the 'sideways' or 'underlying' position of the biological in relation to the social. The point to be borne in mind is the following: with the beginning of work, a new level of human life emerged and acquired ever greater importance, becoming relatively autonomous from the animal base; this new level (and not the biological level) has a decisive effect on the development of everything encompassed by the term of superstructure, and therefore deserves *in this sense* the name of structure or base. The term 'biologism' (in its pejorative meaning) should be used to designate any theory which, denying or underestimating this function of the socio-economic structure, claims to explain in biological terms the division of society into classes, the class struggle, war, institutions, and culture as a whole. But can it be said that man merely had an animal *origin,* but is no longer an animal? Whoever replies in the affirmative to this question runs up against certain obstinate facts which are undeniable and can only be evaded with an old arsenal of sophistical arguments borrowed from idealism. Whoever replies in the negative is not a 'biologist' but simply a materialist, and is unquestionably closer than the first respondent to the mature thought of Marx and Engels. Nonetheless, even the second position, when fully developed (especially with regard to the obstacles to man's happiness created by the persistence of biological man within social man), is

[168] Ibid. pp. 487ff.

not completely consistent with 'Marxist orthodoxy': no more than any of the currents of contemporary Marxism. Consequently we must, in my opinion, reconsider an entire tradition of hedonist-materialist thought which culminates in Leopardi.

Returning for a moment to Sève, I believe that another short-coming in his book lies in its inadequate analysis of the various social and cultural sub-groups which contribute (within the general framework of one's class affiliation) to the shaping of one's indivi-dual person. Each of us belongs to a class, but also to a particular section or stratum of it. Each of us belongs to a family, i.e. to a micro-social entity which often presents major discontinuities with respect to society's general degree of development. Each of us lives in a society in which the classes stand opposed to one another but also influence one another and have periods of partial 'collabora-tion' in which one exercises hegemony over the other. Through the medium of culture, each of us (even without being specifically an intellectual) undergoes influences which come from afar both temporally and spatially. Each of us can become a part of a class different from his or her origins (either as a result of an actual change in socio-economic status or through a transfer of allegiance dictated by 'ideal' considerations), without for that matter ever being able to erase the traces of the past. Each of us under the influence of mystifying ideologies, can feel a national, religious or racial solidarity which overlays class solidarity. The list could be con-tinued. A Marxist theory of the person must confront this entire complex of problems to a greater degree than Sève does, and must attempt at least to sketch the general outlines of a materialist ethics. Sève's book, despite all his aversion for pure psychology, apolitical psychology, is still to too great a degree the book of a psychologist. Besides its under-estimation of the question of the man-nature relationship, it suffers from an inadequate articulation of the concept of 'society'. It remains, however, an important book for the reasons which we have summarized.

What kind of critique from the left will a work like Sève's provoke? An example can be found in the essay by Tony Andreani, 'Marxisme et anthropologie'.[169] Despite the author's lively intel-ligence and sense of the complexity and dramatic nature of the

---

[169] Tony Andreani, 'Marxisme et anthropologie', *L'homme et la société*, xv (January–March 1970), pp. 27–75.

problems involved, it does not appear to me an altogether encouraging example. Andreani is persuasive in the closing pages of
the essay when he argues, if only cursorily, against Sève's anti-
Chinese and anti-Castroist prejudices. It is both interesting and
correct to demand that priority be given to the question of 'needs'
as an impetus to the class struggle and the transformation of
society.[170] It is correct to point out that Althusser's closed theoretical
system becomes translated, on the level of practice, into a form of
*attentisme*.[171] But all of this will fail to lead anywhere as long as
Andreani adheres to that rigidly anti-experimental conception of
science which represents one of the worst legacies of structuralism,
and which can only have the effect of increasing the split between
revolutionary activism and a metaphysical science open only to a
circle of the initiated. However filled he may be with a healthy
rebelliousness towards certain *maestri*, Andreani has religiously
inherited from them one particular teaching: that science must as
far as possible seek 'that which is hidden' – with all the Platonist
and Freudian-Platonist misunderstandings connected with this
conception and with all the anti-materialist consequences to which
it leads. The main objection which he raises against Sève is that his
psychological categories 'remain at the level of the visible and,
essentially, at the level of lived experience'. Sève 'does not go
beyond a surface description'; his analysis 'does not lead to intuitive
categories'; his psychology 'is not erroneous, but remains at the
phenomenal level'; and so on and so forth. But this is not enough;
even Lévi-Strauss, despite his love for hidden Reason, still remains
too attached to the surface for Andreani – better Foucault and
Lacan.[172] Science is no longer a search for truth which, to this end,
makes use of abstraction and a detachment from sense appearance.
It is a flight from the sensory as an end in itself and a descent into
Mithraic mysteries. For reasons we have stated repeatedly, we do
not feel inclined to associate ourselves with such speleological
undertakings.

It is hardly necessary to say that the accusation of empiricism
made against Sève and more or less everybody else is followed up
by accusations of biologism and 'mechanism'.[173] Even though Sève

[170] Ibid., pp. 40–41 and *passim*.
[171] Ibid., pp. 40ff., 72ff.
[172] Ibid., pp. 39, 43.
[173] Ibid., pp. 37, 51, 53.

is excessively concerned, as we have seen, with subordinating the biological to the social, this does not spare him the usual harangue from Andreani about the inseparability of the biological from the social: 'What could the social and the biological ever be in their pure state? . . . The social is always present, inserted within the biological, which itself is also a relationship between the organism and its environment.'[174] We are still dealing here with the typical scholasticism of the professor or student of philosophy who, in any discussion involving a relationship between A and B, is capable – even though he may know nothing about either A or B – of 'objecting' that A and B cannot be considered separately from one another. And although an 'objection' of this kind (which at most is useful as a *general warning* to avoid rigidifying distinctions) does not carry the discussion further in the slightest, there are always those who find it very perceptive.

Even the question of 'needs', which, to Andreani's credit, is taken into consideration and could lead to a new synthesis of materialism and hedonism, ends with one more attempt at a Freudian Marxism, not much more convincing than those which Andreani himself rejects. In his concept of a 'system of libidinal propulsions' all distinction between structure and superstructure is lost. Andreani falls into the illusion of those who believe that the eradication of this distinction (rather than a more precise articulation of it) would serve to restore a revolutionary impetus to Marxism.

It appears, therefore, that post-structuralism – with only a few partial exceptions – is destined for the time being to remain in that closed circle of various alternating forms of idealism in which, for a number of decades now, western culture has been revolving and from which only a new socio-political situation can release it.

[174] Ibid., pp. 33–4.

# 5

# Karl Korsch and Lenin's Philosophy

In 1938 Anton Pannekoek published in Amsterdam a mimeographed essay, *Lenin als Philosoph,* under the pseudonym of J. Harper, in which he passed judgement on the Lenin of *Materialism and Empirio-Criticism.* Karl Korsch wrote a long review of it in English, signed with the initials l.h.¹ and entitled 'Lenin's Philosophy', which expressed similar views in still harsher terms. Pannekoek, together with Herman Gorter and Henriette Roland-Holst, had been among the most combative and intelligent of the Dutch 'ultra-leftists'. Lenin had written *'Left-Wing' Communism, An Infantile Disorder* (1920) in large part (although not entirely) as a polemic against them. Lenin's book is certainly filled with that 'impassioned sarcasm' (the phrase is Gramsci's) which characterizes all of Lenin's polemical writings. But this is a sarcasm accompanied by a deep feeling of sympathy (seen in the title itself) and by an awareness that there was only one enemy within the worker's move-

---

¹ He wrote this for a Chicago journal *Living Marxism* (November 1938, pp. 138–44), edited by the German Spartacist Paul Mattick. Over the years Korsch and Mattick found themselves together as exiles in the United States, and *Living Marxism,* which later became *New Essays,* carried many articles and reviews by Korsch between 1938 and 1943. Mattick, who is still alive (his activities in the German workers' movement began in his early youth), has increased his activities as a theorist and writer in recent years. The new edition of Pannekoek's essay, which also contains Korsch's article translated into German, has a preface by Mattick: Anton Pannekoek, *Lenin als Philosoph,* Frankfurt 1969 (English translation, *Lenin as Philosopher,* New York 1948, new edition London 1975). Mattick's preface first appeared in *New Politics* (New York), Winter 1962, pp. 107–14. Mattick's preface – though, like almost all his writings, very interesting in other respects – is inspired by an anti-Leninism which seems to me aberrant. But it goes without saying that such ideas should be discussed, and not excommunicated in a Stalinistic manner. For Korsch's collaboration with the journals edited by Mattick, see the bibliography appended to the Italian edition of *Marxism and Philosophy* (Milan 1966, pp. 188–90).

ment, social-democratic opportunism. Thus the extremists were not 'rightists parading as leftists' (as was later and still is claimed by official post-Leninist Communism), but bona fide comrades who had committed certain errors in their way of organizing the struggle against the bourgeoisie.

The immediate reasons for the dispute had been the Dutch refusal to engage in political activity within the unions and their support for parliamentary abstentionism. But the controversy was based on a much more important and serious question: Was the Bolshevik path to revolution valid also for the countries of Western Europe, or was it only a *Russian* path, suited to a semi-Asiatic country with limited industrial development? Was there a need in the West too for a strategy of class alliances, even if on significantly different terms (the study of these differences and similarities played a major part in Gramsci's thought)? Or alternatively, was the working class in the West faced with an absolutely compact opponent which could not be broken down into its different parts? Pannekoek and Gorter favoured the second option. The consequence was a political vision which was both exalting and despairing; exalting because the revolution could be carried out by the working class in order to realize socialism, without any intermediary 'democratic' stages and without any delegation of powers by the masses to their leaders; despairing because the 'ultra-leftists' had an acute and basically pessimistic awareness not only of the isolation of the working class (the phrase, 'the working class is alone', recurs throughout Gorter's reply to Lenin's *'Left-Wing' Communism*), but also of its social-democratization, against which they could only recommend efforts at propagandizing and condemnation from the outside.[2]

Almost twenty years after those events, Pannekoek's critique of Lenin the philosopher (i.e. Lenin's *Materialism and Empirio-Criticism*, published in 1909 but translated and disseminated in the West only in 1927) was a faithful reproduction of the critique he

[2] Cf. Herman Gorter, *Riposta all'Estremismo di Lenin*, Rome 1970. The original German text can be found in A. Pannekoek and H. Gorter, *Organisation und Taktik der proletarischen Revolution*, ed. H. M. Bock, Frankfurt 1969. In the Italian volume are published also the counter-replies of Trotsky (who was quick to point out the pessimism present in Gorter and Pannekoek's position) and of Bela Kun. With regard to this entire controversy I shall make only passing references, since the 1920 debate on extremism represents simply a prelude to the subject matter discussed in this article.

had made of Lenin the revolutionary strategist. *Materialism and Empirio-Criticism* is not a book of Marxist philosophy, according to Pannekoek; rather, it represents a radical-bourgeois philosophy, just as the Bolshevik Revolution was nothing more than a 'Jacobin' revolution. The proletariat of Western Europe basically had nothing to learn from either Leninist theory or Leninist practice. Pannekoek saw in Stalinism and the developments in the Third International after Lenin not a degeneration of Leninism but a coherent continuation of it, interpreted as a form of bourgeois radicalism.

Korsch came from political experiences similar to those of Pannekoek. He too was one of the great defeated men of revolutionary 'Western Marxism'. He had become aware of his own anti-Leninism a few years later than Pannekoek and Gorter; but once he had become aware of it he developed into an even stronger anti-Leninist, in part because his philosophical background was much more decidedly idealist than that of Pannekoek. Thus, the article of 1938 shows us a Korsch who, although in fundamental agreement with Pannekoek's book, still finds it insufficiently critical in relation to Lenin the philosopher. As Rusconi has written, the article represents the 'final unpolished document of Korsch's rejection of Leninism'.[3]

The year in which the article was written is the same one in which the English edition of *Karl Marx* appeared – a work of the mature Korsch and one to which he was to return ten years later to make revisions and additions. Among Italian students of Korsch, Giuseppe Bedeschi has stressed particularly the distance separating the early *Marxism and Philosophy*, still heavily imbued with idealist activism and an aversion for the natural sciences (going so far as to suggest that a shadow of 'scientistic' and social-democratic involution lay over *Capital*), from *Karl Marx*, in which Korsch

[3] Cf. G. E. Rusconi's introduction to the Italian edition of Korsch's *Il materialismo storico (Anti-Kautsky)*, Bari 1971, p. lxi. (The original German title is *Die materialistische Geschichtsauffassung*, originally published 1929, new edition Frankfurt 1971). Rusconi's introduction, beginning with its title of 'Contro Kautsky, contro Lenin', is a very good characterization of Korsch's position. See also Rusconi's book, *La teoria critica della società*, Bologna 1968, pp. 99ff., 189ff. The critical remarks which Rusconi addresses to Korsch's anti-Leninism concern the oversimplification found in the latter's political argument, and therefore its utopian character. Not enough attention is given, however, to a critique of Korsch's anti-materialism, which is closely connected with his utopianism. Cf. also below, note 10.

allegedly overcame his anti-materialism and attained a full understanding of Marxism as science.[4] Giuseppe Vacca, on the other
hand, has insisted on the fundamental continuity in Korsch's
thought; he arrives, however, at a generally positive assessment
of it, and attempts to differentiate it from the early Lukacs (despite
the obvious similarities and the explicit statement of Korsch
himself).[5] We find, however, that the 1938 article, with its
exasperated anti-materialism (in addition to the anti-Leninism),
takes us right back, despite its date, to the Korsch of *Marxism and
Philosophy* or, even more, to his *Anti-Kautsky* (1929) and *Anti-
Critique* (1930) – which he used as an introduction to the second
edition of *Marxismus und Philosophie*.[6] It seems to me, therefore,

---

[4] *Karl Marx*, London 1938, revised edition New York 1963. *Marxism und
Philosophie*, Leipzig 1923, English translation *Marxism and Philosophy*, NLB
1970.

[5] Cf. G. Bedeschi's introduction to the Italian edition of Korsch's *Karl Marx*,
Bari 1969; Giuseppe Vacca, *Lukács o Korsch?*, Bari 1969; in opposition to the
latter, see C. Pasquinelli, 'Né Lukács né Korsch', *Critica marxista* (1970), No. 4,
pp. 178ff. With regard to the early Korsch's hostility towards the natural sciences
and the way in which certain strains of this 'obscurantist Marxism' were developed
by the Frankfurt School, see especially Lucio Colletti, 'Marxismo e filosofia'
in *Problemi del socialismo* (September–October 1966), pp. 776ff. An overall
interpretation similar to that of Bedeschi is given by L. Ceppa, 'Lo sviluppo del
pensiero di Karl Korsch', *Rivista di filosofia*, LX (1969), pp. 341ff. In Ceppa's
article there are also some interesting remarks about the influence which American
philosophic-scientific culture had on Korsch.

See also Ceppa's long essay, 'La concezione del marxismo in Karl Korsch',
in *Storia del marxismo contemporaneo*, pp. 1239ff. A striking, but also isolated
and non-generalizable, indication of the political and ideological shift of ground
which Korsch underwent at least for a period of time while in the United
States is represented by his 1939 piece on American science, published in
*Alternative*, No. 41 (April 1965), pp. 76ff. One should bear in mind, however,
that this is a passage from a private letter which Korsch never published and
which was printed only after his death. The interview with Hedda Korsch on
her husband, published in *New Left Review*, No. 76 (November–December
1972), pp. 35ff., is particularly interesting with regard to Korsch's early cultural
background and his last years spent in the United States; it is obvious that the
interview should be regarded and evaluated as the statement of someone who
shared the dramatic and sorrowful experiences of Korsch, and not as a critical
assessment of his thought. The interview makes no explicit reference to Korsch's
anti-Leninism. He is presented simply as a critic of Stalinism and post-Stalinism,
and as someone who recognized the need to revitalize Marxism so that it would
not lag behind the development of capitalism and bourgeois science. As is
obvious, debate on this question still goes on – not, however, on the question of
the need for such revitalization (a need profoundly felt also by Lenin), but on
the question of how to orient and concretize it.

[6] For the *Anti-Kautsky*, see above, note 3. The *Anti-Critique* can be found in
*Marxism and Philosophy*, op. cit., pp. 89–126.

that the question of the continuity or discontinuity in Korsch's thought should be formulated somewhat differently from the way it is by Vacca and Bedeschi. On the one hand, there is a Korsch who is more debatable and, in my opinion, more unacceptable on a theoretical level; that same Korsch is, however, more vibrant and authentic, for he remains clearly 'dated' in that he is linked to that phase of revolutionary radicalism (with its Luxemburgian matrix, but with an exasperation of idealist and voluntarist themes which, at least in that form, are not to be found in Luxemburg) which had been at the centre of his experience in post-war Germany and which had been decimated by the failure of revolution in the West and by the elevation of Stalinist dogmatism into the official ideology of the Third International.[7] On the other hand, there is a Korsch who, though more 'mature' in some respects, is in reality only more bland, and who is represented by *Karl Marx*. The 1938 article shows clearly enough that there is no chronological development from the one Korsch to the other; rather, there is a difference in 'literary genre' and in the audiences to which the various writings were addressed. *Karl Marx* is predominantly an expository work, even though it is of a high level; and so it is natural that many controversial points are glossed over.[8] But Korsch never ceased to be decidedly anti-materialist. And if he appears in *Karl Marx* to have come to a reconciliation with science and to acknowledge a certain analogy between the method of Marxist social science and the method of the natural sciences, it is only because he is thinking of the anti-materialist epistemology which has become predomi-

[7] The era of 'Stalinist dogmatism' (and of the bureaucratic power which was the basis of that dogmatism) begins in many respects immediately after Lenin's death, and even in the final months of Lenin's life. On the fact that Lenin was well aware of the danger, one need only cite the short work by Moshé Lewin, *Lenin's Last Struggle,* New York 1968. Zinoviev himself, before he became a victim of Stalinism, was one of its forerunners, and it is to him, as Secretary of the Third International, that we owe the official condemnation of *Marxism and Philosophy* and *History and Class Consciousness*. This condemnation was generally correct in its content; but the procedure adopted was already 'Stalinist' – pronouncing an official excommunication to stifle debate.

[8] Rusconi is right when he remarks that *Karl Marx* and the various reformulations contained in it remained essentially a work for 'the uninitiated', that it did not correspond 'to the formulations the author was developing in his own private itinerary', and that these new formulations represented not just a break with Leninism alone but also a greater detachment from Marxism in general; see his introduction to Korsch, *Dialettica e scienza nel materialismo,* Bari 1974, p. viii.

nant in the twentieth century. A fuller study of the late Korsch's interest in logical neo-positivism – an interest which the cultural milieu in the United States certainly helped to foster – would enable us to understand better and to reassess from a Marxist standpoint his favourable attitude towards a science which is very different from the one the early Korsch had opposed. The 1938 article itself contains a long paragraph which argues against a polemic waged by an English Marxist (M. Black), in that same year, against Carnap; to Korsch this polemic appeared, though much more 'refined' than the one Lenin had waged in his time against the empirio-criticists, still to contain 'the same old Leninist fallacy'.[9]

\*　　\*　　\*

We find clearly in Korsch a theory which he never modified (despite a few belated and very ambiguous and isolated expressions of esteem for Lenin's 'anti-dogmatism', accompanied, alas, by esteem also for that of Sorel[10]), and which today has again become

[9] Korsch, 'Lenin's Philosophy', *Living Marxism*, IV (November 1938), p. 143.
[10] Cf. Rusconi, op. cit., p. xxviii. To a greater degree than in his previous writings, Rusconi in this essay analyses with a great deal of subtlety the unresolved ambivalences and tensions in Korsch's thought. No doubt, in comparison with Rusconi's work, my essay must appear to give a somewhat schematized picture of Korsch's personality. Nonetheless, I do not entirely regret this schematism, both because it remains necessary to grasp the fundamental tendency – above and beyond all the commotion and waverings – of a writer's thought, and because the aim of the present essay is not a characterization of Korsch's theory and political action in all of its tortured developments but a discussion of the relationship between 'Western Marxism' and Leninism. In any case, it seems to me hard to deny (and here I disagree with Rusconi, ibid., p. xxix, n. 13) that anti-materialism remains a constant throughout Korsch's thought, although Rusconi is right to point out that anti-materialism for Korsch, as with many philosophers and epistemologists of our century, does not mean opposition to science. As Rusconi notes, Korsch's rejection of Leninism does not stem from simply gnoseological interests, but also from a retrospective reflection on Leninist 'Jacobinism' and on the worker-council experience (which still remains, with all its limitations, Korsch's greatest merit in the history of the workers' movement). However, it was precisely in this interpretation of Leninism as bourgeois radicalism that we find the weakest point in Korsch's thought, as I shall attempt to show below. It is interesting to note that Brecht, as he began to develop an overall judgement of Lenin clearly different from that of his 'master of Marxism', developed a different position also with regard to the specific question of Jacobinism. Cf. Brecht, *Me-Ti: Buch der Wendungen*, p. 19: 'The master Sa taught: Liberation comes like the eruption of a volcano. The master Lan-Kü taught: Liberation is achieved through a surprise attack (*Uberfall*). Mi-en-leh taught: Both elements are necessary – something that erupts and something that attacks.' That Sa and Mi-en-leh are the 'Chinese' disguises of, respectively, Rosa Luxemburg and

fashionable. According to this theory, not only is Stalinism the necessary offspring of Leninism, but Leninism in turn is alleged to have its roots and substance in Kautskyism and behind Kautsky's misrepresentation of Marxism there allegedly lie those great misunderstandings of Engels. The only point in all this which Korsch appears to have revised is the extension of this '*ex post facto* trial' back to the Marx of *Capital*. But the fundamental antithesis which Korsch thought he detected in twentieth-century Marxism, the one which he stressed again and again, was the following: on the one hand, a basic common ground shared by Social Democracy and Leninism (however unconscious it may have been) extending to the extreme but self-consistent form of the Stalinist degeneration; on the other hand, a revolutionary and anti-dogmatic Marxism which found its theoretical expression in the works of Korsch himself and in *History and Class Consciousness*, and which was suppressed both by the post-Leninist Bolsheviks and by the Social-Democrats.

This is an antithesis which is perfectly intelligible in historical terms. It goes back to the tragic fate of revolutionary Western Marxism, which did indeed suffer expulsion at the hands of both Social Democracy and a 'Leninism' which, on the very morrow of Lenin's death, was rapidly moving towards dogmatization and the subordination of world Communist strategy to the interests of the Russian state. Nevertheless, it is an antithesis which is objectively false, which does not begin to do justice either to Lenin the political strategist or to Lenin the philosopher.

In 'Lenin's Philosophy', the strong language used by Korsch in criticizing *Materialism and Empirio-Criticism* indicates how he saw Lenin's book of 1908, in a certain sense, as the basic cause of the lack of understanding and the condemnation which befell *Marxism and Philosophy* during the twenties. He talks about 'a considerable amount of misinterpretation, misunderstanding, and general backwardness' in Lenin's book. While it is certainly superior to the pseudo-philosophies of fascism and nazism (a generous concession!), it is much inferior to the most advanced European thought, even that which had a bourgeois foundation. And he talks about Lenin's 'general unfairness' towards modern

---

Lenin is well-known. I do not know if it has been pointed out before that Lan-Kü is Blanqui.

science and his 'complete unawareness of the real achievements made since the days of Marx and Engels in the field of modern physical science'.[11]

This final accusation is perhaps even today the one most frequently repeated. As everyone knows, *Materialism and Empirio-Criticism* does indeed contain a number of inaccuracies with regard to particular physical theories. An accusation of this kind is, however, condemned to insignificance, since Lenin's book is not at all a defence of classical physics against more recent scientific achievements and the methodological changes they require. Rather, it is a critique and an unmasking of the *ideological use* (whether reactionary or reformist) made of these achievements and of the ensuing 'crisis of fundamentals' by bourgeois philosophy (often represented by the scientists themselves, who were great scientists but bad philosophers).[12] This point alone would be enough to distinguish Lenin from the subsequent Stalinist con-demnations of the theory of relativity or quantum mechanics or Mendelian–Morganian genetics. Not only is there not the slightest repudiation on Lenin's part of the 'new physics', but there is even a full awareness (akin to Engels's prior recognition) that the new physics makes it necessary to carry out an epistemological revision which 'is not only not "revisionism", in the accepted meaning of the term, but, on the contrary, is demanded by Marxism'.[13] As a consequence of the distinction and connection he makes between absolute truth and relative truth,[14] Lenin manages to redeem the historicity of science as well as its objective truth. Those who are frightened off by the term 'absolute truth' (conceived as a limiting concept), are forced to reduce science to ideology and lapse either into agnosticism or into the mysticism of an absolute Subject (and this kind of 'absolute' is indeed metaphysical).[15] Those who use the

[11] Korsch, 'Lenin's Philosophy', pp. 139, 141.

[12] Lenin never neglects to make this distinction. See, for example, *Materialism and Empirio-Criticism, Collected Works*, Vol. 14, Moscow 1962: 'Henri Poincaré is an eminent physicist but a poor philosopher' (p. 164); 'a very great chemist and very muddled philosopher, Wilhelm Ostwald' (p. 168 and cf. also p. 269).

[13] *Materialism and Empirio-Criticism*, p. 251.

[14] Ibid. pp. 122ff.

[15] With regard to Lenin's concept of absolute truth, see especially *Materialism and Empirio-Criticism*, p. 136. This point is elucidated very well by Eleonora Fiorani in *Che fare* (May 1972), pp. 122ff and especially pp. 127–8. The best overall account of Lenin's philosophy is given by Ludovico Geymonat, *Storia del pensiero filosofico e scientifico*, Milan 1972, Vol. VI, Chapter 4. Certain parts of

critical revision of the concept of matter as a basis for maintaining that matter *does not exist*, that thought is independent of the brain, and that the chronological priority of inanimate nature with respect to living beings (and of the more elementary living species with respect to man) must be either denied or 'interpreted' in a more or less sophisticated manner so that it can by rechanneled into idealism – such individuals are not 'up-to-date' scientists. Rather, they are the ideological extrapolators and mystifiers of scientific results.

With regard to those who accuse Lenin of lapsing into vulgar materialism, of not placing enough emphasis on the 'active side' of the knowing process, etc., replies from a variety of commentators have pointed out how Lenin himself openly acknowledges the *intended* one-sidedness of his book. Whereas Marx and Engels had had to focus particularly on what distinguished *their* materialism from the apolitical or reactionary forms of vulgar materialism which were relatively widespread throughout the bourgeois culture of their time, the situation was profoundly changed by the beginning of the twentieth century. By that time a neo-idealist movement was in full force and, although it was highly differentiated within its own ranks, it was unanimous in its anti-materialist bias. At the same time, there was an ongoing attempt to give an idealist interpretation of Marxism, focusing on a tendentious reading of the *Theses on Feuerbach* (a highly creative and stimulating text, but one not devoid of ambiguities, especially when considered apart from the then unknown *German Ideology* and from the subsequent evolution of Marx and Engels's thought) and representing Marx's philosophy as a kind of voluntaristic activism.

---

this and other chapters of the concluding volume to Geymonat's work were already anticipated by the above-cited number of *Che fare*. But the editorial committee of this journal should come to realize that it is not possible to adopt a position in 'political defence of Stalin' (p. 8) at the same time that one takes a critical position towards Stalin's cultural politics and the distortions of Leninism made by Stalin on the theoretical level (see Fiorani, op. cit., pp. 137ff.). The cultural degeneration which took place under Stalinism is too closely connected with the political degeneration. And even if one were to assume that it is possible to separate them, it would not make much difference to a Marxist if such a hypothetical Stalinist regime benignly permitted avant-garde cultural and artistic expression while at the same time the working class continued to be excluded from the actual exercise of power. This is a dilemma which sooner or later the various parties and groups defining themselves as Marxist-Leninist must resolve – even if, in so doing they have to break with certain positions of the Chinese Communist Party.

Hence, according to Lenin, the need to give particular emphasis to materialism, even to that element in materialism which is undeniably shared by both Marxism and bourgeois materialism.

This defence of the 'one-sidedness' of Lenin's book is correct. It runs the risk, however, of being interpreted in an altogether too reductionist fashion. For example, when Luciano Gruppi says that *Materialism and Empirio-Criticism* can be properly evaluated only if it is situated within the framework of the historical period and the political struggle in which and for which it was conceived', and when he contends that Lenin's notion of absolute truth represented a 'Platonic hypostatization of the concept of truth and a relapse into metaphysics',[16] he is conceding far too much to the anti-Leninists (or to those 'Leninists' who maintain that the true Lenin is found in his political action, which is conveniently free from the scholasticism which casts a shadow over his philosophic writings). Unquestionably, *Materialism and Empirio-Criticism* is *also* a response to the immediate needs of the struggle within the Russian worker's movement, which had been penetrated by empirio-criticism through Bogdanov and Lunacharsky with particularly deleterious political effects. But the book has another, primary polemical target which is much broader: i.e. the entire restoration of idealism at the end of the nineteenth and beginning of the twentieth centuries. This is a polemical target which even today, more than sixty years after the book's publication, is far from demolished; for today again we find ourselves in the midst of such flourishing partnerships as Marxism-neo-positivism, Marxism-pragmatism and Marxism-structuralism. And again today the common denominator of all these philosophical pastiches is anti-materialism. The 'historical period' which justifies that measure of one-sidedness which can be found in Lenin's work is, therefore, a *long historical period* already encompassing almost half of the twentieth century and with no sign that it has come to a close. Gruppi himself, with his attempt to equate materialist objective truth with Platonism and metaphysics, provides proof of the need to continue the materialist crusade undertaken by Lenin.[17]

[16] Luciano Gruppi, preface to the Italian edition of *Materialism and Empirio-Criticism*, Rome 1970, p. 9. Cf. the same author's *Il pensiero di Lenin*, Rome 1971, p. 122.

[17] Lenin has already identified and unmasked the sophism according to which, from an agnostic-subjectivist viewpoint, materialism is simply a form of metaphysics; cf. in particular *Materialism and Empirio-Criticism*, pp. 311, 347–50.

It should be added that Lenin saw with particular insight – and, in certain respects, foresaw – that empirio-criticism was only the first phase in an involution towards forms of 'fideist' spiritualism, which would lead from a methodological critique within science to the negation of science itself or a falsification of it in a teleological or providential direction. Behind the empirio-criticists were the so-called immanentists, to whom Lenin makes frequent polemical references. Behind Poincaré was Le Roy,[18] Bergson and Blondel had already made their presence felt, Italian neo-idealism was well along in its development, etc. When Pannekoek accused Lenin of forcing an idealistic interpretation of the texts of Avenarius and Mach, i.e. of refusing to accept their stated intentions, he was partially correct from the standpoint of the history of philosophy in a strict sense. The historian of philosophy certainly has a greater responsibility to differentiate the positions of the individual thinkers; for example, he should bring out the differences between Avenarius and Mach in their cultural background and philosophical conception; he should stipulate that Mach went *only so far* in his anti-materialist reaction and not beyond, and that he was not responsible, therefore, for the open idealism of his successors. Nevertheless, while Pannekoek, like many others who came after and were worse than he, thought he had demolished Lenin's book with criticisms of this kind, he failed to grasp the underlying truth of that so-called trial of intentions and that method of 'lumping them all together'. In other words, he did not grasp the fact that the book represented a polemic against the *entire* anti-materalist shift.[19] If Lenin had confined himself to a minute discussion of just the theories of Avenarius, Mach and their Russian followers, then indeed his book would be almost completely out of date today!

[18] *Materialism and Empirio-Criticism*, pp. 290–91.

[19] Note the clarity with which Lenin justified his own intended simplification (*Materialism and Empirio-Criticism*, pp. 268, 272): 'Thousands of shades of varieties of philosophical idealism are possible and it is always possible to create a thousand and first shade; and to the author of this thousand and first little system (empirio-monism, for example) what distinguishes it from the rest may appear important. From the standpoint of materialism, however, these distinctions are absolutely unessential. . . . Bogdanov may dispute as much as he pleases with the "empirio-symbolist" Yushkevich, with the "pure Machists", the empirio-criticists, etc. – from the standpoint of the materialist it is a dispute between a man who believes in a yellow devil and a man who believes in a green devil. For the important thing is not the differences between Bogdanov and the other Machists, but what they have in common: the *idealist* interpretation of "experience" and "energy", the denial of objective reality . . .'

Equally reductionist is the 'symptomatic' reading (i.e. an arbitrary one which prides itself on its own arbitrariness as if it were a virtue) of *Materialism and Empirio-Criticism* given by Althusser in his *Lenin and Philosophy*,[20] which gives the impression that the book dealt only with a refutation of subjective idealism. A Platonistic objective idealism of the kind Althusser has borrowed from his non-Marxist mentors is no less anti-materialist and no less contrary to Lenin's concept of science, which certainly is not that of a vulgar empiricism. Rather, it implies a strong accentuation of the experimental element, which is precisely what Althusser and Co. reject. Furthermore, in Althusser's essay Lenin represents little more than an excuse for announcing the advent of Althusserian philosophy (always with the air of someone who is about to make great revelations, but never does so). In this case, Perlini is right in referring to 'Althusser the juggler';[21] or even better, he could have said that this polemical sortie of Althusser's was nothing more than an episode in the rivalry between Parisian jugglers and Frankfurt jugglers.

We can see, then, how mistaken are both the opinion of Pannekoek, who in Chapter VIII of his book claimed that the only way of justifying *Materialism and Empirio-Criticism* was by ascribing it to the backward social-cultural situation of Tsarist Russia, and the opinion of Korsch, who regarded Pannekoek's judgement as still too lenient. Convinced more than ever of the continuity between Leninism and Stalinism, Korsch saw Lenin's book as the first sign of a tendency harmful to *all* of the international proletariat – a tendency to prefer 'immediate practical utility' to 'theoretical truth'.[22] Of course, in the 1938 article Korsch recalls that Lenin, when informed after the victory of the October Revolution that Bogdanov persisted in his teaching of empirio-criticism, did not

[20] Louis Althusser, *Lenin and Philosophy*, NLB, 1971.

[21] T. Perlini, *Lenin: la vita, il pensiero, i testi esemplari*, Milan 1971, p. 126. I indicate 'in this case' because on the whole Perlini's short work represents a total misreading of Lenin's thought and, in particular, of *Materialism and Empirio-Criticism*.

Just as deficient – and perhaps even more so – is the essay by Helmut Fleischer, 'Lenin e la filosofia', in *Storia del marxismo contemporaneo*. Anyone who has such a banally pragmatist conception of Marxism (a conception which is revolutionary only in appearance) is already far removed from the 'Marxism of Marx'; thus, his criticisms of Engels and Lenin become just a diversionary manoeuvre.

[22] Korsch, 'Lenin's Philosophy', p. 143.

'deliver him to the GPU to be instantly shot for this horrible crime' and contented himself with a 'spiritual execution' rather than a physical liquidation of his opponent.[23] But if there was a difference in the degree of their repressive ruthlessness, Lenin and Stalin were alike, according to Korsch, in their intolerant mentality, which was unfriendly towards any innovations and vulgarly political-propagandistic.

Without entering into a discussion on the general question of the continuity or discontinuity between Leninism and Stalinism,[24] we must point out that only an extremely prejudiced reading of Lenin's book could have led Korsch to those conclusions. If there is an animating force behind *Materialism and Empirio-Criticism,* it is the concern for objective truth – that objective truth which precisely Western Marxism undertook to downgrade, equating it with alienation and bourgeois 'reification'.[25] For Lenin, idealism is reactionary because it is untrue, and not vice versa. Thus, he can adhere to certain scientific results of the materialism of the heroic age (results which are not destined to pass away with the passing of the bourgeoisie, precisely because they are scientific), at the same time needs make no concessions to the reactionary ideologies intertwined with them: e.g. biologism, racism, the unmediated identification of human history with natural history.

*   *   *

Western Marxism made an assessment of the revival of idealism which was different and, in large part, the opposite of Lenin's.

[23] Ibid. p. 142.

[24] It is obvious that I stand on the side of non-continuity, in the sense in which Franco Belgrado and I have attempted to make clear in our short article published in *Giovane critica* (Spring 1972), p. 57. See also, however, the important essay by Lucio Colletti, 'The Question of Stalin', NLR 61 (May–June 1970), pp. 61–81. A very interesting contribution to the study of the different conceptions, Leninist and Stalinist, of socialism has recently been made by a broad-ranging debate over the question of the 'transition to socialism'; because they are particularly rich in general theoretical implications, I wish to single out the essays by Valentino Gerratana, *Ricerche di storia del marxismo,* Rome 1972, chapters 6–8, and Attilio Chitarin, 'Considerazioni "ideologiche" sulla transizione', *Problemi del socialismo* (1972), pp. 328ff. and *Lenin e il controllo operaio,* Rome 1973.

[25] An excellent treatment of this serious misunderstanding on the part of revolutionary Marxism in the West is to be found in Marzio Vacatello, *Lukács,* Florence 1968, chapter 2 (with regard to Korsch in particular, cf. pp. 39–49). But see also the conclusion to Colletti's review cited in note 5 above.

Whereas the great revolutionary rejected the illusion that pragmatism and voluntaristic idealism could be anything other than a kind of *revolutionary stimulant* with short-lived effects – a stimulant incapable of providing a solution to the problem of a mass proletarian revolution[26] – Western Marxism saw in these new tendencies a real support for the refounding of an authentic Marxism, emancipated from any positivistic dross.

For those who proposed to amend orthodox Marxism 'from the right', this cultural operation was not without coherence. It was natural, for example, that Bernstein, or the Austrian Marxists (in varying degrees), or later De Man, should advocate a rapprochement between Marxism and the most modern currents of bourgeois thought – a rapprochement based on the assumption that capitalism was 'humanizing' itself and that, therefore, sufficient economic and political margins existed to allow a collaboration between proletariat and bourgeoisie and to relegate all revolutionary perspectives to the realm of utopias. As the proletariat became more and more assimilated within the bourgeoisie, it made sense to do away with the 'crudities' of materialism. The extent to which this apparently reasonable outlook has shown itself to be illusory has been demonstrated by two world wars, by the fascist régimes between the two wars, and today by the pseudo-progressive barbarism of contemporary capitalism. Nevertheless, once those

---

[26] This polemic against 'voluntaristic idealism' (*Materialism and Empirio-Criticism*, p. 192), despite everything that has been said to the contrary, links Lenin the philosopher to Lenin the political strategist. Indeed, this is demonstrated by the fact that it reappears many years later (without there having been any disavowal during the interim) in the writings and speeches of 1918 in which he polemicizes with Bukharin and other Communists of the far left, and also in '*Left-Wing' Communism, An Infantile Disorder*. One should not forget, however, what was stated at the beginning of this article with regard to Lenin's 'anti-extremism'. In this connection, I find it necessary to point out the shortcomings of the article by Gian Mario Bravo, 'Sull'estremismo contemporaneo', *Critica marxista* (May–June 1972), pp. 262ff., in which the author ends by lumping together into a single condemnation of 'petty-bourgeois' extremism everything which today is to the left of the 'official' Communist Parties. Despite the correctness of his analysis in many of its individual remarks against the present-day *gauchistes* and their anti-Leninism, the article remains highly one-sided and tendentious; and it is all the more so in that it is not accompanied by any critique of present-day revisionism, apparently implying that the USSR and the Italian Communist Party today follow the most rigorous Leninist line. One would not have expected such direct and simplistic political exploitation of everything he knows on the subject from one of the most serious and well-informed students of pre-Marxist communism!

reformist presuppositions were accepted, the interpenetration of Marxism and neo-idealism appeared as a necessary consequence.

But for Western Marxism, which was *revolutionary* and rigorously classist, the accounts did not balance so readily. It was necessary to explain how it was that the anti-materialist ideologies of the twentieth century – the cultural expressions of an increasingly aggressive and imperialistic bourgeoisie – could also be used by Marxists in order to rediscover the revolutionary kernel of Marxism. The need to overcome quietism and vulgar evolutionism was an insufficient explanation. If it was true that those positions had unquestionably indicated a loss of revolutionary trenchancy on the part of the workers' movement, neo-idealism, on the other hand, was also a genuine offspring of bourgeois society – indeed, of a bourgeoisie become even more virulent.

Attempts were made to reply to this embarrassing question. But the considerable diversity in these replies on the one hand, and the limited importance placed on them on the other, are already significant. One almost always has the impression that they would like to liquidate the question without bringing out its seriousness.

This subject requires a more exhaustive treatment than I can give it here. For the moment, I should like to compare the replies of Gramsci and Korsch, bearing in mind also that Pannekoek's position is more nuanced. According to Gramsci, the similarity between certain features of twentieth-century idealism and Marxism results from the fact that the neo-idealists (i.e., for Gramsci, primarily Croce and to a lesser extent Gentile) have carried out an astute operation involving the absorption and remetaphysicization of Marxism, which enables them to 'vaccinate' bourgeois culture, making it more battle-ready and less immediately refutable. In this way the leaders of the intellectual bourgeoisie have acquired a temporary advantage over those scholastic Marxists who have succeeded only in banalizing Marxism by disregarding its originality and contaminating it with a bourgeois philosophy now old and discredited in the eyes of the bourgeoisie itself: positivism. Croce has made an intelligent use of certain features of Marxism, adapting them to the interests of the bourgeoisie; Bukharin (but Gramsci was certainly thinking also of Engels, as is apparent from some of his remarks, although he did not adhere to that particular form of extreme anti-Engelsism) has vulgarized Marxism and, therefore, made it less effective in its competition with the more modern forms of bourgeois philosophy. The *Anti-Croce* planned by Gramsci was to be an unmasking of that Crocean operation, a ferreting-out and restoration to its original revolutionary meaning of the para-Marxist content in Croce and Gentile.

It is a highly intelligent reply, and undoubtedly accurate in part (both Croce and Gentile first appeared as idealist revisionists of Marxism, although they took very different paths in this revision). And yet it is an unsatisfactory reply, at least in the way in which Gramsci tends to develop it. In order to unmask the Crocean and Gentilean operation in its entirety, it would be necessary to rid oneself of Croceanism and of a certain unconscious Gentileanism to a greater degree than Gramsci was able to do. Gramsci reaches his greatest detachment from Croce and his most creative elaboration of Leninism in his reflections on the relationship between dictatorship and hegemony; in his rejection of the classist separation between a 'religion of freedom' for the educated and the continued use of Catholicism for the masses; in his analysis of the function of the party, the relationship between state and 'civil society' in the countries of mature capitalism and the social position of intellectuals. These cursory remarks are sufficient to indicate that the author does not belong to the ranks of the 'anti-Gramscians of the revolutionary left', but rather agrees with those who claim Gramsci for the revolutionary workers' movement. The fact remains, however, that in Gramsci there is a lack of materialism which, moreover, cannot be explained by his supposed provincialism. Rather, as Eugenio Garin has noted,[27] it is to be explained on the basis of his adherence to idealistic Western Marxism, or at least to certain of its features which Italian idealism (itself far from devoid of 'provincial' characteristics) had in common with almost all European and American philosophical culture of the early twentieth century. It turns out, therefore, that in his attempt to redeem Marxism from Croce's instrumental use of it Gramsci ends by giving pre-eminence to precisely those features of Marxism (the primacy of praxis, the struggle against vulgar materialism and biologism, etc.) which had been selected out and isolated by neo-idealism (and therefore interpreted in a tendentious fashion). The existence of the external world independently of a knowing and acting subject is regarded by Gramsci as popular prejudice derived

[27] Eugenio Garin, 'La formazione di Gramsci e Croce', in *Prassi rivoluzionaria e storicismo in Gramsci,* special issue of *Critica marxista* (1967), pp. 119ff.

from the Christian religion. It would appear that the only alternative is between theocentrism and anthropocentrism, between a world which is *objective because it is created by God* and a world which *exists only insofar as it is known and transformed by man*.[28] Once one accepts the sophism of the idealists that materialism and positive religion are both forms of 'transcendence' and 'metaphysics' (a sophism which Lenin had decisively rejected, cf. above, note 15), it was inevitable that Gramsci would become to a certain degree a party to that absorption of Marxism within idealism which it had been his intention to oppose. At other times Gramsci refers to a different justification for popular materialism (and determinism). Materialism is no longer viewed as a pre-bourgeois residue of Catholic education, but as an ideology of an initial, and still predominantly 'rebellious' and unorganized, phase of the proletariat's struggle – like that of every preceding oppressed class – for its own emancipation. If one were to paraphrase Gramsci, materialism would be communism's infantile disorder. In the people's own 'good sense' there is presumed to be something salvageable, i.e. a kind of embryonic experimentalism and the first step towards a scientific and demythologized conception of reality.[29] But Gramsci

[28] From among the numerous passages one could cite, see especially *Quaderni del carcere*, Valentino Gerratana (ed.), Turin 1975, II, p. 1456f: 'Common sense affirms the objectivity of the real insofar as reality, the world, has been created by God, before and independently of man. Thus, it represents an expression of the mythological conception of the world. . . . Without man's activity, which creates all values – even that of science – what would 'objectivity' be? Complete chaos, i.e. nothing.' (See also the statements which follow this passage.) Between an objectivism in which religion and materialism come to be equated with one another, and a subjectivism which, as far as the relationship between man and nature is concerned, Croce is presumed to inherited from Marx, *tertium non datur*. The only correction of Croce which has to be made with regard to the latter question is presumed to be simply an accentuation in a pragmatist direction. Cf. also ibid., p. 120, also found in *Selections from the Prison Notebooks,* London 1971, p. 420: 'In common sense it is the "realistic", materialistic elements which are predominant, the immediate product of crude sensation. This is by no means in contradiction with the religious element, far from it.'

[29] On the question of determinism, cf. *Selections from the Prison Notebooks,* pp. 336–7, etc. 342; on the question of 'good sense' or 'common sense', cf. ibid. p. 348. Massimo L. Salvadori, in his *Gramsci e il problema storico della democrazia,* Turin 1970, rightly asserts the revolutionary character of Gramsci's political thought. Because he mistakenly believes, however, that Gramsci's antimaterialism was an indispensable component of the struggle against the quietism of the Second International, he is forced to blur Lenin's materialism as much as possible. Thus his chapter on 'Gramsci and the Relationship Between Subjectivity and Objectivity in Revolutionary Praxis' is the weakest of the whole book.

was quick to add that these were attitudes which had to be over-come, and not in the sense of a more rigorous materialism, but in the sense of a 'philosophy of praxis'.

We have said that Gramsci's explanation of the penetration of idealistic elements into twentieth-century Marxism still concedes too much to idealism. But if we compare it with Korsch's attempted explanation, we see immediately how much more inadequate and improbable the latter is. The 'crudeness' lies much more with the Mitteleuropean than with the Sardinian!

In his *Anti-Critique* of 1930, Korsch takes up Lenin's opinion about the need to concentrate one's fire on the adversaries of materialism in order to counteract 'the surging idealist tendencies of bourgeois philosophy'. His response is the following. 'What I have written elsewhere shows that I do not think this is really the case. There are some superficial aspects of contemporary bourgeois philosophy and science which appear to contradict this, and there certainly are some currents of thought which genuinely do so. Nevertheless, the dominant *fundamental orientation* in contemporary bourgeois philosophy, natural sciences and humanities is the same as it was sixty or seventy years ago. It is inspired not by an idealist outlook but by *a materialist outlook that is coloured by the natural sciences*.'[30]

'What I have written elsewhere' refers, as indicated by one of Korsch's own notes, to his *Anti-Kautsky*.[31] Here we would expect to find an explanation of what this 'fundamental orientation in contemporary bourgeois philosophy' is – an orientation which, despite 'some superficial aspects', continues to be inspired by materialism well into the twentieth century. But our expectations remain completely unsatisfied. In his *Anti-Kautsky* as well, which is primarily a polemic against Kautsky and not against Lenin, Korsch expresses himself with the same generality and is careful not to mention the name of even one contemporary bourgeois materialist. The Korschologists may claim that Korsch had neo-positivism in mind (which, however, cannot at all be defined as materialist, and had among its precursors precisely the empirio-criticists attacked by Lenin; furthermore, as we have indicated, it already enjoyed the sympathies of Korsch at that time). Or else they may say he was thinking of a certain vulgar biologism which

[30] Korsch, *Marxism and Philosophy*, p. 114 (translation modified).
[31] Korsch, *Die materialistische Geschichtsauffassung*, pp. 29ff.

was to furnish the pseudo-scientific arguments for Hitler's racism (but Korsch does not appear to be referring to tendencies such as these, which had no connection with Kautsky's Darwinian Marxism and were not regarded by him as representative of most of twentieth-century bourgeois philosophy, as is clear in the passage cited above from the 1938 article). One is left with the clear-cut impression that Korsch has unwittingly invented a straw man. In order to represent his own idealism as authentic Marxism, he had to overlook the idealist shift in bourgeois thought which took place at the end of the last century, and which had a great influence on Korsch's own thought as well as on that of the early Lukács. He also had to represent the work of the senile Kautsky, *Die materialistische Geschichtsauffassung* (1927), as representative of social-reformist thought of the twenties and thirties, whereas in reality that work was no more than a fossil. During the period between the two wars, the fashionably current reformists were influenced by idealism. They talked about Kantian ethics, voluntarism and humanism. Convinced that he was far ahead of Lenin, Korsch was actually far behind him. He was waging an anachronistic battle against nineteenth-century bourgeois philosophy, whereas Lenin had understood the fallaciousness and dangerousness of the new bourgeois philosophy some fifteen years before Korsch began his philosophic activity.

At the beginning of the *Anti-Critique* Korsch does not conceal his displeasure with the fact that *Marxism and Philosophy*, the work of a revolutionary who had always presented himself and acted as such, had been the object of condemnations by Kautskyites and Bolsheviks, while it had received the praise of bourgeois philosophers.[32] On a personal level, Korsch had every reason to repudiate this praise. Nonetheless, however tendentious and distorting it may have been, it was not due to a mere misunderstanding. It was directed towards Korsch's anti-materialism, and represented a refutation of the proposition he desperately clung to – namely, that twentieth-century bourgeois thought was materialist.

Connected with this misconception is another one. In his *Anti-Kautsky* Korsch maintains that the 'obscurantist and reactionary' tendencies present in twentieth-century philosophy were actually 'pre-bourgeois', and that they were supported by bourgeois

[32] Korsch, *Marxism and Philosophy*, p. 89.

philosophers and scientists 'both in earnest and in bad faith', or at times advanced 'in a revolutionary "socialist" guise'.[33] If Korsch meant by this that Bergson, or Blondel, or the pseudo-socialist Sorel, or Croce and Gentile in reality signalled an involution with respect to the great age of bourgeois thought spanning the Renaissance and the Enlightenment (and, in certain regards, with respect to nineteenth-century bourgeois materialism, taken not so much in its mediocre philosophic systematizers as in a Darwin), he would have been correct. But this involution was the involution of a class which had already entered into its imperialistic phase; it no longer had any 'enemies on its right', nor did it have that measure of 'universality' (if only in a mystified form) which it had incarnated in its ascendant phase. To designate such an involution 'pre-bourgeois', to represent the ideological expressions of an increasingly aggressive and exploitative bourgeoisie as medieval or feudal 'residues', meant that any serious Marxist analysis of twentieth-century idealism was precluded. Korsch's complete lack of understanding of the bourgeois culture of his time is confirmed by his proposition that idealism and spiritualism could be espoused by bourgeois philosophers 'in bad faith'. Were these philosophers, then, materialists pretending to be spiritualists in order to confuse the theoreticians of the proletariat and induce them to embrace materialism?

*      *      *

Was Korsch simply in error, then, in thinking there was an affinity between the thought of Lenin and that of Kautsky? No. We all know that with regard to certain features of his philosophic and political thought Lenin owed a genuine debt to Kautsky (as well as to Plekhanov). We know too that his break with Kautsky and with the whole of his own optimistic assessment of German Social Democracy's ideological and organizational strength cost him a great deal of effort and suffering – and came somewhat late. But there is, after all, at least *one* reason for Lenin's excessive attachment to Kautsky which is to his credit: materialism. It is possible to attribute a scholastic spirit and a relatively uncreative orthodoxy even to the early Kautsky. In my opinion, however, one cannot ascribe to him a vulgar-materialist falsification of Marxism, a

[33] Korsch, *Die materialistiche Geschichtsauffassung*, p. 30.

reduction of Marx to Darwin.[34] Thus with a hundred good reasons for anti-Kautskyism on the part of Korsch and the early Lukács, there was one bad one, and this was precisely anti-materialism. From this standpoint, it was natural that Lenin should appear to Korsch a Kautskyite, even after his violent rift with Kautsky the 'renegade'. But in this case the fault lay entirely with Korsch's idealism.

Human history has specific characteristics which distinguish it from the evolution of the animal species (and of man himself *qua* animal). Marxism must not be dissolved into Darwinism. On this question there can be no argument. But Korsch and the other Western Marxists were not satisfied with this; they wanted to reduce nature to a mere object of human praxis. The compilation of a kind of enormous Marxist-evolutionist handbook which would begin with the formation of the solar system and end with the advent of communism – thereby encompassing (and also dogmatizing) the entire spectrum of human knowledge – this is a mirage of the old Kautsky. It is contradictory to the very spirit of Marxism and represents also on the level of practice (whether consciously or not does not matter) a false objective which serves to sidetrack revolutionaries from their primary task of preparing and carrying out the revolution. On this question too there can be no argument. And if by the term *Weltanschauung* one means dogmatic-encyclopedic claims of this kind, then one is perfectly right to deny that Marxism is a *Weltanschauung*. If, however, one means by this that Marxism is only a revolutionary sociology, such that a Marxist could indifferently opt for the Ptolemaic system or the Copernican system, creationist biology or evolutionism, religion or atheism, etc., then one is denying one of the fundamental requirements of Marxism itself. For not only must the problems of theoretical critique and practical, revolutionary supersession of bourgeois society be placed *at the centre* of things; it is also necessary to re-examine all the other fields of human culture and all aspects of man's place in the world,

[34] Cf. above, Chapter III. In his introduction to the Italian edition of Rosa Luxemburg's *Lettere ai Kautsky*, Rome 1971, pp. 18ff., Lelio Basso makes a plausible case for the argument that there was a re-emergence in the late Kautsky of that positivism which went back to his early background and antedated his embrace of Marxism. This does not alter the fact that Western Marxists have had, and still have, a tendency to regard as vulgar-materialist even what was simply Marxist in the writings of the better Kautsky.

using this centre as one's point of departure. One could say, there-fore, that Marxism is a dynamic *Weltanschauung*. In this sense, one must concur with Lukács in his 1967 Postcript to *Lenin* (whatever other critical judgement one may wish to pass on Lukács in his late years), in which he regards as too narrow the initial definition of his 1924 essay: 'Historical materialism is the theory of the pro-letarian revolution'.[35] This was a definition, however, to which Korsch continued to subscribe. While he obviously refused to pay Stalinism the price exacted from Lukács during the thirties and twenties, he ended up paying another heavy price, not just in terms of his political isolation but also in his lack of understanding of Marxism and Leninism.

The reduction of Marxism to revolutionary sociology has often been represented (by Korsch and at times by Gramsci) in a form which at first view is alluring. Marxism, it is said, is a self-sufficient theory; it does not need 'integrations' of any kind. This statement is completely correct as a warning against facile pastiches of Marxism and the latest fashionable bourgeois theory, without a prior inquiry into the scientific (objectively true) and ideological (incompatible with Marxism) elements in such a theory, and without a full awareness of the completely new relationship between theory and practice established by Marx. But the state-ment is incorrect if its intent is to restrict Marxism solely within the sphere of the critique of political economy and to draw Marxists away from study of the man-nature relationship, or to claim that this relationship can be entirely absorbed within the 'social relations of production'. In such a case, one need only call to mind that the first 'integrationists' were Marx and Engels themselves, with their interest in Darwin and Morgan. In short, Marxism seeks to arrive at a coherent vision of the world and of man's place in the world (without which not even Marxism would be exempt from the charge of anthropocentrism); a vision of the world which is equally distant from agnosticism and from a statically conceived *Weltanschauung*. This explains the need for contact with the natural sciences and also for polemics against all idealistic and biologistic elements in the philosophies which have arisen from reflection on the natural sciences alone. It was the failure to recognize this need which led Korsch to identify Lenin with Kautsky, and which then caused him to be surprised at the approbation he found among

[35] Georg Lukács, *Lenin*, NLB 1970, p. 90.

neo-idealist bourgeois philosophers.

From this standpoint, the 1938 article does not signal any real advance over the *Anti-Kautsky* and *Anti-Critique* written almost ten years earlier. It signals merely an attempt to 'adjust' to a new situation. According to the proposition put forth by Pannekoek (and accepted by Korsch in the final part of his article), Leninist materialism had become the ideology of the 'popular fronts'. Precisely because these fronts were not anti-capitalist but only anti-fascist, and represented an alliance between the progressive bourgeoisie and the proletariat at the expense of the latter's specific class interests, they borrowed from the bourgeoisie *its* ideology – i.e., needless to say, materialism. In more precise terms, materialism is here represented as the ideology of the petty and middle bourgeoisie, whereas 'the upper and hitherto ruling strata of the bourgeois class' adhere to 'idealistic philosophies'.[36]

As one can see, there is a slight correction with respect to the perfect equation 'bourgeois ideology = materialism' which Korsch had previously espoused. Besides being due to the self-evidence of 'stubborn facts', the correction is also very likely a consequence of his having read Pannekoek's book. One should bear in mind that although Pannekoek rejected Lenin's materialism, he had attempted in his 1938 book to maintain his distance from bourgeois neo-idealism as well. He came to regard it correctly as 'the ideology of a self-contented, already declining bourgeoisie'.[37] In contrast with Korsch, whose basic background had been alien and hostile to the natural sciences in general (and who achieved only very late a reconciliation with a science which by then had been neo-positivized and rendered impervious to any suspicion of materialism), Pannekoek was an astronomer by profession and in his early years had had a lively interest in the relationship between Darwinism and Marxism. Thus Pannekoek had no intention of expressing a clear-cut preference for idealism, but rather of holding to a semi-idealistic position and making what use he could of those anti-materialist glimmerings present in Dietzgen.[38] His defence of

[36] Korsch, 'Lenin's Philosophy', p. 144.
[37] Pannekoek, op. cit., p. 72; cf. also pp. 31, 39, 47.
[38] In *Lenin as Philosopher*, the entire fourth chapter is devoted to Dietzgen. While he recognized Dietzgen's genius, Lenin was frequently concerned with the anti-Marxist uses to which Dietzgenism was put (cf. *Materialism and Empirio-Criticism*, pp. 243ff. and *passim*). See also P. Vranicki, *Storia del marxismo*, Rome 1971, pp. 260ff.; and on Pannekoek, see pp. 351ff. of the same volume.

empirio-criticism was, therefore, much more *engagé* than that of
Korsch, who was far more interested in attacking Lenin than in
defending Avenarius and Mach. Korsch regarded the latter as the
last and most sophisticated epigones of 'bourgeois philosophic
materialism', rather than as the first neo-idealists.[39] 'Neither
bourgeois idealism nor petty-bourgeois materialism' – this could
have been Pannekoek's motto, which the Korsch of 1938 appears
to approve. But even this formulation bears little correspondence
to reality, for materialism was not at all the ideology of the petty
bourgeoisie of the thirties, any more than it is today. Nor was
materialism the ideology of the popular fronts and anti-fascist
unions (to the extent that one can talk about a predominant or
unitary ideology with regard to such socially and culturally multi-
farious formations). Rather, their ideology was, if anything, an
abstract, progressive 'humanism'. Korsch's past experience as an
'extremist' – with all the errors but also with all that was positive
in the German worker-council communism of the twenties – led
him to an incisive political assessment of the inter-classism of the
popular fronts and of 'that state capitalism which, for the workers,
is nothing more than another form of enslavement and exploitation'.[40] But his idealism prevented him once again from making

[39] Korsch, 'Lenin's Philosophy', p. 141.

[40] A major limitation of Korsch, as well as of Pannekoek, remains the fact
that they regarded the USSR as simply a variant of the 'bourgeois state', without
analyzing in depth the specific characteristics of Stalinism. The superiority of
Trotsky's analysis is clear-cut. The same criticism, in an even stronger dosage,
can be made of Althusser's attempt at a 'theoretical' analysis of the 'Stalinist
deviation', which is to be found in his remarks appended to *Réponse à John Lewis*,
Paris 1973. For Althusser, Stalinism represents a revival (under changed circumstances) of the Second International's degenerate form of Marxism, which had
bequeathed to Stalinism the 'couplet of humanism and economism'. The
charge of displaying a professorial air while giving short shrift to politics, which
is Althusser's heavy-handed critique of Lewis, is also perfectly applicable to
Althusser's own criticism of Stalinism. A. Chitarin, in his introduction to the
Italian edition of Victor Serge's *Memorie di un rivoluzionario*, Florence 1974,
p. xxx, n. 84, correctly remarks: 'It actually seems as if this professor has never
heard of the price scissors, bureaucracy and the failure of the German revolution'.
The equation of Stalinism with Social-Democracy is correct in certain regards,
but it is more incisive as part of a present-day *gauchiste* polemic against the
*post*-Stalinism of Brezhnev and Berlinguer than as a way to understand Stalinism
in all its specificity; nor is it any more effective in understanding Stalinism in all
its array of pseudo-theoretical positions (varying from economistic to exag-
geratedly voluntarist), which were dictated from time to time by contingent
political motives. A duly harsh judgement has been passed on this essay of
Althusser's by Lucio Colletti, 'A Political and Philosophical Interview', NLR 86,
p. 17.

a balanced assessment of Lenin's philosophy.

★     ★     ★

Finally, it is interesting to consider Korsch's position on Lenin's *Philosophical Notebooks*, which date back to the years of the First World War and were published, in an incomplete form, at the beginning of the thirties. The question of their continuity or discontinuity with *Materialism and Empirio-Criticism* is still much debated. Most present-day Marxists in the western countries insist, more or less emphatically, on their discontinuity. Just as Lenin in his politics is supposed to have abandoned (at last!) his position as a 'left Kautskyite' when faced with imperialist world war and the collapse of the Second International, he is supposed to have done the same in his philosophy. He gives up vulgar materialism and for the first time comes to a serious reckoning with the dialectic. He comes to realize (to repeat a sentence which, according to many Marxists, sums up the *Notebooks*) that 'intelligent idealism is closer to intelligent materialism than stupid materialism'.[41] Only a few scholars – among whom should be mentioned Christine Glucksmann and; more recently, Ludovico Geymonat[42] – have given more emphasis to the continuity. Another position, apart from both of these, is represented by Lucio Colletti, who in his introduction to the Italian edition of the *Philosophical Notebooks* perceives a regression in the late Lenin with respect to *Materialism and Empirio-Criticism* and even more with respect to *What the 'Friends of the People' Are*.[43] But in *Marxism and Hegel,* although he maintains and accentuates his negative judgement on the *Notebooks,* Colletti is much less favourably disposed towards *Materialism and Empirio-Criticism*.[44]

None of these recent positions on the *Notebooks* and their rela-

[41] Lenin, *Philosophical Notebooks*, in *Collected Works*, Vol. 38, Moscow 1963, p. 276.

[42] Cf. Christine Glucksmann, 'Hegel et le marxisme', *La Nouvelle Critique* (April 1970), pp. 25ff.; Ludovico Geymonat, *Storia del pensiero filosofico e scientifico,* Vol. 6, pp. 103ff., 112ff. Geymonat rightly remarks that if the *Notebooks* represented a genuine turning point, one would not be able to account for the fact that Lenin republished *Materialism and Empirio-Criticism* in 1920 with a brief new preface in which he reaffirms its validity.

[43] The introduction also forms the first part of the Italian text of *Il Marxismo e Hegel,* Bari 1969. (NLB).

[44] See the English translation of the second part of ibid.: *Marxism and Hegel,* NLB 1973.

tionship with the preceding works of Lenin can be traced back to the judgement expressed by Korsch in his 1938 article. Korsch was convinced that all of Lenin's thought was archaic bourgeois thought, and he saw in the passage from *Materialism and Empirio-Criticism* a re-run, step by step, of that same itinerary over which Central-European bourgeois philosophy had travelled a century earlier and with much richer cultural baggage: from Holbach to Hegel, and from eighteenth-century mechanistic materialism to the absolute idealism of the early nineteenth century. And according to Korsch, this showed a more perfect parallelism between Lenin the philosopher and Lenin the political strategist than even Pannekoek had been able to perceive. 'Both in his revolutionary materialist philosophy and in his revolutionary jacobin politics, Lenin had concealed from himself the historical truth that his Russian revolution, in spite of a temporary attempt to break through its particular limitations in connection with the simultaneous revolutionary movement of the proletarian class in the West, was bound to remain in fact a belated successor of the great bourgeois revolutions of the past.'[45]

At first view, everything appears to enter perfectly into this schema. On re-reading Korsch, however, one realizes that the old voluntarist revolutionary paradoxically presents us, in disdain for Lenin, with a kind of Menshevik justification of Stalinism. In pre-bourgeois Russia nothing more advanced than bourgeois political and philosophic thought could emerge. The 'temporary attempt' at extending the revolutionary movement to the advanced capitalist countries (which was precisely the 'attempt' of Lenin and Trotsky and which failed – certainly – because of great objective difficulties, but also because of the victory in Russia of the anti-Leninist theory of socialism in one country, and in the West because of the support given to capitalism by the Social Democrats and because of the mistakes caused by 'extremism') is here represented as pure utopia – an attempt that could not help but meet with failure. And after he had fought so much (not just in his early writings but even in *Karl Marx*) against a mechanical conception of the relationship between structure and superstructure, it is precisely to this kind of conception that Korsch has recourse in his polemic against Lenin.

[45] Korsch, 'Lenin's Philosophy', p. 143.

He stresses how Lenin's thought could not have risen above the socio-economic backwardness of Russia, how it could not have been ahead of its socio-economic setting in any way, and how it was therefore condemned to reproduce (belatedly and with a good measure of provincial crudity) the development of bourgeois thought in its heroic age.

In Korsch's anti-Leninism of 1938 there is, as we have said, an understandable resentment – that of the 'extremist' betrayed, incapable of distinguishing between Lenin's anti-extremist polemic (which remains entirely within the framework of a class and internationalist perspective) and the genuine betrayal perpetrated by Stalin. But at the same time there is an emergence (probably unconscious) of social-democratic themes. Anyone who has lived through the historic tragedy experienced by Korsch and the other revolutionary western Marxists certainly does not have the right to adopt a posture of moralistic and professional censure vis-à-vis these waverings (which, moreover, never led Korsch to politically unworthy positions). One can only note that during these terrible years there was only one great European revolutionary who managed to struggle against Stalinism with all possible vigour and lucidity without lapsing into social-democratic politics or into a 'revolutionary Westernism' reduced to mere wishfulness: this was Trotsky.

How then are Lenin's *Notebooks* to be interpreted? Certainly no answer can be sketched in just a few lines; one can only indicate certain points as a basis for further discussion. Korsch's opinion is unacceptable because of the simple fact that Lenin's thought, as we have attempted to show (certainly not for the first time), cannot be strictly confined either to a Russian geographical ghetto or to a pre-Marxist chronological ghetto. Korsch appeared to overlook completely the long exile in the West experienced by Lenin, Trotsky and other Russian revolutionaries – an exile which served as a great school for their 'deprovincialization'. Equally unacceptable is the position of Hegelian Marxists, according to whom the *Notebooks* show us a new Lenin, freed at last from vulgar materialism and Kautskyism. One need only point out against this position that Lenin's reading of Hegel is clearly and expressly an Engelsian reading. It is Engelsian in a good sense, in its materialism, in its insistence on the historicization of nature, and in Lenin's famous 'laugh' at the idea that nature represents the 'submersion of the Notion into externality'.[46] None of these things is accepted by present-day Hegelian Marxists, and they should be led to the conclusion (if they were completely self-consistent) that Lenin greatly misunderstood Hegel. It is also Engelsian in a bad sense, in its simplistic belief that one need only 'turn on its head' Hegel's dialectic in order to transform it into a materialist tool – a belief which was shared, moreover, by Marx.

It seems to me that there is an element of continuity between *Materialism and Empirio-Criticism* and the *Notebooks* which is represented not just by the common grounding in a materialism never repudiated, but also by the anti-agnosticism and opposition to subjective idealism. This opposition, which was completely justified in the wake of the new empirio-pragmatist wave at the beginning of the twentieth century, had already led Lenin in *Materialism and Empirio-Criticism* to a kind of identification of Berkely, Hume and Kant with one another, and to an identification of the latter with the empirio-criticists. He was led also to a guarded reassessment of Hegel, who, although an idealist, was at least not a subjective idealist. He even went so far as to state that 'Hegel's absolute idealism is reconcilable with the existence of the earth, nature, and the physical universe without man, since nature is regarded as the "otherness" of the absolute idea'.[47] In fact, the least convincing points in *Materialism and Empirio-Criticism* do not at all consist in its presumed vulgar materialism (from which Lenin always keeps his necessary distance), but are two quite different defects.

First, there is a certain wavering between the need for an integral *materialism* and the tendency to fall back on a mere *objectivism* or *realism*. When Lenin presses his opponents on the question of the existence of nature before man and on the question of the relationship between thought and the brain,[48] when he states that 'sensation depends on the brain, nerves, retina, etc., i.e. on matter organized in a definite way' and that 'sensation, thought, consciousness are the supreme-product of matter organized in a particular way',[49] when he exposes the religious and obscurantist elements which exist in even the most up-dated 'immanentism', he demonstrates an

[46] Lenin, *Philosophical Notebooks*, p. 186.
[47] Lenin, *Materialism and Empirio-Criticism*, p. 73.
[48] Ibid., Chapter 1, sections 4 and 5.
[49] Ibid., p. 55.

awareness that materialism is much more than a gnoseological theory. Materialism entails also the recognition of man's animality (superseded *only in part* by his species-specific sociality); it is also the radical negation of anthropocentrism and providentialism of any kind, and it is absolute atheism. Thus it represents a *prise de position* with regard to man's place in the world, with regard to the present and future 'balance of power' between man and nature, and with regard to man's needs and his drive for happiness. This feature of Lenin's thought (which predominates in *Materialism and Empirio-Criticism,* both from a purely quantitative standpoint and in terms of the polemical force of his argument) finds its natural complement in his writings on religion.[50] When, however, he is more concerned with combating *subjective* idealism than the spiritualist reaction in its entirety (and his concern was justified by the fact that the most immediate opponents of his argument were subjective idealists or semi-idealists), and when he seeks to make it clear that the crisis of materialism as such has not been the consequence of a change or deepening of our ideas about the structure of matter (and this point too is altogether correct), then Lenin tends to confine his argument to a purely gnoseological framework. 'The *sole* "property" of matter with whose recognition philosophical materialism is bound up is the property of *being an objective reality,* of existing outside our mind';[51] 'the concept of matter expresses nothing more than the objective reality which is given us in sensation'.[52] Of course, even this narrower objectivist argument is entirely correct and necessary, for Lenin had to do battle *also* on the specific terrain of the gnoseology of the sciences and of its pseudo-philosophic extrapolations. But the two arguments tend to intertwine with one another in *Materialism and Empirio-Criticism,* without sufficient clarity about how they differ and relate to one another. And this fact explains how it was possible at times to misinterpret Lenin's book as a work which dealt only with anti-subjectivist gnoseology; in such a case, it was necessary to ascribe to him a certain number of 'relapses' into materialism, as if one were dealing with inconsistencies or naïvetés. In my opinion, however, a close reading of the entire book is enough to dispel this misconception. Someone who is simply a realist and not a

[50] See V. I. Lenin, *On Religion,* Moscow 1966.
[51] *Materialism and Empirio-Criticism,* p. 261.
[52] Ibid., p. 267.

materialist does not agree with Lenin, even if he may give his approval to a few individual statements in the latter's book.

The second weak point in *Materialism and Empirio-Criticism* is Lenin's belief that the profound transformations in the traditional concept of matter, which the new idealist tendencies used to justify themselves, could be accommodated through the concept of the dialectic.[53] This view is correct only if one understands by the dialectic not the logic of the unity of opposites but simply a kind of energetic, dynamic materialism, non-creationist and not 'evolutionist' in a necessarily gradualist sense. One must, however, bear in mind that the dialectic in this sense is only a modern form of Heraclitanism, which is valid as a general schema for conceptualizing and investigating reality but must be complemented by a great number of epistemological elaborations and refinements as to detail. Otherwise it may turn out that the dialectical materialist not only does not have any difficulty in dealing with the crisis of the old dualism of matter and energy, but also does not have any difficulty in accepting as valid the pseudo-phenomena and pseudo-experiments of alchemy, spiritualism, more or less far-fetched vitalistic biology, etc! Lenin is far away from dangers such as these (which were to become reality with Lysenko, for example). But he is far away thanks to his materialism, to his vigorous experimentalism, and to the connection and distinction he always maintains between science and ideology and between science and history; *not* thanks to such Hegelianism or generic hostility to 'common sense' as has always remained an inherent part of the Marxist dialectic.

We have seen, then, that the element of continuity between *Materialism and Empirio-Criticism* and the *Notebooks* is represented by their anti-agnosticism and anti-subjectivism (an anti-subjectivism which, as Colletti has rightly pointed out, takes its toll on Kant to a greater extent in the *Notebooks* than in the earlier work, in which the realist side to Kantianism was still recognized), and that the dialectic does not represent a decisive basis for distinguishing the two phases of Lenin's thought from one another. However, the need Lenin felt to come to a more direct reckoning with Hegel's thought and to study the possible applications of the dialectic to the analysis of socio-political situations and to revolutionary action

[53] See especially the conclusion to Chapter v of ibid.

did provide a partially new element. Confronted with the crisis of the Second International, Lenin felt the need to launch an even more vigorous opposition against, on the one hand, gradualist and quietist evolutionism of the Plekhanov or Kautsky kind, and on the other hand, the over-simplifications of revolutionary comrades who denied the continued existence under the imperialist phase of capitalism of national questions, conflicts between proletarians of advanced and backward countries, and class antagonisms – including within individual states – inside the generically anti-capitalist front.[54] For the Lenin of World War I and later of the Revolution, 'not to understand the dialectic' meant essentially to lapse either into reformism or into an over-simplified revolutionism; this is the significance of the criticism he was to make of Bukharin in his so-called 'testament'.

It is undeniable that Lenin's enthusiasm for certain Hegelian propositions is excessive in the *Notebooks;* that his criticisms of Hegel are directed predominantly against the more openly theological features of Hegelianism; and that on the whole his brilliant early writing, *What the 'Friends of the People' Are,* displays a more perceptive awareness of the intrinsically idealist character of the Hegelian dialectic (which is beyond redemption through any 'standing on its head', 'breaking the shell', or other metaphorical operations of the kind).[55] But one should bear in mind also that this Hegelian moment of Lenin's is the first attempt at an 'emergency

[54] See in this regard L. Gruppi, *Il pensiero di Lenin*, pp. 165–71.

[55] For too long now Marxist exegesis has attempted to squeeze more from these metaphors than they could give, and from time to time has given preference to one over the others (usually for the purpose of showing that Marx alone, and not Engels, had succeeded in completely superseding Hegelianism). It is all the more discouraging to see how Althusser's essay on 'Lenin Before Hegel' (*Lenin and Philosophy*, NLB 1971, pp. 107ff.) for the most part still amounts simply to a twiddling with such metaphors and utterly trivial variants on them. Althusser's great discovery is supposed to be the realization that 'Lenin did not read Hegel according to the method of "inversion", (but according to) the method of "*laying bare*"' (p. 114). Althusser goes on to add that this had to be a 'radical *laying bare*'; and to clarify matters further, he states that 'the extraction needs to be laboriously laid bare' ('think of a fruit, an onion, or even an artichoke'). A reading of these pages confirms my belief that Althusser has been taken too seriously not just by the Althusserians but also by most of his critics. On the relationship between Hegel and Marx (and implicitly, therefore, also the one between Hegel and Lenin), one of the most rigorous and intellectually forthright positions has been expressed by Jean Fallot, *Marx et le machinisme,* Paris 1966, Appendix III. Fallot is, in my opinion, the most serious and original Marxist philosopher that France has today. His aversion for the coquetry of

resolution' of those problems of imperialism and revolution
alluded to above. Furthermore, insufficient attention has been paid
to the important fact that as Lenin advances in his reading of Hegel
(and especially when he moves from *The Science of Logic* to the
*Lectures on the History of Philosophy* and *on the Philosophy of History*),
his critical notations – and often harshly critical ones – become
more common. I think it can be shown that Lenin had an *initial*
enthusiasm for Hegel, which gradually began to wane. Finally, and
related closely to this last point, it should be pointed out that it is
impossible to dissociate the *Notebooks* from the two 'finished'
philosophical writings of the late Lenin: his 'Karl Marx' written
for the *Granat Encyclopaedia* and the article 'On the Significance of
Militant Materialism'.[56]

In 'Karl Marx', Marx's materialism is strongly emphasized and
the dialectic is presented in substance as a 'revolutionary evolutionism' (i.e. one not excluding sudden and catastrophic transformations). Contradictions are described in terms of conflicts
between forces, not in terms of the identity of opposites; and the
Hegelian 'trichotomies' are regarded as idealist rubbish, 'which it
would be absurd to confuse with materialist dialectics'.[57] We are
once again not far removed from the formulations of *What the
'Friends of the People' Are*. Similarly, in 'On the Significance of
Militant Materialism' – at first approved by Korsch, who like Lukács
misinterpreted it as a mere exhortation to raise the backward
Russian people to an admittedly elementary level of bourgeois
culture, and later liquidated by him in his 1938 article, where he
included it in his negative interpretation of all Leninism[58] – Lenin
explicitly accords a positive value to that materialism based on the

structuralistic Marxism and Husserlian Marxism – predominant today in the
culture of the French revolutionary left – and his detachment from the fossilized
orthodoxy of the French Communist Party have meant that his thought has
not yet received the recognition long overdue him.

[56] Lenin, 'Karl Marx', in *Collected Works*, Vol. 21, Moscow 1964, pp. 43ff.
(originally written in 1915); 'On the Significance of Militant Materialism', in
ibid., Vol. 33, pp. 227ff. (originally written in 1922).

[57] Lenin, 'Karl Marx', p. 55.

[58] The reductionist interpretation of this article of Lenin's which was made
by Lukács in *History and Class Consciousness*, London 1971, pp. 221–2, n. 65,
and by Korsch in the *Anti-Kautsky* (*Die Materialistische Geschichtsauffassung*,
p. 30, n. 17), has rightly been rejected by Vacatello, *Lukács*, pp. 45–7. But in the
1938 article Korsch abandons even this interpretation; the few references to
Lenin's article are clearly disparaging, and the very suggestion of a 'militant
materialism' is regarded as an anachronism.

natural sciences which has not yet arrived at a Marxist perspective (and for that reason has remained 'idealist' with regard to its conception of man in society), but which nevertheless performs a clarificatory function in favour of secularism and against providentialism or anthropocentrism. Within this framework, Lenin says, the 'militant atheist literature of the late eighteenth century' still has an indispensable function to perform.

In the second part of this article we again find Lenin's concern (already present in *Materialism and Empirio-Criticism*) to distinguish the new scientific achievements – not in themselves anti-materialist – from the anti-materialist use to which they have been put by bourgeois philosophy. (Lenin refers in particular to the theory of relativity, which in those years, through no fault of Einstein's, had brought forth a swirl of inanities on the part of philosophers ignorant of physics and journalistic dabblers in scientific matters.) 'Natural science is progressing so fast and is undergoing such a profound revolutionary upheaval in all spheres that it cannot possibly dispense with philosophical deductions.'[59] These are certainly not the words of an enemy of twentieth-century science or someone who, as Korsch says in complete misunderstanding, wishes to defend a primitive materialism 'by any means, extending even to the exclusion of modifications made imperative by further scientific criticism and research'![60] Rather, as one can see from the entire preceding page of that same article, they are the words of someone who was well aware of the dangers threatening Marxism should it lose its contact with the natural sciences.[61] Thus here too Lenin

---

[59] Lenin, 'On the Significance of Militant Materialism', pp. 229 and 234.

[60] Korsch, 'Lenin's Philosophy', p. 142.

[61] And not just with the natural sciences, moreover. With regard to political economy too, Lenin had clearly asserted, as far back as *Materialism and Empirio-Criticism*, on the one hand its 'partisanship' ('taken as a whole, the professors of political economy are nothing but learned salesmen of the capitalist class') and on the other hand the need to know how to use the most up-to-date techniques of the bourgeois economists ('you will not make the slightest progress in the investigation of new economic phenomena without making use of the works of these salesmen', pp. 342–3). And he had put his emphasis on the crucial question: in every relationship between Marxism and bourgeois culture, the question is to see who hegemonizes and who is hegemonized. In reply to Lunacharsky, who lauded the lack of dogmatic close-mindedness towards empirio-criticism on his part and on the part of his comrades, Lenin wrote: 'You do not go with your, i.e. Marxist (for you want to be Marxists), standpoint to every change in the bourgeois philosophical fashion; the fashion comes to you, foists upon you its new falsifications adapted to the idealist taste, one day *à la* Ostwald, the next

shows himself to be much more profound and modern not only than Stalinist dogmatism but also than 'Western Marxism'.

---

day *à la* Mach, and the day after *à la* Poincaré. . . . The infatuation for empirio-criticism and "physical" idealism passes as rapidly as the infatuation for neo-Kantianism and "physiological" idealism; but each time fideism takes its toll. . . .' (p. 343). If we were to substitute the words 'structuralism' and 'phenomenology' for 'empirio-criticism' and 'neo-Kantianism', Lenin's words would be a perfect diagnosis of the situation of present-day Marxism.

# Postscript

Re-reading this book nearly ten years after the appearance of the first Italian edition, I find little in it that is out of date, apart from references to particular political events or particular comrades and friends. I remain, of course, well aware of the real limitations and 'pre-philosophical' character of the essays it comprises; but I believe that the book expresses ideas and requisites that deserve not to be ignored, but rather examined, deepened, and if need be, refuted by philosophers (and, as regards the third chapter, by linguists and anthropologists).

There is, however, one aspect of the book that belongs to an era that now seems long past: its more narrowly and directly political side. Many things have happened during the past ten years, both in Italy and throughout the world, and many people who were 'more revolutionary' than I ten (or even five) years ago have set sail for other points; neither I nor some of the other comrades mentioned in this book (and others not cited) have any intention of following them.

There is, to be sure, a genuine and serious crisis of Marxism. Many of the concepts and predictions of Marx and Engels must be revised. Indeed, even at the time of its publication, my book was not at all 'orthodox', although its 'heterodoxy' was quite different from most other varieties. (In this regard the reader should consult the remarks made by Perry Anderson in his *Considerations on Western Marxism*, London, NLB, 1976, pp. 60n and 91n, with an accuracy and comprehension for which I am most grateful). But it does not seem that the most recent critics of Marxism are striving to ground on more solid foundations a new revolutionary theory and a new path to communism in the developed capitalist countries. Their aim is rather to annihilate (some wittingly, some not) not only Marxism, but any prospect of the advent of a classless society. Once again, as so often before in the history of the workers' movement, necessary and urgent 'revision' is fast becoming 'revisionism'.

The Italian Communist Party (PCI) is now so entrenched in this road that it will be impossible to deviate from it so long as the party is directed by the present leadership group. But the PCI has not become a Social Democratic party, even though it is partly fulfilling typically Social Democratic functions. It is rather a new phenomenon: a party whose internal structure and the mentality of whose leaders and intermediary cadres remain Stalinist, but which strives to participate in the direction of the capitalist state not in order to change it in ways favourable to the working class, and still less to destroy it, but instead to manage it through methods even more authoritarian, repressive, and intolerant than those of traditional parliamentary democracy, in accordance with the exigencies of 'law and order', conformism, and unanimity increasingly characteristic of contemporary capitalism. The greater part of the Italian working class no doubt continues to support the PCI; but the party's bureaucratic structure and long decades of political and ideological miseducation render it incapable, at least now and for a long time to come, of reclaiming its own independence, of becoming the *subject*, and not the *object*, of political action. There are some intellectuals who are studying Marxism and its problems seriously and whose ideas are not purely and simply 'revisionist' in the pejorative sense (many of them are mentioned favourably in this book). But what is the use of even the best 'academic Marxism' if it bows to all the orders of the party leadership? It serves only to deceive other intellectuals, lending the party an external appearance of 'theoretical respectability' behind which the worst political machinations detrimental to the working class are the more easily concealed.

Many comrades of the far left of 1968–1969, whose attitude towards the PCI was perhaps even too sectarian, have now become – today, when the PCI has undergone further degeneration – disciplined party activists, chattering about the working class 'becoming the state' (without bringing down capitalism!) and perceiving enemies exclusively on their left. These new PCI members and sympathizers who have come over from the far left are perhaps the worst elements of the party, for they feel compelled, with the zeal of the converted, to atone – to themselves and to their leaders – for the 'errors' of their youth.

Then there are others, more consistent, who no longer consider themselves Marxists and aver that 'compared to the police state' to which they hold any socialist revolution must inevitably lead, 'stand on the side of liberal-democratic institutions, however imperfect and deficient they may be'. These are the words of Lucio Colletti, reprinted in his recent volume *Tra marxismo e no* (Bari, 1979, p. 149). The case of Colletti is particularly painful to me, for I learned much from him, as did the entire far left of the sixties and early seventies (however ungrateful to him they have often been), both in Italy and (through NLB and *New Left Review*) in Britain. I have always admired the Enlightenment inspiration of Colletti's Marxism, his struggle against the penetration of irrationalism into Marxism, his 'anti-dialectical' position (which I share in part, though I would argue that it is too one-sided, while none the less polemically and theoretically fertile), his defence of the objective, ideologically neutral character of science, without which there is only obscurantism and 'religious' anti-capitalism, incapable of defeating capitalism in any event. Even ten years ago I disagreed with him on some, not at all secondary, questions, as is apparent in chapter 3 of this book. But these were disagreements between two comrades striving together for a communist society. At that time, Colletti was convinced that the dialectic was an aberration of Hegel and Engels of which Marx was happily innocent. Once he finally realized that the dialectic was present in the work of Marx as well, he drew the conclusion that communism was a utopian dream at best; any attempt actually to implement it would result in abominable tyranny. He has thus opted to live under the protection of bourgeois-democratic freedoms. But are the exploitation of the workers, inequality, and the purely formal character of bourgeois freedoms (not purely *illusory*, but *insufficient*) irrationalistic 'dialectical' inventions, or are they realities experienced daily by the working class? Must we resign ourselves to all this, and compel others to so resign themselves, on the pretext that the states that call themselves communist are in many respects, even worse? It seems to me that Colletti, who is so readily disposed to deem illusory any attempt to inaugurate a society in which exploitation and inequality no longer exist, is indulging in strange illusions (strange for *him*, for he has so well understood and taught certain things) about the possibility of reforming capitalism. Capitalism, of course, is indeed conducting *its own* reforms; but these consist in an ever greater authoritarianism, in a fortification of the 'police state' that Colletti correctly perceives in the Eastern countries but fails to see growing and becoming ever more dominant in his own back yard. Capitalism increasingly regards bourgeois freedoms, the alternating rule of political parties, and parliamentary institutions as encumbrances to be jettisoned. This is not the first time this has happened, but the forms always differ, and the prospect that now looms before us is not of classical fascism, but of so-called authoritarian democracy, based on mechanisms of 'compulsory consensus' more refined than those employed by fascism and more 'peaceful' wherever possible, but always embodying a fundamental intolerance of opposition and a disguised violence that becomes open as the need arises (and the need is often felt).

Nor does insistence on the objectivity of scientific knowledge – which is essential to materialism and is upheld continuously throughout the present book – justify closing one's eyes to the criminal use of science by capitalism and to the constantly rising tendency of scientists to debase themselves to faithful servants of the rulers of society. It is this daily experience of the degradation of science from an instrument of liberation to one of oppression that gives rise to the (one-sided and mistaken) reduction of science to ideology. To close one's eyes to this reality and to polemicize against those who deny the neutrality of science as though they were merely irrationalist devotees of mediaeval obscurity amounts to 'Enlightenmentism' in the narrow, petty, and pejorative sense of the word. Every passing day brings us news of labour processes highly noxious to the workers, which continue to be used with the connivance of physicians and political leaders, and of a 'peaceful' employment of atomic energy that increasingly threatens the premature death of millions of human beings, quite apart from the danger of nuclear war. The ecological 'suicide' of all humanity is no wild prospect of science fiction. This is the new and greater irrationality and 'anarchy' of capitalism (and of the pseudo-socialism of the countries of the East), much greater than the irrationality and anarchy of production of which Marx spoke. Granted, the far left has committed grave errors and now finds itself, in Italy as more or less everywhere, in a state of deep crisis and fragmentation. Yet it is only the reconstitution of the New Left that holds out hope for the survival of humanity and for a freer and less unhappy society.

Condemnations of 'utopia' must avoid schematism. As is clear in this book, I have never had anything to do with so-called Frankfurt Marxism. But certain Marxists and 'scientific' ex-Marxists have now wound up including Marx, Engels, and Lenin among the Frankfurt School! If by 'utopia' one means not religious-like ideologies and comforting evasions of reality, but rather rejection of the prevailing situation, rejection of the supposedly absolute and inviolable character of the laws of the capitalist economy, and aspiration for different human relations (even outside the strictly political domain), then it must be said that it is impossible to contest capitalist barbarism without *this* 'utopia', which in no way conflicts with science. Clear positions on 'violence' are also required. I am convinced that terrorism is a senseless and savage practice, profoundly anti-Marxist and useful only to strengthen capitalism. But after condemning terrorism, we must ask ourselves why it is that this phenomenon, non-existent ten or fifteen years ago, does exist now. The answer, in my view, is clear. Once any mass opposition to capitalism, any communist project, fades from view, why should it be surprising that some people, out of desperation, become convinced that the only way to combat this society is through blind terrorist violence? Just as others, through a psychological process that is no different at bottom, cede to drugs and alcohol. The ones primarily responsible for terrorism are those who have renounced political opposition to the capitalist system. Moreover, one must not close one's eyes to the violence of the employers, who lay off thousands of workers, or of the police, who under the pretext of fighting terrorism slaughter peaceful citizens, always with impunity. It must not be forgotten that this violence exists alongside the violence of the terrorists (which every Marxist, I repeat, must condemn). Finally, we must never forget – as Chile should have taught us once again – that the bourgeoisie, 'democratic' so long as its power is not in danger, is ever prepared to unleash the most savage violence and to quash all freedoms the moment it is faced with a genuinely socialist government that threatens its most vital interests, *even if that government came to power through free and peaceful elections*. It is this experience, much more than any theoretical considerations, that prevents liquidation of the question of the dictatorship of the proletariat as a 'Jacobin' crotchet long since obsolete. As I am well aware, the dictatorship of the proletariat has yet to come into existence anywhere, save in a few *initial* revolutionary moments of brief duration. Instead we have seen the dictatorship of a bureaucratic group *over* the proletariat. There is no cure for this degeneration except the reinforcement of the *soviets*, of council democracy, of control from below. It is difficult, I know, to effect this cure; but whosoever condemns it as 'utopian' serenely prepares for atomic death, while composing hymns to the beauty of bourgeois freedoms.

Let me conclude with a self-criticism. I never shared the enthusiasm for Maoism that enthralled the far left, with the sole exception of the comrades of the Fourth International, during the period of the Cultural Revolution and even after (although I understood this enthusiasm as an emotional reaction to the barbarism of capitalism and the dismal bureaucratism of the USSR). This is shown by what I have written in the prefaces to the present book (pp. 9 and, especially, 23–26) and, even earlier, in the review *Nuovo Impegno* of Pisa (volume II, no. 9–10, August 1967–January 1968, pp. 59–66). Nevertheless, I freely admit that the events that occurred in China after the death of Mao (and are still occurring) represent a 'new course' far worse than the Cultural Revolution and compel a much more critical assessment of the Cultural Revolution itself than I advanced at the time. There were even fewer mass initiatives than I believed (by which I mean conscious and independent mass initiatives, and not outbreaks of fanaticism), since otherwise it would be impossible to explain how the same masses, in the space of just a few months, could have accepted without resistance (or with sporadic but easily isolated and repressed resistance, which undoubtedly did occur) renunciation of the equalitarian and anti-imperialist slogans and the inauguration of a productionist and technocratic ideology and practice. Thus, although in 1975 I wrote that 'unquestionably, a revolutionary militant faced with a choice between the USSR and China must unhesitatingly opt for the latter' (see above, page 23), in 1975, in the light of the most recent developments in Chinese internal and international policy, which today, even more than in the past, supports some of the worst fascist regimes in the world and has even committed armed aggression against Vietnam, I believe that it is no longer possible to recommend such 'options'. We can no longer refer to any model of socialism either realized or on the road to realization in the world today. With the advent of Stalinism in Russia during the 1920s and with its diffusion through the world communist movement (while even earlier, in 1914, Social Democracy was stained with the worst cowardice and crimes), the very notion of communism suffered an obfuscation from which it has yet to recover. But the crisis cannot be overcome by taking refuge in a bourgeois democratism that has been abandoned by the bourgeoisie itself and that, even during its brightest periods, was always marked by a regime of oppression, inequality, and exploitation of the proletarians in the Western countries and of the masses of peoples in the underdeveloped countries. And the renovation of socialism, however much it may diverge, even in important respects, from the vision of Marx, Engels, Lenin, and Trotsky, will not be able to ignore some of their teachings that remain fundamental. Whoever speaks of a socialism that must be 're-invented wholly anew' winds up inventing something very old: capitalism.

S.T. 1979

# Index